WITHDRAWN

INFORMER
001

INFORMER 001

THE MYTH OF PAVLIK MOROZOV

YURI DRUZHNIKOV

TRANSACTION PUBLISHERS

NEW BRUNSWICK (U.S.A.) AND LONDON (U.K.)

Library of Congress Catalog Number: 96-42466
ISBN: 1-56000-283-2
Printed in the United States of America

Library of Congress Cataloging-in-Publication Data

Druzhnikov, ÍUriĭ, 1933–
    [Voznesenie Pavlika Morozova. English]
    Informer 001 : the myth of Pavlik Morozov / Yuri Druzhnikov.
        p. cm.
    Includes bibliographical references and index.
    ISBN 1-56000-283-2 (cloth : alk. paper)
    1. Morozov, Pavlik, 1918–1932. 2. Soviet Union—Politics and government—1917–1936. 3. Informers—Soviet Union—Biography. I. Title. II. Title: Myth of Pavlik Morozov.
DK268.M66D7813   1996
947.084'092   96-42466
[B]—dc20   CIP

Contents

Preface: A Dangerous Subject

The glory of Pavlik Morozov surpassed the fame of many heroes. For decades he has been known to everyone, young and old alike, in Russia and in the so-called friendly republics, i.e., the now independent states of Eastern Europe. Hundreds of works have been published about this boy in various genres, from poetry to opera. His portraits hung in picture galleries and graced postcards, matchbooks, and postage stamps. Vast amounts of paper, film, canvas, and paint exalted him. Bronze and granite statues of him stood in various cities. Schools named after him had special Pavlik Morozov hall-museums, where children were ceremoniously accepted into the Pioneers.[1] Plaster busts of the boy were awarded to the winners of sports competitions. Ships and libraries were dedicated in his honor. And his official title was "Hero-Pioneer of the Soviet Union Number 001."

In 1982, the year marking the fiftieth anniversary of the heroic death of Pavlik Morozov, the press called the boy "an ideological martyr."[2] The place of his death was described as a sanctuary and the child was depicted as a saint. In the atheistic Soviet press such overt hagiography rarely occurred, but it significantly demonstrates the fundamental power of spirituality in communist ideology. In the history of mankind, this kind of official glory had never been bestowed upon a child-informer.

The following summarizes the deed that glorified this hero: In the early 1930s, a boy by the name of Pavlik Morozov informed the OGPU (the governmental secret police later called the KGB) that his father was an "enemy" of the Soviet regime. With this action Pavlik helped promote communism in the Soviet Union. His father was soon arrested and disappeared in Soviet concentration camps. "Enemies" of the party later killed the boy, whereupon the people proclaimed him their hero. Since then, every schoolchild in the Soviet Union has learned Pavlik Morozov's biography in order to follow his example.

This young informer and betrayer of his own father was made the national hero of a huge country with a thousand-year-old history. His story was published so many times in the Soviet press that it would seem that there could not possibly be any vagueness about it. I easily found a side street in Moscow named after Pavlik Morozov. I also found a park named after him; it possessed an impressive bronze monument immortalizing the boy, who proudly holds a red banner.

While reading book after book, however, I was amazed to discover contradictions regarding every "fact." How old was Pavlik Morozov at the time of his heroic death? In different publications his age was indicated variously from eleven to fifteen. And where was he born? The place of Pavlik Morozov's birth, Gerasimovka, was called a "village" in some sources, in others a "town." Depending upon the source, it was located in the Koshuk district of the Tobolsk province, or in the Irbit district of the Obsko-Irtish province, or in the Omsk province (located in Siberia), or in the Verkhnetavdinsk region of the Ural province, or in the Tavda region of the Sverdlovsk province (located in the northern Urals).

Photographs of the hero in various publications, when compared, turned out to be of different people. The circumstances of the hero's death seemed even stranger to me; he was not killed alone, but together with his brother, also an informer, who for some reason did not become a hero. The piles of books I read grew larger. I found different people named as the murderers of the Pioneer; according to my count, the total number of murderers was no fewer than ten.

My amazement grew even more profound when I turned to the historical archives. The answer was always the same: "There are no documents on Pavlik Morozov." I headed for the Zauralye in Western Siberia, to the boy-hero's home in Gerasimovka. But even there, in the memorial museum of Pavlik Morozov, not one personal item, not one sheet from his school notebook, not one family relic was found. I visited other Pavlik Morozov museums. Instead of documents, there were pictures, books, and newspaper clippings on display. The preserved relics of thousand-year-old saints are regularly found on exhibit; such was not the case in the more recent twentieth-century story of Pavlik Morozov. Perhaps the boy never even existed and was just another of the idealized characters that make up Soviet literature.

One last thread remained: live witnesses.[3] However, while attempting to find out more than was displayed in the museum, I met with obvious resistance: "Tourists should not meet with villagers," explained the guide.

"The peasants misunderstand everything and might not say the right thing. The museum workers organize these groups so that visitors can view the famous places of Pavlik Morozov and leave the village right away."

I didn't leave "right away." But I couldn't talk to people or take photographs because I was constantly followed. I did eventually leave the village, returning later and going from home to home in order to avoid the attention of officials. Despite this precaution, the peasants who spoke with me either refused to answer or avoided my pointed questions, evidently afraid of being too candid.

To my surprise, however, the testimony of eyewitnesses regarding what transpired in the village of Gerasimovka added much unexpected information to the hero's biography, familiar to all since childhood. They explained that mysterious events kept occurring even after the murder of Pavlik Morozov. The house in which the boy lived burned to the ground, but the arsonist was never found. Pavlik Morozov's grave had been secretly moved at night from one place to another. One official text after another turned out to be false. When I managed to find an original, unpublished photograph of Pavlik Morozov, it became clear that portraits of the hero were false in every encyclopedia and schoolbook, on every postcard and postage stamp.

In order to find out what happened nearly fifty years ago, I needed to make haste. The oldest living witnesses of this tragedy were almost 100 years old. Many had moved to different cities. Private inquiries were always extremely difficult to make in the Soviet Union, and since the subject was officially untouchable, any risky question or deviation from established norms could bring serious consequences for the overly curious. I had to make my inquiries very carefully, and the reader will understand why from the following pages. The official propaganda had done its work. Morozov's biographies had been greatly embellished during the half-century after his death, and Pavlik's schoolmates remembered him mostly from reading about him. Even the hero's eighty-year-old mother, Tatyana Morozova, who provided me with a great deal of otherwise unavailable information about her son, tellingly stipulated, "What is written in the books is correct." One of Pavlik Morozov's remaining classmates summarized the relationship between truth and myth even better: "I will tell how it was, but you yourself add what is needed. It can't be done otherwise." Thus, even barely educated people have mastered this peculiar type of ideological literacy.

Later, in the humble home archives of some of the participants in the bloody tragedy in Gerasimovka, I found miraculously preserved documents that compensated for the incompleteness of human memory. Luckily, I also found unique secret archival documents, without which this book on one of the most vulnerable aspects of the Soviet system would have remained mostly conjectural.

What deeds did this boy actually accomplish, this boy whose life became an example and an imposed model for several generations of Soviet people? Who killed Pavlik Morozov, and with what motive? Why was the informer made into a national hero?

I begin my inquiry by reporting three absolutely reliable facts. First, the legendary Pavlik Morozov actually existed. Second, he really was murdered. And, although it is not known when he was killed, his funeral did take place on September 7, 1932. Everything else remained to be investigated.

* * *

This book was first published in Russian by Overseas Publications (London, 1988) and then translated into some East European languages. This is the first publication in English, with one additional chapter.

Several friends and colleagues helped me with many questions about the translation. I particularly thank Robert Crummey, Jackie DiClementine, Jim Gallant, Wendy Goldman, Sidney Monas, Daniel Rancour-Laferriere, Mark Steinberg, Beatrice Stillman, Irene Stevenson, Kenneth Straus, Carolyn Waggoner, Bob Weinberg, and of course my wife Valerie. My especial gratitude goes to my son Ilya Druzhnikov who spent long hours editing the manuscript. I appreciate the warmth and good humor these people always accorded me.

Notes

1. Andreeva and Kutakov (1978: 1–3). For items listed without a date, refer to Archival Materials/Unpublished Memoirs and Personal Archives listed at the end of this book.
2. Balashov (September 1982).
3. For a list of witnesses whose tape-recorded statements I quote throughout this book, see Testimony on Tape at the end of this book.

Cast of Characters

All of the following names are true. The ages of the participants, unless otherwise specified, are given at the time of Pavlik Morozov's death in 1932. Those persons indicated by an asterisk were living at the time this book was being researched. Fifty years after the events took place, they provided me with their testimony.

Peasants of the Village of Gerasimovka

The Morozov family:
   Sergei, 81: Head of the household and Pavlik's grandfather.
   Ksenya, 80: His wife and Pavlik's grandmother.
   Trofim, 41: Their son and Pavlik's father (possibly still alive).
   Tatyana,* 37: Trofim's wife and Pavlik's mother.
   The children of Trofim and Tatyana: Pavlik (Pavel), about 14; Alexei,*
      10; Fyodor, 8; Roman, 4.
   Ivan, 45: Trofim's older brother and Pavlik's uncle.
   Danila, 19: Ivan's son and Pavlik's first cousin.

The Kulukanov family:
   Arseny, 70: Pavlik's godfather.
   Khima, about 40: His wife, daughter of Sergei and Ksenya, and Pavlik's
      aunt.

Mezyukhin, Vladimir, age unknown: An inhabitant of the neighboring
village of Vladimirovka and friend of Sergei Morozov.

The Ostrovsky family:
   Onisim, 45: Pavlik's uncle.
   Malanya, 35: His wife, Tatyana's sister, and Pavlik's aunt.

The Potupchik family:
   Ustinya, 50: Daughter of Sergei and Ksenya, and Pavlik's aunt.

Ivan,* 20: Ustinya's son, Sergei and Ksenya's grandson, and Pavlik's first cousin. Officially a member of the Society for Assistance to the Police, in reality an informer for the OGPU.

The Shatrakov family:
Anton, about 60: The Morozovs' neighbor.
The children: Dmitry, about 18; Efim 20–40; Efrem 20–40.

Silin, Arseny, 33: Pavlik's uncle.

Witnesses Living at the Time of this Book's Writing

Baidakov, Lazar,* 12: A distant relative of Tatyana Morozova's.
Berkina, Vera,* 35: A peasant woman and Tatyana's cousin.
Kabina, Zoya,* 18: Pavlik's last teacher.
Korolkova, Matryona,* 13: A distant relative of the Morozovs and Pavlik's classmate.
Pozdnina, Elena,* 19: Pavlik's first teacher.
Prokopenko, Dmitry,* 13: Pavlik's classmate.
Sakova, Elena,* 50: A peasant woman and one of Gerasimovka's first inhabitants. She died in 1984.

The Investigators

Bykov (first name unknown), about 30: An authorized agent of the regional OGPU, or secret police.
Kartashov, Spiridon,* 29: Assistant authorized agent of the Special Section of the OGPU.
Titov, Yakov, 24: District police inspector.

The Authorities

Arkhipov, Vasily, about 25: Assistant Chairman of the Central Bureau of the Children's Communist Organization of Young Pioneers.
Kabakov, Ivan, 41: First Secretary of the Ural Regional Party Committee.
Kosarev, Alexander, 29: General Secretary of the Komsomol.
Poskryobyshev, Alexander, 40: Head of the Special Section of Stalin's personal secretariat.

Postyshev, Pavel, 45: Secretary of the Central Committee and Politburo member.

Shcherbakov, Alexander, 31: Central Committee worker, later Secretary of the Soviet Writers' Union.

Stalin, Joseph, 53: General Secretary of the Central Party Committee.

Stetsky, Alexei, 36: Head of the Department of Culture and Leninist Propaganda of the Central Committee.

Zolotukhin, Valentin, about 30: Chairman of the Central Bureau of the Children's Communist Organization of Young Pioneers.

Arkhipov, Kabakov, Kosarev, Postyshev, Shcherbakov, and Stetsky were liquidated during the repressions; the others died.

Creators of the Myth of Pavlik Morozov

Antonov, V. (age unknown): Correspondent for the Sverdlovsk newspaper *Na Smenu!*.

Babel, Isaak, 38: Writer.

Balashov, Vladimir*: Modern publicist of Pavlik Morozov's deeds.

Eisenstein, Sergei: Film director, began work on a film about Pavlik at the age of 37.

Gorky, Maxim, 64: Writer, first chairman of the Soviet Writers' Union.

Gubarev, Vitaly, 20: Correspondent for the Moscow newspaper *Kolkhoznye Rebyata*, later an editor of *Pionerskaya Pravda*, and author of many books about Morozov.

Mikhalkov, Sergei,* 20: Poet, author of the first song about the informer, later laureate and winner of the Stalin and Lenin prizes, Hero of Socialist Labor, and Secretary of the Soviet Writers' Union.

Rzheshevsky, Alexander, 31: Playwright.

Shchipachev, Stepan: Poet, began to write about Pavlik Morozov at the age of 50.

Smirnov, Elizar (a.k.a. William), 24: Correspondent for *Pionerskaya Pravda* and public prosecutor for the Central Committee of Komsomol at the Morozov murder trial.

Solomein, Pavel, 25: Correspondent for the Sverdlovsk newspaper *Vskhody Kommuny* and author of the first book about Morozov, which was entitled *In the Kulaks' Nest*.

Yakovlev, Alexander: Writer, novelist, author of nonfiction, who began to write about Morozov at the age of 50.

Athough living, neither Balashov nor Mikhalkov would provide testimony.

Of the fifty-three main participants in the events connected with the name of Pavlik Morozov, twenty-one were denounced and arrested for political reasons, one was arrested for the rape of a minor, three succumbed to mental illness, seven died of alcoholism, three were probably poisoned, and nineteen were executed. The fate of two of them, Antonov and Bykov, is unknown.

The literature and materials from the investigation and trial contain a great number of mistakes, some more intentional than others. Among the lesser infractions, spelling ranks highly. Pavlik's uncle, Arseny Kulukanov, is variously identified as Kukanov, Kudukanov, Kodukanov, and, probably deriving from its phonetic resemblance to the word kulak, Kulakanov. The neighbor Dmitry Shatrakov is called Shitrakov, Shiprakov, Shartikov, and Shatronov. The brothers Dmitry and Efim Shatrakov sometimes bear their own first names but different last names (e.g., Efim Shitrakov and Efim Shirokov). Silin is dubbed Simin. Danila Morozov's name is combined with Arseny Kulukanov's to form a new personage, Danila Kulukanov, who maliciously sabotages grain shipments. Danila appears in documents as Danil and Daniil. Ksenya Morozova is referred to as Aksintya and Aksenya. The teacher Zoya Kabina's name is often masculinized by dropping the feminine ending, resulting in the peculiar Zoya Kabin, who writes in "his" articles about Pavlik's childhood. To avoid further confusion, all names have been restored to their proper spelling and transliteration.

1

A Scripted Trial

Tavda is a small district center in the taiga. It has crooked side streets, ramshackle houses, and a filthy railroad station congested with timber-laden freight trains. Among the sparse villages that surround Tavda is Gerasimovka, where Pavlik Morozov was murdered. A half-day's journey by train from Tavda and you find yourself leaving Siberia for the Ural province and its capital, Sverdlovsk, the trans-shipment point from the Asiatic part of Russia to Europe. But for many, leaving Tavda is not always simple: the region teems with forced labor camps. Even now at the stations and on the trains you can find police in civilian clothes whose expressions reflect their calling. Tavda was like this a half century ago at the start of a typical Siberian winter in 1932. The events then taking place there were, however, most extraordinary.

On November 24, 1932, an announcement appeared in bold print in the local newspaper, *Tavdinsky Rabochy* (The Tavda Worker). It ran thus:

ATTENTION
ON NOVEMBER 25, 1932, AT 6 P.M.
IN THE STALIN CLUB

A SHOW TRIAL AGAINST THE MURDERERS OF
THE PIONEER MOROZOV WILL BEGIN.
THE REGIONAL ASSIZE COURT WILL BE IN SESSION.
ALL ARE WELCOME.

At that time the large wooden Stalin Club on Stalin Street had been hastily rebuilt after a fire. The sound of axes chopping wood could be heard day and night. Demonstrations of workers were organized in the city before the start of the trial, and posters demanding the death of the murderers of the Pioneer Pavlik Morozov were everywhere in evidence. Approximately one thousand children, including students from every school in the district, attended a rally outside the club during which they brandished posters demanding that the accused be shot. The military signal corps set up five hundred loudspeakers to broadcast the trial, and crowds of curious listeners gathered around them.

There is no need to exaggerate the enthusiasm of the masses; the newspapers did well enough in following their orders. Pavel Solomein, a young correspondent for the Sverdlovsk newspaper *Vskhody Kommuny* (Cornshoots of the Commune) who participated in the spectacle, states in his unpublished writings that everything regarding the trial was planned, ordered, and organized in advance. Instructions from above descended upon every village in the district. The District Party Committee and the District Executive Committee sent out telegrams specifying, "Hold a rally," "Send delegates to the trial," and "Organize a patriotic transport of grain as a donation to the state." These telegrams also indicated in advance how many people were "expected" to assemble and just how many bags of grain were to be "volunteered."[1]

On the eve of the trial agitational brigades and a brass band arrived in Gerasimovka. Vodka was sold from makeshift stalls without restriction. After a "live" newspaper (something like an oral magazine) and choral singing, the merrymaking reached its peak and it was announced that the show trial would begin the following day. As old-timer Grigory Parfyonov told me, "They came for us early with ten wagons and a red flag. The temperature was around minus thirty degrees Centigrade, and the horses ran friskily. Several of us only found out why they were taking us once we were on the road. They promised a free buffet to those who at first did not want to go."

The start of the trial, scheduled for evening so that peasants from the surrounding villages could manage to get there, was delayed for about an hour and a half. Members of the secret police armed with rifles stood around the club, which they opened after the rally in front of the building had finished. Entry was selective: only those delegates named on special lists were admitted.

Intended to hold six hundred, the club was packed with roughly one thousand spectators.[2] Newspaper accounts claiming there were two thousand present are clearly exaggerations. Nevertheless, people sat close together in the aisles and stood along the walls. There were also many children in the hall. In the second row, in front of the judges, sat the mother of the murdered boys Pavlik and Fedya, Tatyana Morozova, with a third son Alexei in her arms. In spite of the fierce cold, the hall was not heated. Nor was it ventilated, in order to preserve whatever warmth the crowd generated. A stench filled the air.

The spectacle as it was presented to the audience made such an impression that even a half century later witnesses remember it in detail. A black curtain was slowly unfurled, revealing red slogans. A portrait of Pavlik drawn by a local amateur artist served as the backdrop. To the left of the portrait was the appeal, "We demand the murderer be shot." To the right, "Let's build an airplane called 'The Pioneer Pavlik Morozov.'"[3]

Guarded by an armed military escort, the five defendants sat on a bench. Accused were Pavlik's uncle, the peasant Arseny Kulukanov; Ksenya and Sergei Morozov, Pavlik's grandparents; Pavlik's cousin, Danila Morozov; and another uncle, Arseny Silin. Only one of the defendants, the schoolboy Danila Morozov, could haltingly read the slogans hanging on the stage. Three others, instead of signing the proceedings of their interrogations, dipped the index fingers of their right hands into ink and made a mark. The fifth, Arseny Silin, was also illiterate, but he managed to make a scribble with a pen.

The three judges sent from Sverdlovsk—Chairman Zagrevsky and People's Assessors Klimenkova and Borozdina—made themselves comfortable behind a table covered with red calico and adorned by a narrow piece of black cloth for mourning. To the right were the people's prosecutors—the representative of the Central Bureau of Young Pioneers and the newspaper *Pionerskaya Pravda* (Pioneer Truth), Elizar Smirnov; the representative of the Ural Regional Komsomol, Urin; and Prosecutor Zyabkin. To the left sat the defense lawyer, Ulasenko. The minutes of the trial were recorded by the secretary, Makarydina. Together they made up the itinerant session of the District Assize Court.

Tavdinsky Rabochy provided the most detailed daily coverage of the trial. On the basis of this local paper's account, it becomes obvious that the trial was not a judicial examination in the accepted sense of the phrase. Officially it was a political trial; in practice, however, it was a club performance with designated roles, intermissions, a buffet, and a concluding act, or finale—the verdict.

I managed to gain access to *File of Investigation No. 374 on the Murder of the Morozov Brothers, prepared by the Secret Political Department of the Ural OGPU*. OGPU is an abbreviation for Unified Main Political Directorate—the secret police. This dossier includes the *Indictment* prepared by the secret police for the trial. *The Decision of the Ural Court* was published on November 30, 1932, in *Tavdinsky Rabochy*. In order for the reader to understand the official interpretation of the murder, I will provide excerpts from both of these documents.

From the indictment: "Pavel Morozov, having become a Pioneer during the course of the current year, conducted a staunch and active struggle with the class enemy—the kulaks [rich farmers] and their henchmen—and spoke at public meetings where he time and time again unmasked kulak swindles and frauds..."

From the decision: "In the village of Gerasimovka, where until recently there were neither Party nor Komsomol cells and, despite the presence of one hundred peasant households, up until now no kolkhoz, the active effort made by the Pioneer Morozov to fulfill the campaign...elicited malicious fury on the part of his relatives..."

From the indictment: "The kulaks feared that Pavel Morozov would make further denunciations to the authorities and set out to threaten the Pioneer Pavel Morozov with reprisals. Regarding Pavel Morozov, Kulukanov and Silin said, 'This pioneer, a snotty communist, has made life impossible for us and, whatever the cost, we must have him wiped off the face of the earth.'"

From the decision: "The murder in question was planned long before it was committed, and the very act of reprisal...was but the willful carrying out of a decision settled on long ago."

From the indictment: "The kulak Arseny Kulukanov, having found out that Pavlik Morozov, along with his brother Fyodor, had gone berrypicking in the forest, arranged with Danila Morozov, who came to his house on September 3, that the latter would assist in the murders of the Pioneer Pavel Morozov and Fyodor. After giving Danila thirty rubles, Kulukanov asked him to invite his grandfather Sergei Morozov, with whom Kulukanov had an earlier agreement, to murder Pavel and Fyodor."

From the decision: "After leaving Kulukanov's and finishing harrowing a field, Danila set off for home and told his grandfather Sergei about the conversation with Kulukanov. When he saw Danila take a knife from the table, without saying a word Sergei Morozov left home with Danila and set out along the path that the Morozov brothers would return upon. When the defendants had left the village, Sergei Morozov said to Danila, 'We are going to kill them. See that you don't get scared.'"

From the indictment: "Having come up to Pavel, Danila Morozov, without saying a word, pulled out the knife and stabbed Pavel in the stomach."

From the decision: "Nine-year-old Fedya, who began to cry and started to run away, was seized by Sergei Morozov and stabbed by Danila, who had come running up. Convinced that Fedya was dead, Danila returned to Pavel and stabbed him several more times with the knife."

From the indictment: "After committing the murder, Sergei Morozov shook the berries collected by Pavel and Fyodor from the bag and, together with Danila, placed this bag on Pavel Morozov's head. Next, Sergei Morozov dragged Fyodor's body into the woods, a little way from the path; Danila did the same with Pavel's corpse. Upon returning from the forest after the murder and discovering bloodstains on their clothes, Sergei and Danila Morozov changed clothes and forced Ksenya Morozova (Sergei's wife) to wash the bloodstained clothing in order to conceal evidence of the crime. Having thus found out about the crime, Ksenya Morozova soaked the bloodstained clothes (trousers and a shirt), but did not have time to finish cleaning them: during the search the shirt and trousers were seized while still soaking wet."

From the decision: "Ksenya Morozova does not deny that the next day she found out about the murder of Pavel and Fyodor, but she concealed this fact when the inquiry about their deaths began."

From the indictment: "During the search the knife used in the murder was discovered behind the household icons."

Despite the apparent clarity of motive and deed established by the prosecutors, careful study of the published materials of the trial, of secret documents pertaining to the investigation that was conducted over the course of two and a half months, and of the testimony of witnesses and eyewitnesses reveals many contradictions and discrepancies in both the investigation and trial.

The brothers Pavlik and Fedya went to the forest for cranberries, but neither the investigation nor the trial ascertained when and where they went—or who knew about it. The court did not raise the question of why in the course of three days no one began a search for the missing children. And why hadn't anyone paid attention to the fact that the Morozovs' dog had returned alone from the forest, howling? Several versions of these tragic events exist, but the court never determined which one corresponded to the truth. The precise time of the murder remained uncertain, and not one photograph was taken of the place in the forest where the murder was committed. The investigators did not visit the scene of the crime, did not view the corpses, did not record any evidence, did not even establish the precise setting of the murder. District Police Inspector Yakov Titov wrote and signed the *Crime Scene Report* without witnesses. I discovered a typewritten copy of this report in the archives of the Sverdlovsk Historical and Revolutionary Museum. The report, which was handwritten on one page, states that it was composed at 1:00 p.m. on September 6, in the presence of peasants whose signatures are absent. The incident is roughly described in the report, and few details are provided: Pavel lay with his head to the east, and the second corpse, Fyodor, lay with his head to the west. Regarding Pavel, "The flesh of the left arm was cut and the fatal stab was made on the right side of the stomach, where the intestines spilled out. There is a second stab in the chest near the heart." The *Crime Scene Report* indicates that there were three wounds but only two stabs. Later, after the funeral, the newspaper *Na Smenu!* specified, based on the words of the investigator, that Pavel suffered not three, but four knife wounds. Public prosecutor and journalist Smirnov, who observed the trial, would later write, "After the fifth stab in the chest, Pavlik lay dead." But Vitaly Gubarev, a writer and colleague of Smirnov's, recalled thirty years later a testimony that Pavlik's body, according to a judicial-medical examination, had sixteen knife wounds.[4]

The *Report* states the following about Fyodor: "A blow by a stick had been struck to the left temple, and his right cheek was speckled with blood, though no wounds were noticeable. The fatal stab was to the stomach, above the navel, where the intestines had spilled out. Also, the right arm had been cut to the bone by a knife." Gubarev would later state that Fyodor was murdered not by a stick but by a stab to the back of the head.

The court did not establish, although it was noted in the verdict, whether Pavlik was lying with his head in a sack. Witnesses asserted that there was no such sack, stating that his shirt was pulled over his head and stained red. But not with blood. The cranberries that the murderers had poured out of the sack gave off a rich, dark-red juice, and it was this juice that had dyed the sack and/or the shirt. Neither sack nor clothing were examined.

Eyewitnesses revealed that Inspector Titov did not write the report on September 6, but at some later date when he was ordered to do so. In the notebook of Solomein, the first journalist to arrive in Gerasimovka, among the notes of testimony offered by eyewitnesses are the following indignant words of Pavlik's uncle Onisim Ostrovsky: "You know, it's only necessary to describe the wounds. The boys were not robbed, not run over, didn't drink to excess, but were wickedly murdered."[5] A physician's assistant who was in the village at the time flatly refused to perform an autopsy when he was summoned to do so by the relatives, and he was the only person with any medical knowledge who ever saw the corpses. His refusal to perform the autopsy is understandable: given the nature of the times, he simply feared repercussions. Significantly, neither the investigators nor the court ever interrogated him, although he could certainly have given a more thorough account than that provided by the semiliterate policeman in the *Crime Scene Report*. It was known to the court that someone called the village from Tavda and ordered the burial of the children before investigators arrived, but the court never ascertained who issued the order to bury them so quickly.

Witnesses at the trial described the solemn funeral of the Pioneer. Eyewitnesses told me, however, that the corpses were driven up to the village in a muddy wagon. "They laid the dead children on the floor near the door without anything at all, without clothes," recalled Zoya Kabina, Pavlik Morozov's last teacher. "The mother saw her dead children and lost consciousness near the wagon. They placed her unconscious in the same wagon alongside the dead children and took all three of them home." The unpublished testimony of eyewitnesses recorded by the journalist Solomein contains the following statement by Onisim Ostrovsky: "There were no nails [with which to hammer together the boards for the boys' caskets]. I found out that there was telephone wire in the village Soviet, and I myself made the nails at a neighbor's smithy. We buried them ourselves. No one helped with the burial. They didn't give any cloth or boards. There weren't enough nails." Oddly, the authorities neglected to participate in the funeral of the murdered hero.

The second edition of the *Great Soviet Encyclopedia* states, "The murderers were caught."[6] "Caught" suggests that a pursuit or at least a search for persons hiding from the authorities had taken place. Neither the investigation, the court, nor the press raised the important question of why the murderers committed a crime so close to the village without attempting to conceal traces of the crime. After all, there was a swamp next to the murder site; the corpses could have been swallowed up, and bears, which were plentiful then, would have been blamed. The court was not surprised that none of the suspects tried to avoid arrest; in this wild country, however, it would have been easy to go to relatives in another village or hide in the vast reaches of the taiga.

The number of people arrested grew from two to ten during the course of the investigation, with one person released before the trial. The court did not seem bothered that these arrests were carried out arbitrarily, without either the sanction of the prosecutor or a shred of evidence. First to be taken into custody was the young peasant Dmitry Shatrakov, who had gone hunting with his dog and rifle on the day of the murder. Then followed the arrest of his brother; after that his father and a third brother were arrested. The arrests were based on an old denunciation—that the Shatrakovs owned an unregistered rifle. "All were beaten up during the arrest," recalled an eyewitness.

A "presumption of guilt" hung over the suspects from the very start. They were expected to prove their innocence to the investigators. Dmitry Shatrakov managed to produce a certificate stating that he had been summoned to the District Military Registration and Enlistment Office in Tavda. The father and the third brother, Efim, found witnesses who testified to seeing them all day harrowing a field far from the place of the murder. The second brother, Efrem, could not quickly supply an alibi and spent more time in jail than the others.

Pavlik's grandfather Sergei Morozov was arrested next, after his grandson, Pavel's cousin Ivan Potupchik, informed on him. As Dmitry Prokopenko, an eyewitness of the events recalled, Potupchik reported that Pavlik and his grandfather had "been at odds with each other for a long time." Potupchik had even offered to arrest his grandfather himself.

The sequence of arrests now becomes more difficult to establish. A relative of Pavlik's mother, Lazar Baidakov, told me, "Across the way from Grandpa Sergei Morozov lived Arseny Silin, who was married to his daughter. When they arrested Grandpa Morozov, they took Silin as well and held him in a barn. They did not seize the grandmother right away. At first she brought them food from the other side of the village." However, Ksenya Morozova had also been arrested, along with her grandson Danila and son-in-law Arseny Kulukanov. Then Vladimir Mezyukhin, who had by chance dropped in on Sergei Morozov from a neighboring village, was arrested. According to the newspaper *Kolkhoznye Rebyata* (Children of the Collective Farm), ten suspects were not enough. The newspaper wrote that "other kulaks and their henchmen from Gerasimovka" were going to be brought to trial.[7]

Even during the trial new defendants appeared. First was the rich peasant Anchov, whom the newspaper *Na Smenu!* characterized thus: "Anchov was the leader and ideological inspiration behind the whole group. There is no doubt about his central role in this vile crime."[8] Afterwards there was no further mention of Anchov. Later they named still another murderer—Rogov. During one of the sessions of the trial an unknown person in a sheepskin coat appeared and announced that Ivan Morozov, who lived in a neighboring village and was Sergei's son and Danila's father, had also been arrested for the attempted murder of a representative of the grain requisitioning committee. Nevertheless, in order to implicate Ivan in the crime, they accused him of instigating the murder of his nephew Pavlik and attempting to destroy community livestock. "Ivan confessed to everything," the schoolteacher Kabina told me, "but he really had nothing to do with it." They then sentenced Ivan separately.

The case of Pavel's and Fyodor's murder was connected to the arrest of their father, Trofim Morozov, whom Pavel had denounced. Yet the investigation did not even try to get testimony from this major participant, who was in a labor camp at the time. Neither was he interrogated at the trial.

The basic proof of the defendants' guilt consisted largely of quotations from Stalin's and his subordinates' official statements on how the class struggle was intensifying in certain areas, and of demonstrating how the accused illustrated the truth of these pronouncements. The prosecutor talked about impending economic changes, through which a classless society would be built and for which all remnants of enemy classes (here he pointed at the accused) had to be destroyed. The public prosecutors did not, on the whole, need to demonstrate guilt. Nor did they try; they simply waved above their heads fat bundles of letters and telegrams from the proletariat of the Urals, from Pioneers, readers of newspapers, and others demanding that the defendants be shot.

The judges addressed the defendants with demeaning familiarity. The notes of the proceedings refer to Ksenya Morozova as "the old woman," and to the eventually acquitted Arseny Silin as "the murderer."

The prosecution had at its disposal two pieces of material evidence that were found in the home of Sergei Morozov: the knife, which was pulled out from behind the icons during the search, and the blood-spattered trousers and shirt—though whose clothes they were, Danila's, the grandfather's, or someone else's, and whose blood was on them remained unknown. The court did not demand a laboratory examination of the blood stains. Nor was there a psychiatric examination of the defendants. Despite all the gaps in the state's evidence, the court did not order further inquiry.

Moreover, instead of hard proof, several "pieces of evidence" from the writings of journalists entered the judicial proceedings. Thus, *Pionerskaya Pravda* reported that kulaks from Gerasimovka had promised to pay gold for the murder. There was no mention of gold in the indictment. But at the trial, according to *Tavdinsky Rabochy*, the theme of compensation sprang up again:

> *Chairman*: Did Kulukanov promise you gold, and did you know that he had gold?
>
> *Morozov, Danila*: I knew. [He did not answer whether the gold was promised to him, given to him, or was taken by him.]
>
> *Chairman*: Tell us frankly, Danila. Is everything that you told the court correct, or are you simply slandering, lying?
>
> *Morozov, Danila*: I am telling it the way it happened. I have nothing to hide. If I'm guilty, then I'm guilty.[9]

If we are to believe the newspaper accounts of the judicial proceedings, the defendants willingly confessed to the murder and exposed each other. The grandmother, "the haughty old woman in black," accused the grandfather and others.[10] The grandfather also exposed everybody else, although more laconically. Danila merrily accused his relatives. I was told, however, by a former resident of Tavda who was present at the trial, Anna Tolstaya, that none of the defendants confessed to committing the murders, and this she remembers perfectly—not one!

Witnesses for the prosecution (about ten people) likewise did not introduce facts but demanded that the court employ the "highest measure of social defense"—execution. In fact, there were no defense witnesses at all. At the trial there was only one defense counsel, but during one of the court sessions he stepped forward and announced to the hall that he was revolted by the conduct of his clients and refused to defend them further. After this the lawyer withdrew with a flourish, and the trial concluded without him. The judges and the prosecutor even demanded that a small boy testify against his relatives. Ten-year-old Alexei Morozov complied; he had been coached beforehand to demand the death of his grandfather and grandmother.

The trial lasted four days. The verdict, which was read in the deathly silence of the courtroom, proclaimed, "We find Arseny Kulukanov, Sergei Morozov, Danila Morozov, Ksenya Morozova guilty of the murder of Pioneer Pavel Morozov and his brother Fyodor because of class antagonisms and, according to Article 58.8 of the Criminal Code and in order to best defend society, sentence all four to execution by shooting."[11] Pavlik's uncle, Arseny Silin, was acquitted for incomprehensible, though for him fortunate, reasons.

Standing behind the crowd, persons not known to the local peasants began loudly singing the Communist party's anthem, "The International." Although journalists wrote that everyone in the courtroom joined in the singing, this detail is extremely suspect: in all likelihood the peasants of Gerasimovka could not even pronounce the name of the hymn.[12]

Thus, without proof of guilt three old people were executed: the grandfather was eighty-one, his wife eighty, and the brother-in-law seventy. Their nineteen-year-old grandson was killed along with them. The peasant Prokopenko assured me that the defendants were shot immediately. They were led to a pit, ordered to take off their good clothes, then riddled with bullets. Agitators from the District Party Committee in the village recounted all this in enthusiastic detail.

The performance that initiated the worldwide fame of Pavlik Morozov had come to an end. In the course of several days the station and streets of Tavda were overflowing with visitors—policemen, soldiers, people in civilian clothes, journalists, and all those who participated in the show trial that had became famous across the entire country.

But why did the authorities need this trial? Who actually was this Pavlik Morozov? And what constituted his heroic feat?

Notes

1. Solomein (Materials...)
2. *Na Smenu!* (27 November 1932).
3. Solomein (1933: 69; 1979: 107).
4. Sokolov (24 September 1932); Smirnov (1961: 71); Gubarev (September 1962).
5. Solomein (eyewitness testimony).
6. Second ed., vol. 28: 310.
7. Gubarev (20 October 1932).
8. Antonov (29 November 1932).
9. *Tavdinsky Rabochy* (28 November 1932).
10. Solomein (29 November 1932).

11. *Tavdinsky Rabochy* (30 November 1932); *Ugolovnoe zakonodatelstvo SSSR* (1957: 48–49).
12. Solomein (1979: 84).

2

How a Son Informs on His Father

According to bureacratic definition, Pavlik Morozov's ancestors were aliens, people of non-Russian descent. They lived in the western part of the Russian Empire, in White Russia, or Belorussia. Pavlik's mother and father were Belorussian by birthplace, by documentation, and by blood. And so was Pavlik himself. This detail could be overlooked if the authorities hadn't felt the need to convert him posthumously into a Russian. The press began to emphasize that Pavlik Morozov was a Russian boy, an "older brother" who could serve as an example for the children of all other nationalities. In order not to leave any doubt, Vitaly Gubarev explained in his article, "The Great Deed of a Russian Boy," that Morozov was born to a Russian mother. Thus, even the hero's parents were made to conform to Soviet ethnic standards.[1]

Later in the Soviet Union heroes were made only after a very close inspection of their backgrounds. Back then the authorities were in a rush, and they overlooked some facts less pleasant than nationality in the foremost Pioneer's biography.

Our hero's great grandfather, Sergei Morozov, fought in the Russian army through several of the previous century's wars, and was decorated six times for his service. After retiring from the army, he went into government service, becoming a prison guard. His son, also Sergei, Pavlik's grandfather, became a policeman. He fell in love with a female prisoner whom he had escorted to jail, and as soon as she was released he married her. Ksenya, Pavlik's grandmother, was, it was said, unusually beautiful—she was also a professional horse-thief. It was a demanding occupation, requiring a quick mind and daring. Grandmother Ksenya had been tried and convicted for rustling twice in her youth. The first time, she spent a year and a half in prison. The second sentence of three years had been reduced, however, because Sergei succeeded in freeing her with

a bribe on the eve of their wedding. Thus, on his father's side, the Pioneer-Hero Pavlik Morozov was the descendant of a policeman and a
professional thief. This fact, of course, has never been publicized.[2]

At the beginning of the century, the Morozovs, along with thousands
of other Belorussians, went off to Siberia in search of their fortune. The
Russian government encouraged the non-Russian peoples of the Empire
to populate the taiga. These newcomers were torn from their native land
and language. But settlement was largely voluntary. The peasants were
given a reduced-fare trip to Siberia, 150 rubles in aid for each male (not
a small sum in those days), and free seed grain each spring. A cousin of
Pavlik's mother, Vera Berkina, recalls:

> I was a nine-year-old girl when I was brought here. We took a train as far as
> Tyumen. There my father bought a horse and a wagon, and we went to where there
> was land. In Belorussia we had very little land, but here you had as much as you
> could take by clearing the forest. Others, also our people, went by steamboat up
> the Tavda River, and then continued on foot. The official in charge of the settle-
> ments registered those who arrived and gave them money. In the places set aside
> for the immigrants, the wells were already dug. The people came, full of life and
> endurance. During those first years they huddled together in sod huts.

I can add to these memoirs of a living witness some information from
an archival source.[3] This entire region of Siberia was settled by Belorussians. In the year 1906, forty families came to this district, and the
eldest of the men was Gerasim Sakov, after whom Gerasimovka was named.
Pavlik's grandfather and his family were registered in Gerasimovka on
October 26, 1910.

Geographically, Gerasimovka is located in the center of Russia; however, it was then and remains now an out-of-the-way territory on a remote frontier. This region is most often called the Northern Urals, although
it is actually a part of Western Siberia.

In the past a peaceful native people, the Mansi, lived on this land.
Russians first came here in the sixteenth century, and the Cossack warriors forced out the Mansi, who left behind them only the names of several villages. Then the Belorussians came, clearing the forests and
cultivating the land they had won from the taiga. Until recently the charred
remains of tree trunks cast a gloom around the village, showing that the
process was still far from complete. Gradually the settlers built huts.
During winters, many went off to earn some cash at the lumber mill
(later, in the 1930s, operated by forced-labor convicts) in Tavda or else-

where in railroad construction. "The people found it rough. Many died before their time," one of the older inhabitants recalled.

Gerasimovka remained an obscure village. In the neighboring settlements churches were built. "We brought icons with us," recollects Berkina, "and went to church only on holidays. Generally, we conducted [religious] services in our own homes."

"And what faith were you?" I asked.

She answered, "We were of the same faith as everyone else. After all, we weren't infidels."

The Belorussians here were, for the most part, Russian Orthodox. Old-timers tell how peddlers used to travel the countryside, trading beads and weapons for furs. Sometimes they were robbed in the taiga. In Gerasimovka, which stood in a complete wilderness, away from the main roads, it was quieter than in surrounding areas. People intermarried during the years of struggle against hardships. The village was quiet, and the people were sober and industrious. Viciousness first appeared alongside "class struggle," after 1917.

The biggest event of 1917 for the Morozov family, however, was not the revolution but the marriage of their second son, Trofim, to Tatyana, *née* Baidakov. These newlyweds were to become the parents of Pavlik Morozov. Tatyana, who was from the neighboring village of Kulokhovka, moved in with Trofim. By local standards, at twenty she was already quite mature. Trofim was twenty-six.

"Trofim was tall and handsome," Pavlik's classmate, Matryona Korolkova told me. "Tatyana also was strong and well built, and her face was regularly formed—one could even say pretty." For Tatyana's parents, the marriage was a joyful thing. They had one son and five daughters, and girls were a burden for a peasant family. The newlyweds built their house next to that of Trofim's parents, on the edge of the village, near the forest. Grandfather and Grandmother gave them some of their own things to help them get started. After a short while, Tatyana and Trofim had their first son.

The child's birth date is the fourteenth of November, according to both the *Great Soviet Encyclopedia* and a publication of the Gerasimovka museum, as established "on the basis of the birth certificate." I did not succeed in finding this birth certificate. According to the monument erected at the site of the home where Pavlik was born, his birthday is the second of December. What is more, even the year of birth given on the monument, 1918, is dubious. Different sources insist that in 1932, at the moment of his death, Pavlik was variously eleven, twelve, thirteen, fourteen, or fifteen years old.[4] Even his mother could not remember the exact date of his birth.

In the fall the roads were so bad that ordinarily it would have been impossible to get to the church in Kushaki even on horseback; as it was, there had been a deep freeze, making it easy go to there and back in a sled. Uncle Arseny Kulukanov carried his godson into the church; he would later pay for this honor with his life. At least we can be certain that Pavlik was born at Gerasimovka; any confusion as to his place of birth was caused by the innumerable post-revolutionary renamings of towns and villages.

They christened the child Pavel (the Russian equivalent of Paul), but called him Pashka. Nobody during his life ever called him Pavlik. *Pionerskaya Pravda* for some time called him Pavlusha, but later they fondly dubbed him Pavlik. The entire media picked up this name. Now, even in the village people use the name Pavlik—a tangible result of the fourth estate's influence on the public.

If we are to believe the books, in 1917 the Bolsheviks arrived in Gerasimovka and elected, instead of a village elder, a Soviet council. Lazar Baidakov, a local peasant, claims, however, that "the village Soviet was only organized here in 1932. The men went out to fight, some for the Whites, some for the Reds. Soviet power was a concept that nobody understood."

The towns to the south of Gerasimovka, bigger and more important, passed from the hands of the White Army to the Red and back again many times, but this did not affect the village politically. Here, in the countryside, people sowed grain, harvested it, and took the surplus off to the market. From time to time armed detachments appeared in Gerasimovka; they took all the food, leaving nothing even for the small children. Because of the village's isolation, however, such incidents were rare.

In summer or winter, it took a day to reach the town on horseback. In the spring and fall, on the other hand, the road turned into a swamp and was almost impassable. The agricultural level of Soviet Russia during the 1930s in villages like Gerasimovka corresponded to that of fourteenth-century England, and the Belorussian settlers eked out a living as subsistence farmers.[5] They disliked outside interference, particularly when it was Russian.

Collectivization was beginning, but the peasants here were not overly concerned with it. In fact, nobody took it seriously. The old-timers were sure that soon everything would be back to normal. Attempts to organize a *kolkhoz* (collective farm) were unsuccessful. It turned out, to the annoyance of the new authorities, that regardless of all the resolutions of the Party and the government, an obscure village could live on as it always had, paying no attention to their directives. The people had learned how to get around the troublesome new regulations, and deceived the government's authorized agents at every turn. In the middle of voting for the kolkhoz, someone would cry out in a heartrending voice, "Fire! We are burning!" Everybody would run out, and there would be no way to reassemble the meeting. In a desperate effort to collect taxes, the authorities brought in the militia, the Komsomol, units of the Red Army, teachers, librarians, and workers from the cities; but the peasants quickly learned to conceal how much grain they produced. Although some tried to meet the State's so-called "iron assignment," or production directives, they soon came to understand the following axiom: if you fulfill the assigned quota, it will invariably be increased.

How did the tiny village of Gerasimovka resist the mighty, grinding wheel of terror that destroyed entire provinces of peasants? It seems to me that there were at least two explanations. First, those who settled here were a special breed, characterized by their pertinacity. Second, the Gerasimovka inhabitants felt that nobody could touch them: this was a country of exiles, an utter wilderness—there was no further place to chase them off to. But here they underestimated Soviet power and its main difference from tsarist government.

The authorities began to exile peasants from the Ukraine and the Kuban to this region at the beginning of the 1930s. In comparison with the earlier times, the number of exiles increased a thousandfold. While the forced labor camps were still being built, convoys brought new trainloads of exiles into the forest and left them there. The virgin taiga itself selected who survived among the exiles. Soon exiled peasants from the central regions of Russia began to arrive. Newspapers wrote that after the removal of the kulaks these districts successfully coped with the task of collectivization. Local Ural leadership took the hint; they, too, had to find and exile those who were blocking progress. Where, then, to send them from this traditional destination of exiles? Of course, to the even more remote frontier of permafrost. In Gerasimovka, the local situation became tragicomic: some were exiled to the region just as others were being exiled from it. And those arriving differed little from those departing. Such was the state of the country when a major conflict arose in the Morozov family in Gerasimovka.

How Trofim and Tatyana Morozov lived is now impossible to establish. They had five children, but one died soon after birth. For about ten years they stayed together, then Trofim went off to live with another woman. This new wife's name was "Sonka" Amosova, according to Solomein; "Lushka" Amosova, according to the schoolteacher Zoya Kabina; and "Ninka" Amosova, according to the testimony of Tatyana Morozova. The confusion over the names resulted from the fact that there were four daughters in the Amosov family, all of them beautiful. Nina (whom Trofim, in fact, chose), was the prettiest of them, with a cheerful countenance, as Matryona Korolkova recalled. Perhaps that was what attracted Trofim to her.

Tatyana Morozova described what happened next:

> Trofim gathered his things in a sack and left. At first he would bring us lard, but then he started drinking and partying. Ninka, the cheap whore, had been married a hundred times before Trofim. All the women hated her because she took away their men. After the war I came to Tavda for some documents, and there at the police department I saw Ninka, who had also come for something. In front of the woman colonel, I told her, "You trash, you German whore! You have children and you don't know whose arm they have, whose nose, whose leg, or whose ass. All of mine are legitimate. You damned vermin! It's because of you all my children are gone, you bitch." The woman-colonel was silent, and did not interfere.

One way or another Trofim left Tatyana and had two families before the conflict with his elder son began. Sometimes he also stayed with his sisters or his new mother-in-law, coming back to his original home less and less frequently.

The very fact that Trofim abandoned his family was extraordinary. A peasant did not normally abandon his wife; that Trofim left Tatyana did not speak in her favor. Solomein, who stayed several times at Tatyana Morozova's home, reasons (and this note was never published either in his book or articles): "She is a slob. The room is dirty, she doesn't clean up. This is a product of Russian lack of culture. Because of this Trofim did not love her and used to beat her."[6]

Books about the drama in Gerasimovka tend to obscure certain motives in Pavlik's decision to inform on his father. "His father left the family," recalls Pavlik's classmate, Dmitry Prokopenko. "The horse and the cow had to be fed, the manure gathered, the firewood prepared; all of these chores fell on the oldest boy's shoulders. His mother helped very little, and the brothers were too young to help. It was physically difficult for Pavlik without his father. And when the chance developed to force his father to come back under the threat of punishment, Pavlik and his mother tried to do so."

"His mother encouraged him to betray his father," Pavlik's teacher Zoya Kabina told me fifty years after the events. "She was an ignorant woman, one who would use any means to get back at her husband after he had left her. She egged Pavlik on to denounce him, thinking that Trofim would become frightened and return to his family." Relatives of the Morozovs also believe that this was the way it happened.

Tatyana Morozova, on the other hand, denied her role in the denunciation, claiming that "Pavlik had come up with the idea. I didn't have anything to do with it because he didn't consult me." Meanwhile, according to those who were present at the trial, Trofim Morozov claimed that Tatyana had coached her son to inform against him. "Let's put it this way," summarized Prokopenko. "If Trofim had not left his family there would have been no denunciation, no murder, none of Pavlik's heroism. But this can't be published."

Soviet writers, ignoring real facts, transformed the domestic conflict between the Morozovs into a political contest. This must be kept in mind as I move on to Pavlik's first heroic deed—the denunciation of his father.

The process of preparing to inform, or how the son went about collecting compromising information about his father, is described in detail in the historical literature. Trofim, who was the chairman of the village Soviet, often came home late and had a drink with his relatives. Sometimes he also worked late at home. According to the journalist Solomein, it all happened like this: When Trofim came home, Pavel peeked through an crack in the door to the room where his father was working and froze— Trofim was counting money. Pavlik did not say anything to his mother. Instead, he decided to keep observing. But this kind of constant observation would have been impossible because Trofim wasn't living at home. In order to make the story consistent, Solomein changed the time of the father's departure to after the son's denunciation. In the second edition of his book the divorce of the parents was removed completely.[7]

In Solomein's book, *Pavka the Communist*, the surveillance is depicted thus: as Trofim works, "quietly, quietly, holding his breath, Pavka got up and walked on tiptoe to the door. From the main room he heard muffled voices. Pavka clung to the keyhole."[8] The boy wants to find out where his father gets the money, and he suspects that it must come from "class enemies." Due to these nighttime vigils the young Pioneer begins to do poorly in school, bringing shame to his detachment; but he is too busy to care. He is completely occupied with spying.

The scene acquires an even more dramatic stature in Morozov's verse biography by the poet Khorinskaya. As Pavlik presses his ear to the keyhole in order to listen and commit to memory everything he hears, his mother awakens. She realizes the importance of her son's work and tells him in rhyme, "Again not sleeping, son? Soon it shall be midnight." And the boy explains in a dramatic aside, "My father has become an enemy, children, and I cannot hide it."[9]

According to the writers, what was Pavlik's father's crime? As chairman of the local village Soviet, Trofim Morozov issued to exiles, dekulakized peasants from the Kuban region brought to the northern Urals to cut down forests for lumber, documents enabling them to return home. The writer Gubarev published the entire text of such a document in *Pionerskaya Pravda* in 1933:

Proof of Identity

This document issued to citizen...confirms that he is, truly, an inhabitant of the village Soviet of Gerasimovka, Tavda District of the Ural Region, and is departing from his place of domicile of his own free will. By his social status, he is a poor peasant. He has no unfullfilled debts to the state. This document is authenticated by a signature and an official seal.

—Chairman of the village Soviet, T. Morozov

This document was composed by Gubarev himself from beginning to end.[10] Fifteen years later he added a changed version to his book. In the first edition, Trofim Morozov typed up the documents on his typewriter, making fifty copies. Later, the typewriter disappeared from this account. The expression "inhabitant of the village Soviet of Gerasimovka" was changed to "inhabitant of the village of Gerasimovka." The district, at that time, was designated "Upper Tavda." Gubarev removed the phrase about "indebtedness to the state" and added the date, July 27, 1932. This date renders the entire forgery absurd, because Pavlik's father by that time had long been convicted and sent to the camps.

Furthermore, Gubarev tells us that Pavlik stole one of the documents from his father in order to take it to the authorities. Thus, it seems, stealing is all right as long as it is for the cause of communism. Gubarev's colleague, the journalist Smirnov, portrays the episode differently: Apparently the father tore up a defective document, but "as soon as the sound of the footsteps outside died down, Pavlik jumped out of his bed and picked up the scraps of torn paper from under the table. Clutching them in his fist, he quickly went back to bed." In the morning, Pavlik took the pieces of paper from his hand and began to piece them together in order to restore the text. In the first few publications the authors wrote that Trofim took money for these documents. Later, they changed the word "money" to "thick wads of money."

Where did Pavlik go to inform on his father? To whom did he speak? Of the many people that I asked, not a single one could remember a thing about it. Each of them recounted information taken from books published after the fact.

Various authors provide equally various accounts. Pavlik told the militia, according to a TASS Bulletin; the members of the village Soviet, according to the writer Korshunov (*Pravda* 23 September 1962); the chairman of the District Party Committee, according to the second edition of the official *Great Soviet Encyclopedia*; the representative of the District Party Committee Kuchin (also called Kochin), according to the booklet at the Sverdlovsk museum; the police inspector Titov, according to numerous sources. The writer Musatov maintains that the boy told the headmaster of the school, who in turn informed the agent in charge of grain requisitioning (journal *Vozhaty*, September 1962). Another possibility is Dymov, an agent of the Tavda District Party Committee, who quickly communicated this to the proper authorities. Or, that the boy told an unnamed agent who, according to Gubarev, "was young, dressed in a white shirt with an unbuttoned collar, and wore creaking boots" (journal *Pioner*, January 1940). In different publications the same OGPU investigator appears under various names: Zheleznov, Samsonov, Zimin, Zharky, among others. One can also read that Pavel informed the investigating agencies (*Pioner*, 5–6, 1933), or the Cheka (*Na Smenu!* 30 March 1972). And two later versions have Pavel "telling the people" (*Pionerskaya Pravda* 7 September 1982), or telling "everyone" (in the collection entitled *Great Deeds Will Live!*). I repeat, all these different sources describe one single denunciation.

The journalist Solomein changed the place where the informing occurred three times in various editions of his books: "Pasha…went to

Tavda and told of his father's activities" (the first report of the location to the newspaper).[11] In the book *Morozov Pavel*, his idea was adopted by the poet Borovin, who chose nighttime for the operation:

> He hurries. Now he will tell it all.
> He is running, rushing to the District Committee.
> And the taiga won't stop him now:
> He is running a race without rest.[12]

However, most authors were forced to reject the idea of the trip to Tavda. The road went through swamps, required crossing rivers, and in the winter was snowbound. Furthermore, the distance to Tavda and back was about 120 kilometers, the equivalent of three marathons. To run that far without rest would have been difficult, to say the least. Possibly for that reason, in the newspaper, Solomein later wrote less specifically that "Pavel told the proper authorities." In his book, Solomein finally has Pavlik denounce his father to a visitor in the village, "a man from Tavda. Military. With a revolver. Comrade Kuchin."[13]

All of the above-mentioned recipients of information, with the exception of the policeman Titov, turn out to have been fictional. Secret police agents could show up in the village under any title, most often as agents of the District Party Committee or the District Executive Committee. It was no accident that in 1932 Solomein jotted down in his notebook the following words of Pavlik's mother, Tatyana Morozova: "When [the secret police] came, Pasha told everything."

But perhaps the boy composed a written denunciation? "He wrote it. Pavlik wrote a communique to the OGPU," insists Prokopenko. "There were always people in the village who would tell him, 'Put your father away in prison for walking out on your family.' Ivan Potupchik, Pavlik's cousin, wanted to become chairman of the village Soviet himself in place of Trofim. He instructed Pavlik how and where to write." I tried to verify this with Ivan Potupchik when I met him: "Did I help him draw up a paper? I don't remember," he answered. "But you can write it that way, if you want."

Gubarev, in *Pionerskaya Pravda*, also initially wrote that Pavel had produced a written denunciation: "'Yasha, give me some blank paper,' Pavel suddenly said, turning his face towards the light. 'Let's write to the OGPU.'" Later, Gubarev turned the denunciation into an oral one. Tatyana Morozova, in one of her discussions with me, said, "Pavlik wrote a letter to the Cheka, and enclosed a photo of his father."

It seems to me that a written denunciation does not necessarily exclude an oral one. A meeting with an agent could have been set up so as to provide supplementary evidence—and to find out more about the voluntary informer for future use. "Pavel came to the village Soviet," writes Solomein in his first book. "A man in a military uniform sat at the head of the conference table. When everyone else had left, Pavel came up to him and said, 'I'll tell you all about it....' The man wrote down everything, and shook Pavel's hand." The writer Alexander Yakovlev filled out Solomein's account. He clarified to whom and how many blank forms Pavlik's father gave out, as well as from whom he got them. Thus, he writes that Pavel denounced many people at once. The agent summarizes: "Even if your own father has become our enemy, we must finish him off."[14]

Note the use of the words "finish him off." The verdict against the father was pronounced by the agent immediately upon receiving the child's denunciation. In the journal *Pioner* Gubarev describes how, while his father sleeps, Pavlik steals the briefcase containing the documents from under his pillow. Waking up, Trofim implores, "Don't ruin me, son!" But the son runs off in the middle of the night to inform, or, as they used to say then in the village, to "prove."

These descriptions are more useful in understanding how a son's denunciation of his father was advertised in the press than in finding out the truth about what really happened. Thirty years after the publication of his first book, Solomein rewrote the entire episode in a new light. Before the denunciation, Pavel was cunning. In school, he stood with a book in his hands: "He only pretended to read it while looking impatiently out the window. Seeing at last that his father had left the village Soviet and headed home, Pavka quickly put on his coat and ran outside." Making sure that he was not being followed (as he was following his father), the boy tried to reach the agent, who had just arrived in the village, without anyone seeing him: "Pavka looked around, went to the window, peered out at the street, and only then carefully sat down on the creaking chair."

On Pavlik's side there was the thirst for a heroic feat; on the agent's part, the pride in his craft. He listened, repeated questions, clarified answers, and took notes. Pavel explained that he was a Pioneer, chairman of his detachment's council, and then the agent began to give instructions. Solomein continues:

"And, you, chairman, can you hold your tongue?"

"I can," Pavka answered firmly, and felt his heart hammering.

"Good. We will get along. First, we will act as if we don't know one another: you didn't come to see me, you were looking for your father. And I don't even know that you are Trofim Morozov's son. Second, you did not talk to me, you only asked where your father was. Understand? And if you see me, even at your home, act as if it is the first time you ever saw me. Is this clear?"[15]

Now he was properly recruited to the new order. And that feeling of belonging to a special kind of people, people who have power over others, was calling him to great new deeds. "Take heed to thyself that thou be not snared by following them, after that they be destroyed from before thee..." These words are not taken from Solomein but, prophetically, from the Bible (Deuteronomy 12:30).

Three or four days after the denunciation, Pavel's father was arrested. The arrest was routine, but the writers of those years turned it into a thriller. In his last book, Solomein describes the scene as follows: "Some old peasants in bast shoes came, prayed, then looked at one another, and at once tore off their wigs. 'You're under arrest, Trofim Sergeevich Morozov,' Pavel heard the familiar voice declare." Another author presents the arrest differently: A policeman whom Trofim does not know is sent to the village Soviet in disguise. "'This is a mistake, comrades. You have mixed something up.' Pasha hears the distressed voice of his father, and he wants to cry out, 'This was no mistake, Dad, no mix-up!'"[16] Tatyana Morozova told me an even more dramatic version: "Pavlik ordered them, 'Take him!' and the NKVD men charged forward."

In fact, nobody was sent undercover. Nor did Pavlik yet have the officer's rank necessary to give orders in the NKVD. They simply came with a search warrant and took Trofim away. The authors of the official myth came up against this problem: If Pavlik Morozov told his father that he had informed, then he would have betrayed the secret of the police; if he kept quiet, how would humanity have learned that the young boy had accomplished an heroic deed? "How in the world did they find out?" the writer Yakovlev asks amazedly in his book. "This is the kind of authorities we have now; one can't hide anything from them."[17] The author was obviously trying to flatter the secret police.

Three months later—thin, dirty, ragged, and bearded (he had always shaved before)—Trofim was brought to Gerasimovka on foot to stand trial. Nowhere in the village could the criminal be fed, although he could barely stand up from hunger. His second wife, Nina Amosova, had left the village and married another man, and Trofim did not want to see

Tatyana and the children. The guards let him go to stay with his father and mother for three days under signed receipt. Here the question came up of who had informed.

Pavlik went to his grandfather's house, where his father was staying, and Trofim asked him about the denunciation. At first the boy denied his involvement, letting his father torment himself with trying to guess who had informed. Having taken pleasure in this, Pavlik then struck the blow, telling his father that, thanks to him, there would be a trial. "Trofim started crying," Solomein recorded from the eyewitness testimony:

> Morozov [the grandfather] jumped up and hit Pashka on the ear, once, twice.... Pashka began to cry and asked,
>
> "What are you doing?"
>
> "I'll kill you, parasite!"
>
> The other peasants took Pashka and led him away.

The trial took place in the village school, in a classroom. At the trial Pavlik was both modest and majestic. In the 1950s the poet Khorinskyaya pictured the boy as being quite content with himself:

> And they were asking me questions,
> What was my name, whose relative I was,
> And the court called me "witness Morozov"
> As if I were a grownup.[18]

I have found twelve different versions of Pavel Morozov's remarkable speech at the trial. I will here only present in full the text from Solomein's archive, because it is the earliest. The trustworthiness and grammatical correctness of the original I leave to Solomein's conscience:

> "Uncles, my father organized obvious counter- revolution, and I as a Pioneer have to tell about this, that my father is not a defender of the interests of October, but tries by every means to help the kulaks get away. He always helped them, and I, not as a son, but as a Pioneer, request that my father be held accountable, so that in the future he does not give that encouragement to others to hide kulaks and openly violate the Party's line, and I would add that my father appropriates kulak property, and took the bed from the kulak Arseny Kulukanov, and also wanted to take from him a stack of hay, but the kulak Kulukanov did not give him the hay, but told him to go fuck himself."

Thus, the father took a bed from his own sister, and wanted some hay with which to pad it. Notice that there is nothing in the speech about falsified documents, nor about bribes, nor a single shred of evidence. The boy mentioned the interests of the October Revolution, then, to prove his father's guilt he threw in the cot and the hay. Later, in his book Solomein would, of course, add the part about the documents given out in exchange for bribes.[19]

I could not establish who gave Solomein the account of the speech that he wrote down. The only reference to the boy's words is in File No. 374, which concerns the case of the murder of Pavel Morozov. This case, entitled "Testimony About the Murdered Pavel and Fyodor Morozov," was signed by employees of the village Soviet. But even this document contains no evidence: "At the trial, the son Pavel described all the details about his father, all his frauds." The versions of Pavel's speech at the trial as published in newspapers, journals, and books all descend from the text composed by Solomein.

The press of the Stalin era presented a picture of the trial with typical cynicism. According to Smirnov's report, when Trofim shouted out "'It's me, me, your father,'" Pavlik told the judge, "'Yes, he used to be my father, but I no longer consider him my father.'"[20] Millions of people repeated these words under interrogation in real life. It is said that Trofim fainted when he heard his son's renunciation. Gubarev, in the account published in *Pionerskaya Pravda*, separated feelings from convictions: "Not as a son, but rather as a Pioneer."[21] *Pionerskaya Pravda* went even further, calling Trofim the "former father": "Remember the speech of Pavlik at the trial of his former father, the kulak's helper."[22]

The poet Borovin, in 1936 rendered one of the versions of Pavlik's speech at the trial in verse:

> "Listen!" Pavka began. "My father
> Was helping kulaks with their tricks;
> Was helping the enemy, giving them documents,
> Disguising them with the mask of poor peasant.
> Yes, now everyone in the kolkhoz knows:
> He wormed his way onto the Soviet for a purpose,
> And, as a Pioneer, I proclaim:
> My father is a traitor to October.
> So that all kulak threats
> Never cause us fear,
> I demand strict justice for my father,
> For the traitor of the kolkhoz."[23]

The sentence was pronounced late at night. Smirnov furnishes it in *Pionerskaya Pravda*: "The father was convicted to ten years of exile." The same verdict shows up in the TASS Bulletin. Solomein's book, however, claims that the sentence did not involve exile, but rather "ten years of strict isolation [in a maximum security forced labor camp], with confiscation of property." The documents I was able to uncover speak only of exile. In a 1938 book about Morozov, Smirnov suddenly announced that Trofim got only five years. The reason for this was that by that time "enemies of the people" were discovered in the judiciary organizations, and word was out that many people were being punished unnecessarily. In accordance with the policy of the day, the writer knocked off half of Trofim's sentence.[24]

What was Trofim Morozov convicted of? Why was the sentence for the falsification of documents so severe?

The official press painted a very unattractive picture of Pavlik's father. The writer Anatoly Aleksin in *Literaturnaya Gazeta* (The Literary Gazette) described Trofim as dull, mercenary, insignificant, and pitiful.[25] The artist Dmitry Nalbandyan wrote in *Komsomolskaya Pravda* (Komsomol Truth) about the "bestial figure of Pavel's father."[26] Gubarev, who at first found something human about him, in later editions of his books ascribed new traits to Trofim: he becomes a drunkard and then a thief, stealing candy from the store while Pavlik proudly refuses to touch it. Still later, Gubarev transformed Trofim into a sly and evil enemy.

In fact, by Gerasimovka standards, Trofim was an extraordinary person. To this day he is remembered as a good soul, in contrast to his wife, whom nobody in the village likes. "Trofim was not an alcoholic, he did not drink at all, those were all lies," the schoolteacher Zoya Kabina told me. "He was tall, well-proportioned though heavy, with a good head of hair. He was an imposing man." Trofim was a brave soldier in the Civil War, wounded twice fighting for Soviet power. Tatyana, the wife he left, told me, "Eight times Kolchak's forces wounded him; a shame that they did not kill him the ninth time." "He was literate, dignified," remembers N. I., a former inhabitant of Gerasimovka. "He was elected to be a chairman of the village Soviet—not the way they do it now, where the vote is unanimous and everyone is afraid to stick his neck out—but with a hope that he would be a fair village headman."

It has been written that several kulaks pushed his candidacy so that he could cover up for them, but this is untrue. The previous chairman of the village Soviet was caught embezzling. Trofim was chosen by the entire village at a meeting, and for a long time he suited both the common people and the new authorities. It was Zoya Kabina, the schoolteacher who proposed his candidacy, and until Trofim's arrest she was on good terms with him; thus it is hardly likely that she advised his son to inform on him, as many sources contend.

Trofim was reelected chairman three times, which indicates that the peasants felt they weren't mistaken in chosing him. Thanks to his intelligence and flexibility, he was able to find some middle ground between the rough pressure from authorities above and, from below, the stubborn reluctance of the peasant farmers to share their grain with the Bolsheviks. Trofim demanded that his fellow villagers pay their "rent"—that is, that they fullfill the grain deliveries to the state. His position was not easy. Agents came to the village demanding information from the chairman regarding who had how much land, and whether anyone was hiring wage laborers. This information was relayed to the authorities, and then the lists would arrive of those to be de-kulakized, or dispossessed.

"He arrested many people and sent them to Tavda," writes Solomein in his first book. The peasants also sometimes threatened Trofim that they would inform against his father to the authorities; apparently, while a supervisor in a prison, he had tortured Bolsheviks. In that case Trofim would have been removed from his position. Denunciation was in the air.

At the same time, the chairman of the village Soviet Council was not very open with the government agents, holding back those who were too aggressive, too eager to take away all of the grain. Trofim was sly; underestimating the stocks of grain, he learned to make vague promises in hopes that the current agent would soon be replaced by a more pliable one. And he wasn't mistaken in this approach: agents were often changed.

"Speaking at meetings," writes Gubarev in *Komsomolskaya Pravda*, "he talked in favor of the kolkhoz, but at home he laughed at what he had said during the meeting."[27] But there came a time when Trofim's restraint began to annoy the representatives sent from above, and it was decided to remove him. The verdict of Pavlik's murder trial describes the circumstances of Trofim's case as follows: "While a chairman of the village Soviet, he became friendly with the kulaks, shielded them from taxation, and, after leaving his position on the village Soviet, he aided those trying to escape from exile by means of the sale of falsified documents." But this quotation implies that he left the village Soviet before his arrest. We do not know whether he was removed by the bureaucrats from the district or resigned himself, refusing to cooperate with the Soviet government. In either case, it was precisely this conflict with the authorities that caused them to initiate criminal proceedings against him.

Let's consider the roots of the crime for which Trofim was tried. Tobolsky Province, in which Gerasimovka is located, had always been been populated by exiles. Various categories of convicts were sent here, but at the end of the nineteenth and the beginning of the twentieth centuries these were generally people convicted for politically extremist activism. Before the revolution of 1917, this province had the largest number of political prisoners in Russia. The Bolshevik newspaper, *Pravda*, in an article entitled *"Bedstviya Ssylnoposelentsev"* (The Anguish of Exiles), argued the following: "In place of exile they had actually received capital punishment. Is it surprising that regardless of the threat of hard labor for attempting to escape, the majority tries to flee their place of exile, often preferring to risk forced labor rather than die slowly in the tundra of Siberia."[28] Under the influence of the exiles, hatred of the existing order percolated down to the local inhabitants, and they helped its victims. One third to one half of the exiles escaped without any special difficulties.[29]

In 1900, the journal *Tyuremny Vestnik* (Prison News, numbers 6–7) announced that by the command of His Majesty, the Siberian exile was revoked; more precisely it was reduced by 99 percent as a legacy of the past harmful to the province in the manner of torture and corporal punishment.[30] Only the most dangerous representatives of underground organizations, including the Bolsheviks, were still being exiled. Stalin, for example, was arrested seven times, exiled five times, and escaped from exile four times. In the inferno of the repression of the 1930s, after Trofim Morozov's trial, the country officially celebrated the thirtieth anniversary of Stalin's first escape from Siberian exile.

Those peasants exiled to Siberia by Stalin himself longed to return home, having no idea why they were brought there in the first place. The number of exiles constantly grew during the Soviet period: in the 1920s cossacks were brought from the Kuban, in the 1930s—Ukranians, in the 1940s—Latvians, and throughout all those years—Russians. And there were always people there ready to help them. But from the Bolsheviks' standpoint, actions that were humane before they were in power now became crimes. Among the people, such a change of view could not take place so quickly; for the Siberian inhabitants, exiles remained martyrs.

One of the exile camps was located twenty kilometers to the north of Gerasimovka. Here thousands of people brought from southern Russia died in the swamps from hunger and illness. They had nothing to lose: those who didn't flee died in the taiga. But not always. "In the penal settlements, the commandant's office kept track of residents," recalls the schoolteacher Kabina. "If a person disappeared, he was trailed with dogs. Twenty people or so were exiled from Gerasimovka. During the summer the exiles would escape from the North, and live in the forest, in huts. The villagers secretly brought them food."

The tsarist government was relatively lenient toward those who aided the exiles. In the thirties, however, accomplices were punished even more severely than the escapees themselves. Under Soviet power, organizations of people who helped escapees had ceased to exist but there still were kind individuals around. Trofim Morozov was not a fighter for the bright ideals of justice, but in helping hungry and dying people return to their homeland he risked a lot. If he did take money, or bribes, to forge documents for escapees, then he used it mainly to ply the district government agents with liquor, calculating that in return they would be kind enough to leave some of the bread for the villagers. Trofim failed to anticipate only one thing—his son's betrayal. But did he, in fact, take bribes?

After Pavlik's murder the newspaper *Tavdinsky Rabochy* asserted: "The criminal ring headed by Trofim Morozov, was tried by the itinerant court convened in Gerasimovka."[31] Pavel's classmate Dmitry Prokopenko recollected, "Trofim and two members of the village Soviet were arrested, then some unknown people, and a new chairman was installed."

It turns out, however, that events were not quite this straightforward, and not at all as they were described by the creators of the official myth. This is what the peasant from the village of Gerasimovka, Lazar Baidakov, told me:

When Trofim resigned as the chairman of the village Soviet, it seemed that documents were being given out just as before. One exile came there and asked for a document. They gave him a blank one and told him to walk to the train station during the night and get out as soon as possible. Well, he went to the station and started looking for someone literate enough to fill out the blank document. He saw a decently dressed passenger waiting for a train. He went up to him, and the passenger agreed to help. "Let's go up to my apartment," said the passenger. "I have a pen there, and ink. I'll write up everything and then you can go." He then took the man to building 39 on Sovetskaya Street, that is, to the district OGPU. It turned out that he was an officer. They immediately began to interrogate him; where, how, from whom. They promised to let him go if he went with them to Gerasimovka and got another one of these documents. Two armed Chekists escorted the poor man to Gerasimovka, gave him some marked cash, and then arrested everybody in the village Soviet. It turned out that they were drawing Trofim's signature. I mean "drawing" it, because they themselves were illiterate.

"It was the OGPU and not Pavlik who followed the members of the village Soviet," the schoolteacher Kabina told me. "But they could not prove Trofim Morozov's guilt until the son came forward and told them that he saw how his father did it. Pavlik was lying because his father was no longer living with them, so the boy could not have seen him falsifying documents. His mother could have known about it, but only from gossip." Vera Berkina supported this view:

> They didn't find any evidence against Trofim, and he would have managed to get out of it in any case. But Pavlik announced that his father had taken bribes. Pavlik was not a witness at the trial, as they have written; he came with his mother. Tatyana testified against Trofim at the trial—that is, she herself denounced him. Then, when Pavel also began to testify against his father even the judge stopped him, saying, "You are too young. Sit down."

And so it is possible that Trofim was never guilty of what he had been accused of. At the very least, his guilt was never proven during the trial. He was no longer working at the village Soviet. The counterfeit documents were being sold by those still working there. Caught redhanded and afraid of punishment, they dumped the blame on Trofim, making him the accomplice.

I would be underestimating the role of the secret police if I suggested that they relied solely on a young boy. It would be naive to think that at the time of the trial, after fourteen years of Soviet power, the OGPU would not have been able to recruit adult informants in this village. All the same, the son's denunciation of his father should be seen as the decisive fact. But Pavlik did not do this for political motives. The real reason behind his denunciation was the burning jealousy of an abandoned woman determined to take revenge on the husband who had rejected her.

Pavlik's father was transported gradually to the far north. Villagers of Gerasimovka remember that he wrote a letter to Tatyana and to her children from a labor camp (not from exile). After the murder of the Morozov children, the director of the village club, who was also the secretary of the local Party cell, composed a response to Trofim under Tatyana's name. It declared that Trofim, as an enemy of the people, should not send letters to Gerasimovka, that he had neither a wife nor children here. On November 28, 1932, the newspaper *Na Smenu!* reported that Trofim had died.

"They sentenced him to death after the murder of Pavlik, just in case," said a peasant from Gerasimovka, who unjustly spent some time in the camps and did not want his name mentioned. When I asked Tatyana Morozova about this personally, she replied, "I wrote to the Supreme Soviet to learn what had become of Trofim. They answered that he had been shot. He himself dug the grave before they shot him."

"How did you find out about this?" I asked.

"I heard it," she said.

One way or another, Trofim Morozov disappeared into the camps.

Notes

1. Gubarev (3 September 1957).
2. Indictment; Solomein (Eyewitness Testimony: 24; 1979: 73).
3. Registration... (1, 29, 31).
4. Eleven in the St. Petersburg Public Library Catalogue; twelve in Bazilevich (1952); thirteen, fourteen, fifteen in *Pionerskaya Pravda* (2 and 15 October 1932; 5 December 1932).
5. Snow (1967: 209).
6. Solomein (eyewitness testimony: 59).
7. Solomein (1933: 13–14).
8. Solomein (1979: 41).
9. Khorinskaya (1954: 11, 16).
10. Gubarev (3 September 1933; 1948b: 31).
11. *Vskhody Kommuny* (8 October 1932).
12. Borovin (1936: 12).
13. *Tavdinsky Rabochy* (27 October 1932); Solomein (1979: 43).
14. Yakovlev (1938: 58).
15. Solomein (1979: 44–47).
16. Ibid. (1979: 48–53).
17. Yakolev (1938: 59).
18. Khorinskaya (1954: 16).
19. Solomein (1979: 56).
20. Smirnov (1938: 53).
21. Gubarev (15 October 32).
22. Smirnov (5 December 1932).
23. Borovin (1936: 12–13).
24. Smirnov (27 November 1932, 1938: 56); Solomein (1933: 20); Special Note...; Indictment.
25. Aleksin (20 December 1952).
26. Nalbandyan (24 January 1953).

27. Gubarev (3 September 1957).
28. *Pravda* (12 April 1913).
29. *Ssylka...* (1978: 66–67, 78–83, 148–49).
30. "K zakonu..." (June-July 1900: 326).
31. *Tavdinsky Rabochy* (27 October 1932).

3

Morozov's Other Feats on Paper and in Real Life

Literary sources agree unanimously that the heroic period of Pavlik Morozov's life began after the denunciation of his father. The desire of many authors to extend this period is understandable; the more feats a hero accomplishes in his lifetime, the higher his merits.

Most sources do not mention the date of Trofim's trial—Pavel's first exploit and the inauguration of his heroic career. The second edition of the *Great Soviet Encyclopedia* places it in 1930. File No. 374 contains three more precise dates of Morozov's denunciation. First, "He turned in his own father in November, 1931"; and, even more precisely, "On November 25, 1931, Pavel Morozov filed a declaration that his father..." In yet another place in the document an expression defining the heroic period specifies, "throughout the current year." That was 1932.[1] Pavlik's teacher, Zoya Kabina, said that Trofim's trial took place in the beginning of 1932.

November 25, 1931, the date the first denunciation was registered, seems to be one of the very few of which we can be sure. We cannot be certain, however, of the identity of the person whom Pavlik contacted to denounce his father. We do know he stayed in the village for a few days. Another three or four passed until the father's arrest. The investigation lasted for three months; then Trofim stayed in the village for another three days before the trial. Because of this, no more than three and a half months had passed between the denunciation and the actual trial. Consequently, the trial took place in March of 1932, which means that the heroic activity of the Pioneer Morozov lasted from March until the beginning of September, when he was murdered—all in all no more than six months.

By the time of the trial, everyone in the village knew who had turned Trofim in to the authorities. Sergei, Pavlik's grandfather, nicknamed the boy "Pavel the little Commie," and the name spread throughout the village. People threw rocks at him, and his relatives cursed and ridiculed him. After Trofim's trial, his father, Sergei, with whom they used to live as one family, not only stopped helping Pavel but also forbade the boy and his mother to come into his house.

The court ordered all of Trofim's belongings confiscated. These possessions were taken from his first family, Pavel's, since the new one, Ninka's, had nothing. Ironically, the denunciation backfired; Tatyana and the kids were left in utter poverty. She was forced to butcher and sell her only calf to the state because there was no food left to feed to the children. The situation at home was becoming more and more complicated.

Authors enjoy describing in their fictionalizations the specifics of a new stage of the young informer's life, the stage that began after his father's arrest. Here, the OGPU agent with whom Pavlik used to deal is promoted and leaves the village. Presently, Morozov spends whole days at the village Soviet listening to the talk of the adults there. "Every visit of the officials from the town, every conversation with them would inspire Pavel more and more," wrote Solomein in the newspaper *Vskhody Kommuny*. In his book he mentions the boy's modesty: "Pavel did not yet fully understand the significance of his heroism."[2]

But according to these same authors, after his first successful denunciation, Pavlik sensed a new power about himself. Solomein wrote, "In the morning, on the way to school, Pavel was walking past the Kulukanov house when he overheard a conversation. Quietly he stood at the entrance gate."[3] He eavesdrops on groups of people who gather in the village, and looks into cracks in the fences trying to find out what is going on on the other side. "These days even the walls have ears," his grandfather once told neighbors. Uncle Kulukanov called Pavel "the number one stool pigeon of the village."

The boy, of course, was manipulated by various adults to the point that he became a mindless pawn in their games. At first, he was involved in the battle between his mother and father; next, in the struggle between his mother, grandfather, and other relatives; and finally, in the conflict between local peasants and the Soviet authorities. If we are to believe the writings of Soviet authors, however, he was far from a mere pawn, but rather a player who wanted to make his own moves.

OGPU agents were obviously seeking something in the village. "Pavlik the activist was right there, guarding the interests of the Soviet rule—he told them everything they wanted to know," said Urin, the representative of the Ural Komsomol organization at the trial. Pavel is the first to show up at the searches, as was expected of any good informant. "His eyes were like arrows," wrote poet Borovin. "And when Pasha's grandfather, Sergei Morozov, helped hide the kulak property," reported *Uralsky Rabochy* (The Ural Worker) correspondent Mor, "Pasha ran to the village Soviet and exposed his grandfather."[4]

Stories have it that Pavlik would go door to door, peddling the state bonds that nobody in the village wanted to buy; supposedly he would not leave until the people bought them. And since all of the peasants were afraid, not wanting to deal with him, they signed up for these bonds. After each successful operation, "Pavel felt like he was in heaven," gloats Solomein in his book *Pavka the Communist*. "Pavlushka worked harder and harder," a TASS bulletin informed.

The authors did not know what to say about the hero's brother, Fyodor, who was killed along with Pavlik. Just in case, they transform him into a spy too: "Pasha, Pasha, I didn't sleep either," whispers Fedya. "Quiet!" warns Pavel. "We'll talk tomorrow."

If Fedya helped Pavlik with his work, it becomes easier to understand why he was killed too. Even earlier, Fyodor had been willingly informing his mother about his father's activities— where he spent time and with whom. And, according to Smirnov and Gubarev, the mother encouraged him to do so.

Pavel supposedly uses Fyodor for minor jobs because everyone in the village regards Pavel with suspicion. The men stop their conversations when he walks by, so it is much easier for the eight-year-old Fyodor to eavesdrop and find out what is going on. Fyodor tells everything to his brother, and the older boy passes the information on to the authorities.

Here is another scenario. At night, while Kulukanov is hiding his grain so it will not be confiscated, Pavel creeps to the door with Fyodor right behind him; they scan the dark silhouettes to figure out who the people are and where they are stashing the wheat. If one believes the imagination of some storytellers, this episode involved Pavel's complete trust of his brother. Together they denounce Kulukanov. During the day, armed men show up at Kulukanov's place, find the cache in a hole in the ground, and retrieve all the grain. Kulukanov was Pavlik's godfather.

The books point out that Pavel was doing his part in the statewide task of exposing the kulaks in the countryside.[5] The problem was that in those days there were no criteria with which to distinguish the poor from the kulaks. According to the newspapers at the time, the number of kulaks increased from day to day. Consequently, the more people Pavel denounced, the more denunciations were expected of him.

Teachers were also expected to participate in this campaign. Since children were more naive than their parents, it was easier to extort information about what was going on at home from them. "The local authorities instructed me to discover, by using children as sources, who was hiding crops at home," admitted Kabina. In the Tavda museum's memoirs of Anna Yermakova, a classmate of Pavel Morozov: "Under the leadership of our favorite teacher, Zoya Kabina, and of Pavel, we found out who was concealing the crop surpluses and where they hid them."[6] The teacher would receive a "list of people to be exposed" from the OGPU agent. This was a tentative list; people on it were suspected of hiding wheat, some due to revelations by the informants and some due to suspicion on the part of local leadership. During class the teacher would ask the children to find out what they could, and then notify her. Some children refused, but in these accounts Pavel always does more than his share.

Many other things become known to the young informant—for example, the fact that Kuzka Silin and Petka Sakov broke the windows of the village Soviet building on the night before the elections and fired sling shots at the pictures of the Soviet leaders in the the village's equivalent of the library, actually little more than a shack. There is evidence, based on the testimony of the villagers and the teacher, that Pavel asked other children to spy on their parents and inform him.

Authors of books about Pavel Morozov continuously invent newer means of denunciation for their hero. Thus Pavlik supposedly offers his friends the opportunity to inform collectively; his idea is that at night they would post signs on people's gates, "Here lives an evil grain hoarder." He himself decides where the signs should be posted. The boy also notes all the details of why people gather, where they pray, and what they sing.

At a school meeting, writes Smirnov, Pavel used to say, "'Among us we probably know about all the kulak hiding spots. But we keep our mouths shut.' 'So what are we supposed to do?' asked Yasha Kovalenko. 'Well, let's expose the hiding spots. Find out where they bury the grain, mark the spot, and inform me or go straight to the chairman of the village

Soviet Council.'"[7] In a story of Solomein's, Misha Kniga tells Pavel that his mother ordered him to rewrite a "sacred letter": "'You tell her that you will do it,' suggested Pavel, 'but give me the letter.'"[8]

Some children hesitated, some talked it over with their parents and refused to be informants, others agreed from fear. The villagers deeply hated those children who informed. They were beaten up, had dogs set on them, and were often struck with clubs. Newspapers and books later dubbed this response "the rise of class struggle in the countryside."

Pavel sneaks around the fences, finding out who owns what, and with whom it is shared. Now, according to Solomein, Pavel is not even happy with the OGPU agent: "'Some guy Svetlov [a fictional name] came, made some trouble, and took off.'" The boy decides to write his letters over the head of the village agent, directly to town.

They try to warn the boy. Trofim's brother Ivan, a provisional member of the Party, comes from a neighboring village to try to reason with Pavel: "You have already ruined your father. Do you want to destroy your uncle and grandfather too? Why did you say that they smuggled rye out and divided it among themselves? Why don't you keep your big mouth shut?"[9] To frighten Pavlik, the villagers play such nasty pranks as oversalting his fish stew, dashing water on him, or poking him with a glowing ember.

People start calling him "commie-bum," "red-ragman," and his mother a "damned commissar woman."[10] Pavel holds the entire village in his hands and, according to Solomein, his mother goads him. One morning she prompts, "At the Silins they are getting the potatoes out of the root cellar. They will take them to the market tomorrow." Pavel goes to school, stopping at the village agent's house on the way to denounce his own uncle.[11]

At that time, Marina Yankovskaya was the OGPU agent in the village; she wore men's clothing, boots, and carried a gun. She shows up at Silin's with a search party and takes everything away on four crates. Here is a combined version of the witnesses' testimony, as recorded by Solomein:

> Silin's wife tells Tatyana secretly that the potatoes are being prepared to be sold at the market. As soon as Pavel hears about it, he immediately runs to the local agent: "The kulaks are selling potatoes, and you are sitting here goofing off.... They're stashing and hiding bread.... Tonight, my uncle Arseny Silin plans to...." At ten o'clock the next morning there is a search over at Silin's. Silin screams, "I won't allow it!" "Well, we will search anyway," answers the young woman, agent of the District Party Committee. "I won't let you!" yells Silin, and punches her in

the face. She falls. Ivan Potupchik is already searching the attic...In two hours they drive away with two confiscated loads of wheat and one load of sheepskins.

There is no doubt that the mother knew about the activities of her oldest son. In the record of the interrogation of September 11, 1932, Tatyana affirms, "Whatever my son Pavel heard or saw of this band of kulaks, he always informed the village Soviet and other organizations." She not only encouraged him, but also did some informing herself. The verdict of Pavel's murder trial reads, "Pavel told his mother about Kulukanov's theft of bales of hay; she, in turn, informed the village Soviet."

Threats only excite Pavel. In the words of the poet Borovin, "He had no mercy and was afraid of no one."[12] Most people in the village were related to each other, but the authorities kept trying to separate people into "allies" and "enemies." For Pavel this is no problem. He feels no personal sympathy—to him everyone is an enemy. And the more intensely the villagers hate him, the more frequently he visits the agent, who notes everything, encourages him, and takes measures.

Many villagers used to hunt; it was never prohibited. Pavel begins to collect information on those who own firearms. He not only finds out who has rifles, but also who keeps them loaded. Yakovlev writes in his book, "Pasha took Titov, the policeman, to the Shatrakovs' house. 'Look for the rifles in the attic or under the fireplace.' Sure enough, twenty minutes later the officer came out with a rifle in his hand."[13] Just whom Pavlik additionally uncovered as owners of firearms isn't quite clear. According to the minutes of different interrogations, the denunciations involved various people, from individuals to even a group of class enemies armed with rifles.

The villagers of Gerasimovka did not want to join the kolkhoz. The old folk used to say that he who joined would lose God's blessing. In the spring, a whole crew came to force people to join. "At the village meeting," the villagers told Solomein, "the chairman of the village Soviet spoke at length. So did the Regional Party Committee representative. The villagers were quiet. They said nothing, either for or against." The press adorns the story further. Suddenly Pavlik gets up and points out the villagers who have stockpiled grain. Smirnov writes in his book, "The representative was quickly taking it all down in his little notebook and smiling in approval." He adds further details in *Pionerskaya Pravda*, "Pavel's hand continues to tap every man's head, 'You have grain! So do you, and you, and you!' Pavel's words ring like a verdict. He points his hand—small, childish, but already firm like a man's—in every direction, and uncovers each enemy of Soviet authority."[14] Obviously a sense of magnitude betrays the author's good sense here; after all, he is only talking about a child.

By now Pavel openly watches everyone. He stops going to school altogether. There is no time for it. Exiles came to the village from the woods to trade their remaining possessions for bread. Whenever Pavel finds out where they were staying, he immediately runs to the authorities; he also tries looking for the escaped exiles himself to turn them in. Whether any of these reports have any truth to them, we will never know. But in his book Yakovlev agrees that this is how one should learn communism. And Pavel learned. According to the poet Borovin, in defending communism from its enemies, Pavel "learned to expose them to the very root."[15]

Here is how Smirnov, journalist and public prosecutor at the murder trial, listed Morozov's victims in his speech, published by *Tavdinsky Rabochy* on November 30, 1932:

> Pavlik has no mercy for anyone. When he caught his father, he turned him in. When it was his grandfather who got caught, it was no different. If the kulak Shatrakov concealed weapons—Pavlik uncovered him too. Silin speculated—and Pavlik made sure he came clean. Pavlik was schooled and taught by the Pioneer Organization.

The Moscow newspaper added a concluding thought to its account of Smirnov's speech, affirming that "He [Pavlik] had grown into a remarkable Bolshevik."[16] Later, Solomein plagiarized the entire passage in his book *In the Kulaks' Nest*.

The village is in turmoil as the seed of betrayal grows and blossoms. Neighbors inform against neighbors, hoping to denounce before they are themselves denounced. Realizing that Pavel is uncontrollable and that, according to the fictional accounts, the only way to get rid of him is through violence, the village turns against the boy. Yakovlev devotes a whole chapter, "The Four Attempts," of his book to this topic.

People try to drown Pavel, but he escapes. His mother goes to the police agent to complain, but he is away in town. At night people bang on their door to give him a scare. He swears at his mother for not waking him up when people were trying to break the door; he could have stepped outside and seen who it was.

To continue denouncing when everyone knows that you are doing it and people threaten you—this, according to one Soviet author, is the ultimate test of courage. Pavel's cousin Danila beats him with a stick. Pavel tells on him. He overhears that his uncle has hidden a cartload of grain in the neighboring village, and the boy denounces him too. Interestingly, Solomein adds in his notebook that the cart was never found.

According to Soviet authors the denunciation of his uncle Arseny Kulukanov seals Pavel's fate. His grandmother Ksenya claims that she wishes she had drowned the boy in his infancy. In Yakovlev's book, grandfather Sergei Morozov summarizes the problem thus: "Pashka is all evil. If he is such a stinker when he is small, he will eat us all alive when he grows up. Just like Soviet life." According to Tatyana Morozova, on the night before his murder cousin Danila tells Pavel, "You are living your last days." Prosecution of the murder and identities of the murderers were deduced from these words.

I must now stress that the real picture was very different from the ones made up by these authors, with their inflated descriptions of Pavlik Morozov's heroic exploits. Here is testimony to that effect: "It is all blown out of proportion," Morozov's classmate Dmitry Prokopenko told me. "Sure, Pavlik was a rotten kid—but that's all. Informing, you know, is serious work. He was…just scum, a small-time hoodlum." His teacher, Zoya Kabina, put it all in a nutshell during one of our conversations: "Pavlik denounced his father, but essentially he did nothing more than that. He never promoted the kolkhoz—didn't know a thing about it." "We can only talk seriously about Pavlik's denunciation of his father," allows his cousin Ivan Potupchik. "The rest was added later, just to adorn the story." Lazar Baidakov, a relative of Pavlik's mother, shared that point of view: "The boy himself was of no importance. To say otherwise is simply nonsense. Why all this hype—well, you know better than I do."

It is important to note, however, that even though the young informer's malicious behaviour has been outrageously exaggerated, because of it real people suffered. The fact remains that Morozov informed; in this particular, Soviet propaganda tells the truth. But even according to the official version of the events, the boy was not killed for his denunciations.

Pavlik's grandfather, grandmother, uncle, and a cousin were all shot in accordance with the infamous Article 58.8. Let us look into *The Criminal Code of the RSFSR*, the 1927 edition, which was in use at the time. Article 58.8 specifies as guilty "[those] committing terrorist acts directed against the representatives of Soviet power or activists of revolutionary workers' or peasants' organizations." A representative of Soviet power is obviously a person employed by a Soviet organization, having certain types of duties and responsibilities. Pavlik was not employed, nor could he have had any official duties. But the prosecution, the court, and the press kept insisting that he was a Pioneer, the representative of a revolutionary organization, and that he was killed precisely for that reason. But was this so? The answer to this question has more than just legal significance. On it rests the entire concept of the Pioneer-Hero.

Notes

1. *Great Soviet Encylopedia* (2nd ed., vol. 28: 310); Special Note...; Indictment.
2. Solomein (27 October 1932b; 1933: 21).
3. Solomein (1979: 47).
4. Urin (29 November 1932); Borovin (1936: 9); Mor (19 November 1932).
5. Smirnov (1938: 17–20, 24, 32, 37); Gubarev (January 1940: 19).
6. Yermakova (memoirs...).
7. Smirnov (1938: 16–22).
8. Solomein (1979: 62–63).
9. Solomein (1933: 40).
10. Balashov (1969: 36).
11. Solomein (1933: 47).
12. Borovin (1936: 4).
13. Yakovlev (1938: 86–87).
14. Smirnov (1938: 62–63; 17 December 1932).
15. Rumyantsev (1953: 62); Yakovlev (1938: 77); Borovin (1936: 4).
16. *Pionerskaya Pravda* (17 December 1932).

4

Was He Ever a Pioneer?

When the first schoolteacher arrived in Gerasimovka in the 1920s, the local village population was almost completely illiterate. The teacher organized a group of students of various ages, and they moved from hut to hut, studying wherever their peasant hosts permitted. Eventually, a local peasant rented his house to them on a temporary basis and moved into a shed. They picked up some used benches and a blackboard from an old itinerant school in a nearby village and added some tables and chairs. The teacher brewed her own ink from black birch mushrooms. Most students came to school in homespun clothes and bare feet; those better off wore bast shoes. They did their written work in the margins of old newspapers.[1]

Pavlik began attending school when he was eleven years old. "But before long," Tatyana Morozova recalled, "the teacher left. She couldn't stand the hardships, and once again the school closed."

Although our hero never succeeded in learning all his letters, his first teacher, Elena Pozdnina, testified to his political acumen and mastery of socialist ideas in her unpublished memoir, preserved in the Sverdlovsk Historical-Revolutionary Museum. At the end of her memoirs, Pozdnina requested that future editors make any corrections necessary to bring her recollections in line with the official story of the boy.[2] Later, when an association with the hero became distinctly profitable, Pozdnina wrote in her job application that her profession was not simply "teacher," but "teacher of Pavlik Morozov." In reality, however, Pozdnina had left the village before she managed to teach our hero to read.

Zoya Kabina, an enthusiastic eighteen year old, arrived in the village after finishing an eight-month training program and became Morozov's next and last teacher. She, too, was horrified by the place and initially wanted to leave, but somehow stayed twenty-five years longer. In place of a salary, she received forty-five pounds of flour—nothing more. She sold part of it to pay a local peasant ten rubles a month for food and lodging.

"Before I came, Pavlik did not go to school," stated Kabina. "He learned to read and write when I arrived in Gerasimovka in the autumn of 1931." At that time, Morozov was thirteen years old.

How did the school actually function? "Kabina was the only teacher in six villages," recalled Pavlik's mother. "Children wandered in and out of school; they came there when they wanted to sit down." Zoya Kabina expands on this state of affairs:

> On paper there were thirty-six students registered in the school. Some days maybe twelve would show up, the next day five, and sometimes there would be nobody at all. The parents were opposed to the school, so I often went from house to house trying to talk them into it. After a while I got tired. The school (a house confiscated from an exiled peasant) was badly in need of repair. The walls were cracked, the roof was tumbling down, and the doors did not close; there were hardly any tables or benches—everything was broken. Collectivization was going on, but the peasants never accepted it. They had come here to live freely, but then Soviet power arrived....

The state considered the school an instrument of propaganda, and the peasants realized its nature. The position of an eighteen-year-old schoolteacher was difficult. The older students—many her own age—ganged up on her and occasionally even assaulted her. Solomein recorded the testimony of an eyewitness: "Yasha Yudov got drunk and attacked the teacher Zoya Kabina. Cursed. What kind of a school is this?"[3]

The peasant Prokopenko recalled, "In 1931 I went to school with Pavlik, but after that we stopped. There was nowhere to study and we had to work at home and in the fields." Kabina remained in the village, but she was busy with other things. The newspaper noted that "special correspondent Kabina reports that the Gerasimovka school is engaged in sowing."[4] At that time freelancers often supplied the newspaper with information. Sometimes Kabina gathered the children and read aloud to them. The entire school library, she remembered, consisted of thirteen books, including primers.

Pavlik Morozov never advanced beyond the first grade of elementary school; he could read a little, copy words, and add and subtract on his fingers. Did Pavlik understand politics with this level of education? Assuming that he did, in what organization did the boy participate? Even to join a troop of Pioneers he had to somehow be enrolled—there must have been a list giving the name and date of each person's membership. At the very least such a troop had to have existed.

Zolotukhin, chairman of the Central Committee of the Children's Communist Organization, in a TASS bulletin named Pavlik Morozov "a Bolshevik." Yet Smirnov in his article "Profile of a Young Leninist", wrote that "Pavlik never entered the Bolshevik Party. Yet all the same, he deservedly carried the proud name 'Communist.'" In fact, he was neither a member of the Party nor the Komsomol. Although the journalist Gusev wrote in his book, *Young Pioneers*, that Pavlik had been "a child of the Leninist Komsomol," Solomein testified that there were no Komsomol members in Gerasimovka at that time.[5]

Fourteen months before Pavlik's death, a decree was passed in Moscow entitled "On the Children's Communist Organization of Young Pioneers." It created the Young Pioneer Organization, whose main goal was to introduce children to Party ideology. Pavlik met the criteria for enrollment in the Pioneers; he was the right age and he had an acceptable social background (the Pioneers only accepted children of workers, kolkhozniks, and poor peasants). Enrollment required some bureaucratic formalities; the young candidate had to be approved in front of the assembled troop of Pioneers, then go through a month-long trial period to determine whether he would obey the rules of the organization. Only after the trial period was the child allowed to take a solemn oath to follow the ideals of the Party. This final rite occurred in the presence of the Party members administering the ceremonial oath. The recruit then became a Pioneer, receiving the right to wear the red Pioneer kerchief around his neck and the special Pioneer pin.[6]

Solomein noted in his book *Pavka the Communist*, that when Pavlik entered school in the autumn of 1931, there were no Pioneers; the first Pioneer group was organized on October 20, 1931, by Kabina, the schoolteacher. The journal *Pioner* (Pioneer) later specified that on this day Pavlik "gave his solemn promise to uphold the ideas of Lenin and Stalin."[7] Solomein's notes, however, tell a different story; Kabina had informed Solomein that the Pioneer troop was organized in November, not October. A triviality, perhaps, but why did Solomein come up with the date in October?

Sifting through the historical evidence, even more glaring discrepancies emerge. Indeed, as early as 1932, after the murder of the child, local organs in Tavda announced in the district newspaper that Pavlik Morozov had never joined the Pioneers in Gerasimovka. *Tavdinsky Rabochy* directly stated in the November 30, 1932 issue that Pavel became a Pioneer outside Gerasimovka. The court sentence reads, "While at the district school Pavlik joined the Pioneer detachment in Tavda, and quickly understood [what was needed]. Upon his return to the village, Pavel Morozov began, with characteristic Pioneer ardor, to put into practice the things he learned in the troop."

Correspondent for the newspaper *Na Smenu!*, Antonov also assumed that Pavel was registered in the Pioneer troop in Tavda.[8] What exactly was meant by "district school" and "troop in Tavda" was never clear. At that time the authorities had to explain somehow the boy's transformation into a Pioneer. This was confirmed by Prokopenko, a classmate of Morozov's: "They explained to us that Pavlik entered the Pioneers in Tavda. Supposedly they brought him to the District Komsomol Committee and registered him there, because we never heard about any kind of Pioneers."

I asked the schoolteacher about this. "He never went to Tavda," said Kabina. "He went to the forest for firewood, plowed the fields, and gathered manure. He also had to pay taxes in wheat. No one had a clue about the Pioneers. I could never have said anything of the sort to Solomein." And Solomein himself wrote in the first newspaper announcement from Gerasimovka, "Neither the District Party Committee nor the District Bureau of the Children's Communist Organization had ever heard of Pavlik."[9] Despite this, the article was entitled "A Twelve-Year-Old Communist." It appears that our hero had not joined the Pioneers either in Gerasimovka or in Tavda.

"I will tell you right away," declared Pavel's old classmate Matryona Korolkova with a smile. "The stuff about his being a Pioneer—they just, you know, wanted it to be true. But up to the time he died, there simply were no Pioneers and we never had any Pioneer detachment." Korolkova's declaration is all the more significant in that she became the first chairman of the Pioneer troop created by the agents of District and Regional Komsomol Committees. But this occurred after Morozov's death. Here is how the schoolteacher, Elena Pozdnina, explained the situation: "No, Pavlik Morozov had never been a Pioneer. But you must understand one thing; it was necessary to believe that he was."

It is clear that someone considered it essential to promote the idea that a Pioneer troop existed in the village of Gerasimovka. Yet, what kind of troop was it supposed to be? How many Pioneers were members?

The most fantastic figures were presented by the writer Alexander Rzheshevsky, who wrote that Pavlik's troop consisted of 150 Pioneers: "Three hundred beautiful kids ran out of the school, half of them wearing Pioneer kerchiefs." Solomein reported in 1932 that "Zoya Kabina organized a small group of kids, too small to be called a detachment." Not long before his death, Solomein wrote in his last book that "fourteen students decided to become Pioneers." Gubarev entitled his article about the Pioneers of Gerasimovka "One of the Eleven." And a publication of the Gerasimovka museum mentioned a troop of six members. Immediately after Pavlik's death, the newspapers cited the two Pioneer brothers, Pavel and Fyodor, although it quickly became obvious that Fedya was only a small child.[10]

Two months after the funeral, Tatyana Morozova told a jornalist, "Fedya was no Pioneer. I put a cross on his grave. But Pasha did not believe in God—so he got a red star." In reality there was never any star. On the cross over Pavel's grave they hung a board with an inscription dictated by his illiterate mother:

SEPTEMBER 3rd, 1932
KILLED BY AN EVIL PERSON WITH A SHARP KNIFE
TWO MOROZOV BROTHERS
PAVEL TROFIMOVICH—BORN 1918
AND FYODOR TROFIMOVICH[11]

And so it appears that the "Pioneer detachment" consisted solely of Pavlik, although he himself was never a Pioneer. Knowing the facts, we can still read in the second edition of the *Great Soviet Encyclopedia*, "When a Pioneer organization was created in the school, Morozov was elected the chairman of the troop." The third edition of the encyclopedia adds even more to his merits: "He was the organizer and chairman of the first Pioneer detachment." An organizer of the detachment which never existed. Later he was even called a Pioneer leader.

After Morozov's death, the job that had been done by many Soviet institutions was attributed to him alone; it was no longer the District Committee, but Pavlik himself who ordered the teacher to organize the Pioneer detachment. The boy communist singlehandedly replaced the propaganda department of the District Committee by composing the texts of Party slogans and inspiring his fellow villagers with tales of a shining future, electricity, tractors, and glass-paned houses.

The young Pioneer even participated in the eradication of illiteracy. His teacher Pozdnina remembered that he once borrowed a primer from her in order to teach his own mother to read and write. One can judge the results of his efforts fifty years later, when Pavlik's mother made a cross in place of a signature beneath the transcribed, typewritten text of our tape-recorded conversation.

What was the point of transforming the boy into a Pioneer after his death? The answer is simple. Despite appeals from above to involve children in communism, the Pioneer movement (based on such organizations as the Boy Scouts, the Young Stormtroopers, and the Spartacus Youth Detachments) developed slowly in the country. "The enrollment lists are here, but where are the Pioneers?" newspaper asked.[12] The secretary of the Central Committee of the Party, Stanislav Kosior, noted in the Central Committee report he delivered to the Fifteenth Party Congress, "There were large numbers of dropouts from the Pioneer organizations, disbandings of some troops and detachments, etc."[13] The hopes for large masses of enthusiastic volunteers were simply not justified by the facts. In many areas, local authorities could not even muster a list of Pioneers on paper. In 1928, there were two million boys and girls in sectarian religious groups.[14] The Pioneers were not able to meet this figure. The increase in the number of Young Pioneers only began when the schools introduced professional, salaried leaders appointed by the Komsomol.

After the murder of the Morozov children, the newspapers immediately declared that they had been Pioneers. When it became clear that this was untrue, local authorities were commanded to remedy these organizational deficiencies. Little Fedya was no good—too young—but the state immediately seized on Pavlik.

Later the press began to favor less specific formulas: "Pavlik was raised and nurtured by our Soviet reality." Sometimes the reports took a mystical turn, as in "The boy became a leader of the Soviet Pioneers after his death."[15] Up until Pavel's death, the Pioneer movement existed mainly in the towns. The countryside persisted, undisturbed, in its age-old way of life. Yet the "Pioneer" Morozov helped the Party to break this deadlock in the villages. "Soon after the death of Pavlik," remembered Morozov's classmate Korolkova, "the first professional, salaried Pioneer leaders appeared, sent by the Regional Party Committee. And they were the ones who really started recruiting Pioneers." Within a month, on October 6, an article appeared in *Tavdinsky Rabochy*; in response to the murder of Morozov brothers, a group of authorized agents had arrived, organized, and registered a Pioneer detachment with ten members under the aegis of the village Soviet.

Why, however, was the troop attached to the village Soviet and not to the school? On the morning of September 3, the day of the murder, what was the Pioneer Pavlik Morozov doing in the forest? Why was he not in school? Surely the school year had begun. Despite all the statements by various Gerasimovka teachers to the contrary, the local school, like the local Pioneer detachment, existed only on paper.

Fifty years later, Soviet newspapers continued to affirm that Pavlik Morozov was a Pioneer. Describing the plaster bust of our hero in the village museum, *Komsomolskaya Pravda* wrote, "No one knows where Pavlik's own red kerchief is now, but one can't help but believe that it is the one now tied on the neck of the stone Pavlik."[16] So, "no one knows...but one can't help but believe." In Solomein's archives I found the frankest acknowledgment of the facts: "If we are to adhere to the historical truth, we must recognize that Pavlik Morozov not only never wore, but never even saw a Pioneer kerchief."[17]

By transforming the boy into a Pioneer, and ultimately into a Pioneer leader and representative of the Revolutionary Organization of Young Leninists, the State was able to claim that his murderers were political terrorists. Accordingly, the trial was transformed into a political proceeding against the enemies of the Party and socialism.

Notes

1. Rostovshchikova (27 August 1967).
2. Pozdnina (memoirs).
3. Solomein (eyewitness testimony).
4. *Tavdinsky Rabochy* (28 April 1932).
5. TASS Bulletin; Smirnov (17 December 1932); Gusev (1948: 40); Solomein (1979: 29).
6. *Detskoe...* (1932: 146–48).
7. Solomein (1979: 32; Materials...: 6); *Pioner* (September 1937).
8. Antonov (30 November 1932).
9. Solomein (27 October 1932a).
10. Numbers of pioneers from one hundred fifty to one were mentioned: Rzheshevsky (1982: 234); Solomein (1979: 32); *Tavdinsky Rabochy* (27 October 1932); *Pavlik Morozov* (1968).
11. Solomein (27 November 1932).
12. *Pionerskaya Pravda* (12 March 1932).
13. Kosior (1932: 166).

14. *Istoria VLKSM* (1978: 161).
15. Chernyshov (1982: 56).
16. Alekseev (2 September 1962).
17. Solomein (manuscripts…).

5

The Family as a Terrorist Organization

No matter how hard the press tried to suggest that the trial in Siberia was concerned with kulakdom as a whole, the fact remained that the victims were two brothers and that the condemned murderers were their grandmother, grandfather, first cousin, and uncle. The majority of the witnesses also belonged to the family.

Pavlik Morozov was not a Pioneer; his ancestors, however, were. They were pioneers in the old, nonpolitical sense of the word—settlers of virgin land, people prepared to suffer hardships for the sake of a better life for themselves and their children. The Morozovs proved themselves pioneers by deciding to move from Belorussia to permanent residence in distant Siberia.

There is no sense idealizing the relations among the Morozovs. It is interesting, however, to observe how external circumstances affected their family. The "child against parent" social model did not come about by chance. The regime profited by, even desperately needed, such a practice. Fifteen years after the revolution, the family, particularly the rural family, still resisted the political demands of the Bolsheviks; instead it asserted and defended itself. A son-informer undermined the family from the inside. His example helped the regime intimidate the peasant who concealed crops, secure in the knowledge that his relations and children would not betray him. The family had to become a component of the state, subordinate to its goals and control. Annihilation of private property and destruction of the family became the single focus of the Stalin era. The trial in Tavda was but an episode in this national tragedy.

Those members of the family on trial were alleged to be kulaks; in reality, they never were. The motive put forward by the prosecution ("class revenge of the kulaks") could not apply to the accused since four of them were poor peasants and the fifth was "moderately poor." "Just between us, what kind of kulaks were they?" asked an official of the modern Tavda City Hall, young enough to be Pavlik Morozov's son. "Everyone knows that kulaks were simply industrious peasants. They had more grain. And since they had more, it should be taken away. That was the idea." Obviously the rationalization is now an acknowledged truism. Thus, even though no kulaks existed in the village, in accordance with instructions from above they had to be exposed and crushed. Grain was needed more than people, and people were obliterated in order to get grain.

To some degree the verdict of the court in Tavda explains the real reasons for the repression associated with collectivization. The county's rising industrialization and the growth of its armed forces demanded an increase of human resources and the grain with which to feed them. There was a shortage of both. Because of this, mass discontent was brewing in the country. A top secret report prepared by Nikolai Bukharin, Politburo member and major Party theorist, declared that collectivization had suffered a failure; the collective farms were foundering, the villages starving, and the country had sunk into poverty. It reeked of a catastrophe that could be blamed on Stalin. In order to hold on to power, Stalin and his followers had to solve four urgent problems: first, to find a cheap or, better yet, free labor force; second, to find, by any means, enough grain to feed the hungry population; third, to suppress discontent in the country; and fourth, of course, to find someone on whom to fix the blame for the existing poverty and hunger.

According to the laws of the time, a peasant could sell or not sell excess grain to the government. Prices, set by the regime, were low and the peasants had little desire to sell their grain for nothing. At that time, in contradiction of its own laws, the government passed a decree that essentially mandated the forceful expropriation of grain if a peasant refused to sell it. Few peasants, in peacetime, had heretofore considered burying their crops in the ground to avoid their being seized.

Beginning in 1928, the courts began to apply Article 107 of the Criminal Code for refusal to sell grain; the prescribed punishment was confiscation of property for "speculation." Politburo member Sergo Ordzhonikidze announced at the Fifteenth Party Congress that nearly fifteen percent of the population would have to be dragged through the courts as a result. Given such numbers, he demanded "speedy execution of the judicial process."[1]

The Kremlin had believed that collectivization would prevent a food crisis. It had the opposite effect; a grave food crisis resulted from the forced collectivization. Stalin, of course, hunted down those at fault; the Party's leader explained the hunger spreading in the country as the outcome of bad weather and "the resistance of kulaks and prosperous elements of the countryside." Grain, according to Stalin, had to be appropriated by way of organized pressure.

In his speech "About the Rightist Elements in the Bolshevik Party" Stalin demanded that the country "liquidate the psychology." Not liquidate people—this would have sounded too crude—merely "psychology." The 1938 edition of the official *History of the Bolshevik Party* explained in the euphemistic terms of that era that the authorities had "released the holds on de-kulakization," or even more euphemistically, that they had unleashed "the creativity of the kolkhozniks themselves," who "demanded that the Soviet authorities arrest and exile the kulaks."[2]

What was a kulak really like? He was, as a rule, a physically fit and enterprising peasant, whose few grown sons worked alongside him. If the head of the household saw that he wasn't able to manage the harvest by himself, he hired another peasant, fed him, and usually paid him with grain. A kulak could be greedy, but he could not be lazy or dishonest. In the kulaks lay the strength of the countryside, its wealth, its initiative, its ability to feed all of Russia, even its chance to sell the excesses of grain abroad. Liquidating the kulaks meant the same to Russia as liquidating the farmers would mean to the United States. Who would then feed America and half the world along with her?

The Bolsheviks sought to annihilate the kulaks as a class, but this presented difficulties as the kulaks could not be separated into a distinct social class—there was only the peasantry who owned small property, property that the Party had not yet had a chance to grab. Lenin himself had announced that peasants were a "petty bourgeois element," and therefore a danger to the dictatorship of the proletariat "many times greater than all [our enemies] put together." Lenin lied, trying to stir up hatred: "A kulak furiously hates the Soviet government and is ready to strangle, to cut the throats of hundreds of thousands of workers." Lenin threatened that those who did not understand the crucial difference between a peasant and a kulak would "be treated as soldiers of the White Army."[3]

Such an outspoken theoretical basis quite suited Stalin. As a result, all the might of the country's repressive apparatus crashed down upon the kulak. In 1919, thirty thousand Party workers went to the front lines of the Civil War. Ten years later the same number of armed city dwellers were sent to institute collectivization in the villages. This constituted, in fact, a second Civil War, at the height of which emerged the Pavlik Morozov affair.

In the spring of 1932, the Seventeenth Party Conference declared its main political goal through the year 1937: "the final liquidation of the capitalist elements and a complete removal of the causes of exploitation." Those "elements" and "causes" were human beings. It is interesting that most sources, concerning the mass repression of the thirties, do not mention that it was planned as one of the most important goals of the second five-year period, on a par with the increased production of coal or metal. It was, in essence, a statewide plan to murder and rob its own citizens. And every stage of the plan's fulfillment was reported to the apex of officialdom.

Paradoxically, on one side, collectivization was instituted voluntarily; on the other, there was always the threat of punishment if deadlines weren't met. The country's split personality, which began to form after the revolution, was now acting in full force. There was always the facade of the rule of law, constitution, and published decree; behind the scenes, however, lurked a myriad of secret institutional instructions contradicting the laws and reflecting the general lawlessness of the communist dictatorship. The ominous figure of the grain-procurement agent, whenever it appeared near any house in the village meant that at night there would be a search, grain taken, and the father of the family arrested.

In order to justify the liquidation of millions of peasants, Soviet textbooks in the seventies began claiming that the Siberian kulaks were connected not only with internal opposition, but with foreign intelligence services and counterrevolutionary organizations.[4] This statement sounds particularly absurd in view of the cultural level of the Siberian village of Gerasimovka.

The modern *History of the Communist Party of the Soviet Union* announces that "In regions of total collectivization the kulakdom was liquidated; kulaks opposing collectivization were removed from their place of domicile. During the period from the beginning of 1930 to the fall of 1932, 240,757 kulak families were evicted."[5]

Such was the unbounded humanitarianism of the Soviet regime. A peasant family usually had many children, four to eight or more. An average family consisted of two old people, six of their adult married children, and four or so grandchildren. Figured in this manner, the numbers of people who suffered during the period of terror reach nine million.

We find the same book claiming the following:

The Soviet government did everything necessary to establish the former kulaks in their new homesteads, to create normal living conditions for them. The majority of the evicted kulaks were occupied in logging, construction, and mining industries, or worked in the kolkhozes of Western Siberia and Kazakhstan. The Party and the Soviet government re-educated the kulaks, helped them become fully enfranchised citizens and active workers [in building] the socialist society.[6]

This text does not need explanation. One comment, however: the *History* speaks of the exile of kulaks but does not mention the numbers of them who died in exile, who were sent to prisons and labor camps, who were shot with or without a trial. Nor does it mention how many poor peasants and peasants of average means were arrested and shot for "cooperation with the kulaks." Various sources place the number of victims of the collectivization campaign at six to twenty-two million people.[7] This includes those who died of hunger, perished in labor camps, or were murdered in prisons or at the transfer points. Tens of thousands of Party employees, OGPU agents, members of the police and military forces took part in the searches, confiscations of property, evictions, and executions. Records concerning these activities were falsified from top to bottom.

As a member of the kolkhoz a peasant became a slave subject to local Party bureaucracy, which in turn received its orders from the city. It meant little more than a return to serfdom. The starving slaves retaliated by stealing kolkhoz property on an unprecedented scale. "The theft of kolkhoz grain began. People stole grain by the kilo, carrying it off in buckets, hiding it in their pockets, shoes, sometimes stealing whole sacks of it."[8] The state stole from the peasants; the peasants paid in coin by trying to steal back a portion of what used to be theirs.

A modern textbook, entitled *The History of the State and Law*, calls the Soviet legal code "the superior form of law." In accordance with this "superior law," the grain expropriations in the thirties were made exclusively on the basis of administrative instructions. Law enforcement agencies prescribed criminal puhishments for noncompliance with the regulations they themselves made. The decree of August 7, 1932 (one month before Pavlik's and Fyodor's murders) declared collective property "sacred," making it the legal equivalent of state property. Having rendered the peasant's personal property meaningless, it would now punish him for theft from the state as it would for the most dire crime. According to this "superior form of law," stealing a cucumber from the kolkhoz field became a manifestation of class struggle against socialism. The same law declared speaking out against the kolkhoz treason.[9]

The authorities tried to create an incentive for the poorest peasants to take part in the dispossession of the kulaks. The law granted 25 percent of any property confiscated to the man who denounced his neighbor for hiding grain surpluses. Theoretically, the rest of the evicted man's property—his cow, farm implements, horse, and so on—would also belong to his betrayer when he joined the kolkhoz since the belongings of the convicted kulak became common property. The quickest way to get rich was to inform; informing thus became an easy alternative to hard work in the fields. Ironically, after making four denunciations, a poor peasant would have received the equivalent of any single kulak's possessions, thus becoming a kulak himself; he could subsequently follow his victims to the labor camps.

Political show trials similar to the one in Gerasimovka instigated mass repression, and this provided Stalin with convenient solutions to all four of his major problems; millions of imprisoned peasants became an unpaid workforce. According to a euphemistic expression in the *Great Soviet Encyclopedia*, "collectivization helped liquidate agrarian overpopulation."[10] Food was supplied to the army and the cities; any organized resistance was eliminated. And there was always a scapegoat. Now opposition inside the Party was accused of obstructing this process, thus providing an excuse for its liquidation. By Stalin's standards this was a truly wise decision.

The Soviet press never mentioned that among other show trials of the thirties—those over Party opposition or involving engineers, top army brass, and other categories of people—there was a separarate show trial conducted over the kulaks. It was historically unprecedented, not only in that a whole family was made into a political terrorist organization but also in that the main audience for which the trial was intended were children and adolescents. Pavlik Morozov was needed for this particular type of show trial, not as a person but as an example.

The first experimental step in the campaign involving the betrayal of parents by their children was taken four years before the Morozov murder. It was called the "Shakhtinsk affair," and was reported by *Pravda*.[11] Among the fifty-three people indicted in connection with the subversive work of a counterrevolutionary organization of engineers were the

Kolodub brothers. Unexpectedly, the court became very interested in the relations between one of the accused and his son. The accused, not suspecting a trap, testified that his son was a Komsomol member who left home because it was more convenient for him to live near the mines. He added that their relationship was quite normal. The father was in prison, unaware that meanwhile the following letter had been published in papers under the title, "Andrei Kolodub's Son Demands Severe Punishment For His Saboteur Father":

> Being a son of Andrei Kolodub, one of the conspirators, and at the same time being a Komsomol member and an active participant in the building of socialism in our country, I cannot condone the treasonous activities of my father and other criminals, who consciously destroyed all that was built by the energy and hard work of proletarian masses. I consider my father a rabid enemy and a hater of the workers, and I add my voice to the voices of all workers who demand a cruel punishment for the counterrevolutionaries. For the past two years I have not had any familial relations with the Kolodubs; I consider it shameful to bear the last name of Kolodub, and so I am changing it to Shakhtin ["shakhta" meaning "mine" in Russian].
>
> Signed: Worker of the mine "Proletarian Dictatorship," Kirill Kolodub.

The family was clearly in the Party's way. At that time there were many articles in the newspapers saying that in the new social order it would be necessary to separate children from their parents. An official circular for teachers, entitled "Childrens' Agricultural Labor," recommended that in order to destroy the nuclear family all children under the age of fourteen be supported by the commune and not by their parents.[12] It was impossible to fullfill this program primarily because of lack of funds.

The events in the Morozov family were a typical example of what was going on in the country. This family had about ten pairs of hands, all busy making bread. Then those hands disappeared. The cancer of betrayal metastasized, reaching into the lives of other families. The people who suffered because of one boy's actions could be counted in the tens of people, but those who fell victim to the denunciations of others numbered in the millions.

Usually, following a denunciation a case would be made against a single family member, most often the father or the grandfather. The other family members would not, however, be spared persecution. The sad irony of it all was that after denouncing his father the Pioneer hero became the "son of an enemy of the people," acording to the definition of the time, and thus liable to persecution himself. It should be mentioned in passing that around Gerasimovka there were scores of corrective institutions for such offspring.

The Shakhtinsk case mentioned above left its mark on all the following show trials, including that of the Gerasimovka peasants. Such cases were planned ahead of time, when the victims and members had no idea about their upcoming participation. The show trial of the case of Pavlik Morozov was prepared clandestinely by the Secret Political Section (SPS). In 1932 the powers of the OGPU were enlarged, and the ordinary police were now under the aegis of the secret police. The spider web of the SPS, especially created for finding and liquidating enemies of the people, embraced the entire country.

The show trials of the beginning of the thirties were spectacles for the masses. They were grandiose not only in the large audiences they attracted, but also in the number of the accused on trial at any one time. Before the trial, SPS agents did not look for the real culprit but, like casting agents, they sought the appropriate type for the part of a murderer or a saboteur. Then, with the help of denunciations, they created a "terrorist group" that consisted of the ideological leader and the founding father, his lieutenants who instigated the crime, the actual person who committed the terrorist act, and those who knew about it but did not inform. At first, a large group of suspects would be arrested and the selection would begin; the investigators sought those who could be broken and forced to inform against the others. Spare prisoners were later released, thus demonstrating the complete objectivity of the trial. Later on, they could be used in other show trials. As a rule, each case became a basis for further trials and accusations.

Children in such trials usually testified against their families. While in the Shakhtinsk case the role of the adolescent was marginal, when it was the Morozovs' turn the children, dead or alive, for the first time became the main accusers. The authorities believed the older generation should be destroyed by the new one, and mobilized to act on that belief.

The directive to complete collectivization in the Urals and Siberia by the fall of 1932 was not working out as planned. Moscow blamed the local government, and the central newspapers wrote about such topics as "dulled Bolshevik vigilance," leftists and rightists in the Party, and the Trotskyites' evil plans. Even though all of Trotsky's followers in the

Urals had been liquidated by 1932, and the struggle against the kulaks was at its highest point, up to that time no major conspiracies or important terrorist organizations had yet been discovered in the area. Such a conspiracy was, however, absoulutely essential.

Ivan Kabakov was thirty-eight years old when he was made the first secretary of the Ural Regional Party Committee; his predecessor, Shvernik, had not been decisive enough in dealing with the opposition and the kulaks. Their educational level was approximately the same; Shvernik had four years of elementary school and Kabakov was a metalworker. Having become the boss of the region, Kabakov, in his own words, set out "to kill Trotskyism." Mass arrests commenced in the cities. At a Party conference in Moscow, while describing his successes in the destruction of the Trotskyites, Kabakov insisted that the liquidation of the kulaks was the central issue of Party policy. The Regional Party Committee promised Moscow that it would collectivize 80 percent of the Ural peasants. Soon they reported that this was nearly completed, with 70 percent collectivized. Then an inspection showed these figures to be only 28.7 percent. The discovery of such deception, in those times, led to certain retribution.[13]

In order to make up for his misconduct, Kabakov, together with Chairman of the Regional Executive Committee Oshvintsev and the head of the authorized department of OGPU in the Urals, Reshetov, began a massive campaign against the villages. In a short time (two months) more than thirty thousand families were exiled, tried, or shot. The total number of victims, including women, children, and the elderly, reached into the hundreds of thousands. The main wave of this terror hit Gerasimovka, heretofore lost in the wilderness. Kabakov insisted that the Ural region was now working under the immediate direction of Comrade Stalin.[14] A directive was sent to the local governments from Sverdlovsk, the capital of the Urals, in April, 1932; it was concerned with the complete liquidation of capitalist elements, which would provide the rapidly developing heavy industry of the Urals with a powerful workforce. This industry would help create a second defense base in the eastern Soviet Union. The instruction quoted Kabakov: "[It is necessary] to uproot resistance inside the kolkhoz."[15]

Local practice, however, seldom supported general theory. There were simply not enough kulaks, so in order to provide the desired number of prisoners the SPS had to arrest the so-called kulaks' "helpers." This term was used to designate any poor peasant who, in theory, should love the Soviet government and yearn to join the kolkhoz, but who, in fact, did not. By prosecuting the kulaks' helpers the authorities rid themselves of discontent in the villages. Newspapers of the time wrote, "The kulaks' helpers and other traitors to Soviet power bawl, spraying saliva till they lose their voices...."[16] *Uralsky Rabochy* insisted that the kulaks and their helpers be shot wherever they were encountered. *Tavdinsky Rabochy* urged the villages to rid themselves of traitors, saboteurs, vagrants, and other suspicious types.

Lazar Baidakov remembers the time well:

> The OGPU looked for the weak points in the village. OGPU agents walked around the train station, pretending to be ordinary passengers, and watched for suspicious-looking people. While a peasant was boarding the train, they would grab him by the sleeve. They told him to come along and pushed him into a dark room. After a while, when he was scared enough, they would question him, ask him who said what against the Soviet government. So he would tell them anything about anybody, just to be rid of them.

The secret police were so deeply involved in the collectivization project that even agricultural plans were printed in OGPU print-shops.[17]

When Stalin sent his personal representatives to the provinces to punish the local authorities for their lack of eagerness, tensions in the Ural Party Committee and the OGPU rose sharply. People in the Party Committee already knew that in the Caucasus and the Kuban the head of the Central Control Commission, Kaganovich, had summarily expelled from the Party about half of the local cadre and enforced mass repressions in the villages. The same was done by the People's Commissioner Molotov in the Ukraine.[18] Fear of Moscow's emissaries forced local authorities to prepare for the arrival of such representatives in their area. Their preparations were soon rewarded; his name was Mikhail Suslov, and he was a representative of the Rabkrin (the Worker-Peasant Inspection). After Stalin's death, Suslov became the head ideologue of the Party, keeping the position for many years. A modest inspector at the time, though possessing wide emergency powers, he accused the local cadre of laziness and began a purge. Suslov demanded that a political show trial be immediately organized. As we know, such a trial soon took place.

In the wilderness, far from even the local capitals, this trial showed the whole world that Soviet power was victorious everywhere. The existence of kulak terrorists supported Stalin's thesis about the increase in the level of class struggle under socialism. The show trial accelerated the fulfillment of a failing grain-shipment plan from the Urals, and provided the basis for other political show trials and mass arrests. All this was done to provide the center of the country with grain and to supply Siberia with an unpaid workforce of prisoners.

The Morozov children's murder furnished a patent excuse to accuse all those whom the authorities wanted out of the village. The authorities were the ones who profited from the murder. Neither the investigators nor the court were interested in the guilt or innocence of the accused. But who was it that really killed Pavlik and Fedya Morozov?

Notes

1. Ordzhonikidze (1928: 69).
2. *Istoria SSSR* (1967, Vol. 8: 448, 557); Stalin (1933: 426–28); *Istoria VKP(b)* (1938: 290–91); *Istoria KPSS* (1960: 444).
3. Lenin (1963, vol. 37: 39; vol. 39: 279; vol. 43: 18).
4. *Kratkaya...* (1972, part 2: 240).
5. *Istoria KPSS* (1960: 440–41).
6. Ibid.
7. Antonov-Ovseenko (1980: 97).
8. *Pionerskaya Pravda* (27 January 1933).
9. *Istoria gosudarstva...* (1981: 81, 84, 88).
10. 3rd ed., vol. 12: 426.
11. *Pravda* (8, 24, 25 May; 30 June; 1, 6 July 1928).
12. *Detsky...* (1930: 6).
13. *Sverdlovskaya...* (1974: 73); *Klassovaya...* (1974: 115); *Shestnadtsaty...* (1930: 162); *Ocherki...* (1974, Vol. 2: 93, 96).
14. Kabakov (1930: 28, 37).
15. *Itogi...* (1932: 4–36).
16. Smirnov (17 December 1932).
17. *Postanovlenie...* (1933).
18. *Istoria SSSR* (1967: 589–90).

6

Posthumous Rehabilitation of the Innocent

Even though ten people were arrested for the murder of the Morozov brothers, it is worthwhile to investigate the participation of other people in the murder.

In print there was proof that Pavlik's killer was his father Trofim Morozov. The writer Victor Shklovsky, in a book published in 1973, maintained that Pavel "spoke out against his father and was killed by him."[1] The phrase "the father—the killer of his son" was often seen in print. But could the father have murdered his son?

During the time of the murder Trofim Morozov was imprisoned in the far north. He could have run away, if he had still been alive at the time. Some say that he wrote a letter to his wife and kids, not even knowing about the murder. If he had escaped, it seems unlikely that he would return to kill two of his own children. The writers who accused the father did not, as I found out, witness the event or know much about it. Their version is more likely of literary derivation (Saturn eating his own children; Abraham preparing to sacrifice Isaac; Taras Bulba, Nikolai Gogol's hero, who kills his own son for treachery). What is more, Shklovsky told me that he read of the father-killer scenario in a movie script.

Could Pavel have been killed by his own mother? This suspicion is not my creation. Tatyana was questioned on September 11 as a witness and on September 23 as a suspect; these records exist. "My kids were killed the third of September while I was not around, having left for Tavda the second of September, and it all happened in my absence," pointed out Morozova during the first questioning.

> Between August 31 and September 1, around midnight, someone came inside our yard, tried to open the door of the hut, but couldn't because the door was strong. It happened again between the first and the second—someone came at night, two male voices were heard. Our dog started barking at them, but then was quiet and

friendly. The dog lives with us and is going to live with Sergei and Danila Morozov, since they lived together.

Morozova couldn't recognize any of her family's voices, but declared that the grandfather and Danila came by, even though family lived in all the neighboring houses, and the dog ran around everywhere and, of course, knew everyone.

The mother's actions during these days might seem a little odd. From what the citizens of Gerasimovka had said, Pavel was threatened many times, especially towards autumn; there was a new harvest and the boy, once again, was caught up with telling who was stealing what and where. So Pavel gets beaten up. Then, for two nights in a row, unknown people break in, and on the following morning the mother goes to the city for a few days, leaving four young children alone, without leaving any food for them or notifying the police of her intended absence. On top of that, knowing the danger her son is in, she convinces him to go, in her absence, to the forest for berries with no companionship except for his little brother. Compounding this dereliction, the children expressed plans to spend the night in the taiga in a shelter made out of sticks and leaves.

Morozova left for Tavda to bring a calf to the purveying center there. Whether she brought the meat to sell on the free market or to the state procurement center, no one checked. If the calf was destined for the free market, then Tatyana's visit was just as illegal as those actions about which she and Pavel told the authorities. By the way, it isn't clear when she left—or when she came back. She wasn't in the village from the day of the murder to the day the bodies of the children were found.

"The mother was bad, uncaring and lazy," remembers her cousin Berkina. "Anyone who happened by fed the kids. The house was dirty, and the family's clothes torn—she not bothering to mend the holes. Afterwards, she hated Pavlik for causing the loss of her husband." Pavlik was threatened, and she could have helped him by sending him away to work or by putting him in an orphanage in the neighboring town. Back then this method of feeding a family was often employed by parents. The writer Musatov, in the journal *Vozhaty*, supported this idea; he maintained that the mother could easily have saved the boy by sending him to work in the city.[2]

Half a century later Morozova told me, "I saw them dead, grabbed a knife, wanted to kill the rest of the kids and myself, but they wouldn't let me, took the knife away. The kids were crying from fright.... At the trial

I said, 'Give me poison, judges, I am going to drink it.' I fell down and don't remember anything after that. They carried me out."

At the investigation Morozova easily agreed to go along with the official version of the murder and was ready to blame anyone. After questioning at the secret-political department of OGPU, her stories became more and more idealized. She remembered, for example, Pavlik's words, "I am at the point, like Lenin said, no steps backward, but forward—two steps at once." Lenin's quote says just the opposite ("one step forward, two steps back"), but what matters here is that Pavlik had become a loyal follower of Lenin. The obvious negligence on the part of the mother in the story of the death of her son definitely played a part in the masquerade. Those who built the case, however, liked the mother better as a victim. They also needed her in the role of witness for the prosecution. This is why, under OGPU manipulation, she went from witness to suspect, and then back to victimized witness.

There is even less reason to suspect Pavel's uncle Arseny Silin. In 1933 *Pioner* printed his picture along with those of the other people who were shot. In the booklet of Sverdlovsk museum he is called "the organizer and the perpetrator of the crime," and also declared to have been executed.[3] That is simply wrong. His guilt, in the prosecution's statement, was never proven: "In winter, 1932, Pavel Morozov told the committee that Arseny Silin, without fully completing his assignment, sold a wagonload of potatoes." It further stated that he was being tried under the same articles as those dealing with terrorist activites. Silin, just like Kulukanov, was on trial a second time (the first involved "the malicious seizing of surplus grain" one year earlier). Silin would not admit his guilt, but at one point, he cried and asked for forgiveness, "Pardon me, judges." Anna Tolstaya, who witnessed the trial, told me of this. Silin had nothing to do with the murder. The jury, to their credit, found him innocent in spite of the OGPU's desires. This was ignored by most of the press; it was as if finding a person innocent somehow compromised the Russian judicial system.

During one of the interrogations, the grandmother suddenly announced that her daughter Khima also tried to talk Danila into killing Pavlik. Khima, Arseny Kulukanov's wife, was nice to Pavel, although she lectured him on the evils of informing. They arrested her during the trial but then let her go. After that, she would hide in a cellar during the day, only coming out to get fresh air at night. She was that afraid they would arrest her again.

In trying to find a wider circle of those implicated in the murder, the prosecution conducted an investigation of the three Morozovs along with a farmer from a nearby village, Vladimir Mezyukhin. Pavlik knew that Grandpa Sergei hid grain at Mezyukhin's. After Pavlik informed on him, they searched his house, but couldn't find the grain. To add to the list of suspects, a theory was proposed that Mezyukhin violently retaliated for this. A week before the murder, Mezyukhin stopped by Morozov's house and stayed for dinner. During his visit, he gave Danila three stamps. The dinner gave the prosecution reason to believe it was a planning session for the murder, and the three stamps, advance payment for the crime. Curiously, all three—Danila, Grandmother, and Grandfather—eagerly supported the issue of Mezyukhin's guilt in this. Later, the investigator rejected the notion of Mezyukhin's participation. Possibly, all this was arranged to test the accuseds' willingness to testify to anything.

Many people were angry at Pavlik. Every person he informed against threatened to beat or to kill him. In the official records of the investigation, however, the only threatening remarks mentioned are those of the accused.

Pavlik's uncle Arseny Kulukanov was characterized as the major organizer and instigator by most of the Soviet press. Sometimes he was called "the main killer."[4] The question of Kulukanov's direct involvement in the murder was ignored by both the investigation and the trial. He was not in the forest the day of the murder. The main accusation consisted of the simple fact that that he was a kulak, as he owned more private property than most locals. Smirnov wrote in *Pionerskaya Pravda*, "Kulukanov played a big part, being one of the kulak leaders." Solomein in his first book referred to him by the less damning appellation of *serednyak* (one who owns a little parcel of land). Before republishing the book the author amended Kulukanov's status to that of a kulak.[5]

The newspapers wrote that Kulukanov had been tried and gotten ready to be sent away, his things had been prepared for confiscation, and he suffered the designated punishment. In the final court statement, however, it states that this punishment was not enforced. By the time of the Morozov trial, the unfortunate Kulukanov was obviously familiar with false accusation and the unfathomability of Soviet justice.

The primary basis for his guilt, as mentioned there, was that he feared "further reports to the secret police from Pavel Morozov." Kulukanov had reason to be afraid; the law had not protected him or anything belonging to him the first time. But the apolitical Kulukanov had no hatred towards the government. It was the government representatives who hated him and publicly insulted him. Kulukanov was Pavel's godfather. After Trofim left his family he took care of Trofim's children and offered them the warmth of his house, which stood across the street from the Morozovs' house. Kulukanov had reason to feel hurt by his godson, who repaid his kindness by informing on him. At the trial they made fun of Kulukanov's contradictory feelings to provide entertainment for the crowd. "Kulukanov insists on his version," reported one account of the trial. "He doesn't want to confess, he wants to play the fool." The newspaper account continues as follows:

> *Urin* (the court prosecutor): "Tell me, defendant Kulukanov, did you love Pavel?"
>
> *Kulukanov*: "I loved him."
>
> *Urin*: "If you did love him, then why didn't you search for him when he and his brother disappeared?"
>
> *Kulukanov:* "I…I…Well, I just simply didn't go, and that's all." (There is laughter from the crowd.)
>   Kulak Kulukanov wants to wiggle out of this situation by pretending to have a complete lack of knowledge abut the occurrences. But this trick won't work. His conspirators give him away.[6]

Is it possible to consider seriously the accusation that this man didn't go to search for Pavlik? Kulukanov was accused of talking others into committing the murder, as well as of paying thirty rubles for the murder, but there was neither money nor witnesses to this transaction. As regards the gold promised to Danila, it could be found only in the newspaper articles. Kulukanov did utter threats against his godson. While threats can be prosecuted by law, there must be sufficient evidence; and it is insufficient cause for execution, especially when concerning those made by relatives.

In the memories of those who knew him, Kulukanov was a hard-working farmer who had two horses and labored just as hard as his animals did. He hired helpers, fed them well, and gave them a fair portion of his harvest in return for their work. Kulukanov was illiterate, but he respected educated people. He housed the teacher who arrived in the province to open a school when no one else would. This teacher, Zoya Kabina, who had lived in his house, told me that "Yes, Kulukanov was against the confiscation of grain, but he did not take part in the murder!"

Understanding that the accusations did not have a solid enough basis, journalist Smirnov, over a month after the execution, in *Pionerskaya Pravda* added to Kulukanov's activities the following crimes: "There used to be Bible reading in his place, and he also made anti-revolutionary speeches."[7] Then he started a rumor in the village to the effect that the Kulukanovs burned their own house, not wishing to give it to the Soviets. In the press different versions of the story appeared, each worse than the next. Kulukanov killed his first wife and bribed a police officer to close the case. Kulukanov used to kill merchants in the forest—and this was how his wealth was made.[8] None of these allegations can be found in the official accusations, nor in any of the witnesses' testimonies.

During the investigation, Kulukanov would not admit to being guilty. The same occurred during the trial. It was written that Kulukanov "lost the gift of speech." It is more likely that he refused to give testimony, understanding well enough the nature of what was going on. Although Kulukanov was executed for murder, one can say with conviction that he never committed the crime.

Neither did the second accused, Ksenya Morozova, Pavel's grandmother, participate in the murder. The court verdict said that she had found out about the murder on the following day. She was executed as a conspirator for covering up the crime—in other words, for not informing. The cover-up consisted of the her soaking the blood-stained clothes and hiding the knife behind the icon. Such evidence raises doubts. It was later shown that the knife was hidden by Danila or the grandfather. As for the clothes, why did such an experienced woman, one who had spent time in prison in her youth, not bother to hide such incriminating evidence for three days? The grandmother helped Tatyana go through labor, and Pavlik was considered her favorite. Solomein did note that the grandmother hated communists. Ksenya did not hide her hatred; neither was she accused of it.

The accusations of Prosecutor Zyabkin were based on the testimony of her grandson, the witness Alexei Morozov. "Ksenya went for berries to the same place as Pavlik and Fedya," concluded Zyabkin. "Therefore, she could hold the children in the forest until the murderers would come."[9] What does "she could" mean? Did she hold them or not? Did she even go to the forest at all? The witness, a ten-year-old child, was at the time sitting in a locked cabin and obviously had no way of knowing this. A legend gave birth to the false idea in the press that the grandmother told the grandfather that Pavlik was going to go pick berries, that she enticed the kids into the forest so that the grandfather could kill them, and when there was a search for the children she purposely pointed "the wrong way." According to the final accusations, however, the children went to the forest by themselves and the grandmother knew nothing about it. The teacher Kabina said the following about Grandmother Ksenya: "She looked like Baba Yaga the witch, all dirty, shabby, and crazy. The village children were afraid of her. But guilty she was not."

Grandfather Sergei Morozov and his grandson Danila, in the concluding accusations, were named "executioners of terror." The grandfather's behavior during the investigation and the hearing seemed quite illogical. Sergei Morozov is named the "primary murderer," but it does not directly state whether he killed one or both of the children.

Grandfather Morozov certainly knew of Pavlik's activities. He would go around the village angrily saying that his grandson had shamed the family name. But a great distance exists between the threats of relatives and the act of murder. "No one beat Pavlik in front of me," Kabina told me. "And if there were threats, well, who doesn't threaten children?"

The accusations maintained that Sergei Morozov hated Pavlik for being a Pioneer. But Pavel wasn't a Pioneer. On the other hand, the grandfather could have hated his grandson for causing his son, who was supposed to take care of him in his old age, to be taken away. Such a feeling could be quite natural given the circumstances. Antonov, the correspondent for the paper *Na Smenu!*, having been in the court room, at one point explained things differently; apparently, the grandfather hated Pavel's mother, Tatyana, because her improper conduct had resulted in the divorce from Trofim. From this, the journalist drew the conclusion that personal hatred developed on the grounds of a family conflict and "grew into a class conflict."[10]

Solomein recorded another accusation; Grandfather Morozov didn't love the Soviet government and spoke up against the collective farms. The tall, slender, white-bearded Sergei Morozov did, as told by those who knew him, like to joke about the Soviet government. He used to come to the local village officials saying, "Comrades, the Soviet wolves ate my colt!"

"What do you mean, Soviet?"

"What else? The colt was mine, but the wolves were Soviet. After all, they live in the Soviet forest."[11] However, all this was only words. He never took any actions against the collective farm because collective farms did not exist during his time. According to the verdict, Sergei Morozov was "a poor peasant, the proprietor of one horse, one cow, and one acre of land." Later, in the newspaper he was called a kulaks' helper and then a kulak himself. The kulak title was necessary to explain the murder's arising from class hatred.

As a former policeman the grandfather couldn't help but know that murder is a serious crime, whether judged by old laws or new. Of course, he recognized the possible consequences. In the forest he could have easily destroyed all incriminating evidence. All his actions went contrary to this logic. He murders the children near the village, right on the road, as if for the specific purpose that passersby would notice the bloodstains and the pile of cranberries spilled from the sack. He doesn't carry away the corpses further down to the swamp, where they would have disappeared, but leaves them in sight. In bloodstained clothes, together with Danila, he appears in the village (possibly only Danila's clothes are stained—it isn't known). The knife—the primary material evidence—he carefully brings with him. Grandpa Sergei doesn't even wipe the blood from it. This indicates that he was carrying the knife in his hands, wrapped so carefully that the bloodstains are preserved. Then he puts the knife in such a place that, during the search of a peasant house, the searchers cannot help but look—behind the icon. What kind of murderer has the main goal of leaving behind as much evidence as possible?

Could Sergei and Danila not have had time to cover up the traces of the crime immediately? They had three days to do so, carefully and calmly. Why did the grandfather have to kill the second grandson? Yes, Fyodor was also an informer, but without Pavel it is unlikely that he would have presented much danger. The investigation, the court, and the press put forth a possible reason; they killed the younger boy fearing the existence of a witness. No, the murderer consciously strove to commit an atrocity, a crime against society.

The season during which the murder took place seems to confirm the grandfather's guilt. The informer is killed in the fall, when the entire village, while filling their storage places with grain, anticipates the next government robbery. They try to hide everything they can, so there will be enough for winter and the children won't starve. The murder could have been, in its own way, an act of self-defense. Revenge would make a fine example to other traitors of peasants' interests. People should know that traitors get what they deserve; those who could have been informed on by Pavel tomorrow sleep peacefully today. Statistics also conspired against Sergei Morozov, maintaining that a large percentage (almost half) of the murders in Russia were committed by a relative. Nonetheless, few facts confirm this data.

Who was capable of bringing Pavel to his senses, explaining that informing is harmful? The father? Trofim had already fallen victim to the evils of informing. The mother? She assisted her son in the project. The teacher? She was constrained by her position. Only the grandfather tried to turn his grandson away from this mean spirited and dangerous pursuit. He did try, but with little success. Does this mean that he decided to kill his grandson? Nor was Sergei just unlucky with Pavel. The grandfather saw that in reality the main informer of the village was his other grandson, from his daughter Ustinya, Ivan Potupchik.

Elena Rostovshchikova wrote in *Tavdinskaya Pravda* thirty-five years later, "Vanya Potupchik stood out especially for his abilities and energy."[12] Ustinya Potupchik, judging by the memoirs of Solomein, had this to say:

One time, old man Morozov came in angry.

"Where's Vanya?"

"Singing songs outside with his buddies."

"Damn you! You had to give birth to a fool. He's so big, but so dumb.... He keeps snooping around, trying to see who's hiding grain.... Got none of his own, but why take away someone else's?"

This episode was moved from Solomein's memoirs into his book, naturally without the knowledge of the mother. What matters here is that if the old man knew that twenty-year-old Ivan was the serious informer, why did he have to kill two small children? Would that have stopped the denunciations?

According to the investigators' account, the day after the murder, Sunday, the old man went to see his oldest son, also Ivan, in the neighboring village to let him know that the deed had been done. This account was later used as evidence in accusing Ivan of being an accomplice. However, in the testimony given by the witnesses and recorded by Solomein immediately upon his arrival in the village, we find quite an important refutation of the allegation: "Morozov came home on Sunday evening with policeman Titov." So it turns out that the old man brought an officer of the law into the village to look for his grandsons even before the mother got back. Thus, according to the report of a fellow villager, the search for the missing grandsons was initiated thanks to the grandfather. For some reason, this fact never appeared in the court records.

From the beginning, the villagers did not consider Old Man Morozov to have been involved in the case. No one took seriously his threats against Pavel. "Having been imprisoned," assures Baidakov, a distant relative of the Morozovs, "the family elder commanded everyone to deny everything before the court proceedings even began. He denied not only his own involvement, but the guilt of all the others arrested as well. Then they started to beat him."

"Even before he was arrested he was beaten half to death," remembers Tatyana Morozova. "Ivan Potupchik especially excelled at this. At the OGPU they were also beaten, so they confessed."

"At the interrogations they threatened to shoot them where they stood," stated the teacher Kabina. "They did not understand what was wanted of them, and would say anything at all in order not to be beaten."

"They kept dragging them to the interrogations," affirms Pavel's classmate Matryona Korolkova. "Sometimes they would confess, and sometimes they wouldn't. The old man was tortured."

As a result of the tortures and the beatings, the prosecution won; before the court, the old man took the murder upon himself.

Tatyana Morozova told me, "In court, the old man stated, 'Your Honors, as I was questioned fifteen guns lay on the table. They hit me with the gun handles till I was half-dead.' The judge asked, 'Who was doing the hitting?' 'The same kind of people as you, only with guns.'"

This is how Solomein describes the end of the trial: "With his head completely shaved, old man Morozov did not look like himself. He spoke quietly. One minute he'd confess everything, and the next minute he'd start clamming up. His answers were muddled. He would frown, wave his hand hysterically, 'It's all the same to me now.... Judge faster.'"

The newspaper report taken from the courtroom reads, "Old man Morozov is trying to make himself look like jesus [newspapers at that time printed Christ's name in lower case letters]. He says, 'I take all sin upon myself as jesus christ did at the trial in Palestine.'" Christ, it is known, was not guilty, and the old man's allusion is quite resonant.

But there are other accounts of the old man's behavior. Later, the writer Yakovlev maintained that the old man never did admit that he committed the murder: "'I didn't even go into the woods, just rested on my couch all day.' 'Then who did the killing?' 'Do I know? I don't know anything.'"

Antonov also maintained that the old man never admitted guilt in court, and that he completely denied the evidence presented at the trial. Antonov wrote, "The mother is crying...The old man is crying, too, but he stays firm and continues to deny his participation in the murder."[13] Neither the judges, nor the prosecutor, nor the witnesses could present any concrete proof that the old man killed anyone. Did anything besides the torture and the beatings cause the hesitations in Sergei Morozov's behavior during the trial? His story changed only because of his grandson Danila, whose testimony was considered major evidence.

"Danila was a little fool," Tatyana Morozova told me. "There was nothing good in him," said Korolkova. "You could trust him as far as you could throw him. But he was not stupid." In Solomein's writing I found the following: "Danila Morozov was short, sullen. He spoke poorly with people...didn't hang out much with the young crowd. Didn't go out with girls." Berkina insists that Danila was "not quite all there." His teachers stated otherwise. Pozdnina assures me that Danila took an interest in his studies and, unlike Pavlik, did not speak Russian badly. At first he even acted as interpreter between the Russian teacher and the Belorussian students. He also treated his cousin Pavlik well. The teacher Kabina remembers similarly:

> Danila and Pavlik studied together in the same class. Danila was not at all like he is portrayed. He was not a bully and he was not a gloomy moron. He mowed the hay, plowed. He was a cheerful, working-class boy—slightly simpleminded. He was of robust build, not too tall, kinder and more generous than Pavlik. Even if he did fight, it was just like all teenagers. Contrary to what is written about him, Danila did not drink. They drank rarely in villages back then, the youth even less frequently. They could not make moonshine because there was not enough grain.

Danila, the son of Ivan who went to live in the neighboring village, was brought up and raised by his grandparents, with whom he lived for about six years. His grandfather was planning on leaving everything he had to Danila. The press called Danila a "kulak" but that is absurd.[14] Danila had absolutely no property of his own even though he was industrious, healthy, and, when grown up, became the support of his older surviving relatives.

The teacher Kabina assured me, "During those days Danila had disappeared." When the arrests started, acting on his grandfather's advice, he ran away to his father Ivan in the neighboring village. Danila was

quickly arrested, but it is unlikely that the grandfather would have tried
to destroy his favorite grandson. According to the investigator, however,
that is exactly how it happened.

"At the time of the arrest," it says in the case, "they were both sitting
in the village Soviet's barn, where the old man Sergei Morozov instigated his grandson Danila Morozov into testifying at the interrogation
that allegedly he, Danila Morozov, killed the Pioneer Morozov, Pavel
and his brother Fyodor." The word "allegedly" shows that it was clear to
the investigator from the very beginning that Danila did not kill the boys,
and the investigator immediately began to pressure the inexperienced
Danila toward exposing his grandfather.

In reality, when the arrested men were being taken from the village to
Tavda, the grandfather again tried to save his grandson. When they had
scarcely reached the forest, the old man whispered something to him, and
Danila took his knapsack off one shoulder in order to throw it off and
dart away. Solomein recorded one witness's testimony, which states that
one of the convoys ordered, "Put it back on, scum, or I'll shoot you from
behind."

Sitting in the holding cell, at first Danila obeyed his grandfather's order
and denied everything. Then, according to the memoirs of Baidakov, who
refers to the stories of the plenipotentiary of the District Committee, Danila
was taken to a separate cell and a prison informer was brought in. The spy
started making friends with Danila, telling him that he had connections on
the outside. And, these "connections" brought the snitch vodka and food,
and both men had a few good drinks. The snitch stressed that Danila would
be shot for sure, but that he might be spared if he would only testify against
his grandfather and the others. The old man would die soon anyway, but
he, Danila, had a long life ahead of him. Still Danila did not back down.

Then Danila was taken over by Bykov, a more experienced plenipotentiary of the secret-political department of the OGPU. Unlike the previous investigators, he had spoken to Danila without threats or abuse at
the interrogations. From Bykov, Danila heard that his grandfather had
named him as the murderer. This trick of the court is as old as time, but
the inexperienced Danila took the bait, testifying against his grandfather
and also, ironically, against himself. A face-to-face confrontation was
set up between them, at which Danila accused his grandfather of being
anti-Soviet and a murderer, while the grandfather, enraged by his
grandson's treachery, claimed that the murderer was Danila. This was

exactly what the investigators were after. In a "Special Note on the Terror Problem," and in reporting the success of the interrogations, all indications of Danila's guilt are absent:

> At the 9/16/32 interrogation of Morozov, Danila, the former testified that the murders of the Pioneer Morozov and his brother were committed by Morozov, Sergei, only because Morozov, Pavel, as a Pioneer, was active in the measures conducted by the Soviet powers and by the Party in the village, and, apart from that, he told the authorities about the old man's kulak tricks. Morozov, Sergei, has always maintained and still keeps up a close relationship with the local kulaks, and is hostile toward Soviet power. When the old man saw the children before the murder indicated above, he habitually threatened them with the words, "Just wait, communist pups, I'll come across you somewhere. Then I'll show you—*I'll take care of you* [italicized in the original]." This he would say in the presence of Tatyana (the children's mother), his wife Morozova, Ksenya, and his grandson Morozov, Danila.

The trial immediately started to move, and Danila became irreplaceable to the investigators. Face-to-face confrontations started coming one after the other. All of the accused denied their guilt; in response, Danila accused all of them himself. Even when he became confused, the investigators would point him in the right direction. That he was housed in a separate cell from the rest also proves that he assisted the prosecution. Even more important, all those political considerations that would be needed for a future show trial were added to Danila's testimony. It became clear that the case was almost ready. The dates prove this as well. Danila gave the necessary evidence against his grandfather on September 16, while on the next day a secret note was sent "upstairs" about the victory. That same day, it was triumphantly reported in the regional newspaper *Smena* (The New Generation) that the investigation was over.

"One has the impression of a simple, quiet country boy," it states in the account of the judicial session. "Standing in front of the judge's table, he said, 'The old man mixed up a lot of things here, saying the truth and lies, admitting guilt, then denying it. I will tell everything like it was.'" The journalist Antonov wrote in *Na Smenu!* that in two and a half months of interrogation Danila reported five or six different versions of the crime, and each time he took back his words.[15] Danila's numerous inventions and retractions caused the court little awkwardness. On the contrary, Danila turned out to be a wonderful find; he neatly signed everything that they placed on the table in front of him, and willingly repeated what they told him to repeat.

In light of Danila's behavior, the grandfather's line of reasoning becomes more understandable. Having lived at liberty throughout the betrayal of three grandsons—Ivan Potupchik, Pavel, and Fyodor—Sergei Morozov defended the remainder of the family. Danila was his last hope, his support, his confederate. And here his fourth grandson sold him to the wolves. This was an unexpected turn of events, and it broke the old man.

We can only imagine the fierce injustice that Danila felt when he received a death sentence just like all the others. But Danila's life was not cut short. The teacher Kabina told me:

> In Gerasimovka there is no post office, not even a mailman. Whoever came out from the city would bring letters and they would lie on the table in the village Soviet. No one would touch the letters—everyone in the village was illiterate. After the trial it was reported in the newspapers that the murderers had been executed. About three months passed. One time I was looking through the mail at the village Soviet. I saw a strange envelope: a sheet of paper torn out of a book, folded and sewn with thread on the side; my last name and address were written above. I opened the letter, started to read, and could not believe my eyes. Danila wrote that the old people had been shot, but that he was still alive. And the letter itself proved that he was indeed alive: I immediately recognized Danila's handwriting—he had been my student!

"So where is this letter?" I asked Kabina, having visited her in the Leningrad hospital where she was staying after having had a cataract removed.

"At first I kept it, but then I got scared. They had officially announced that he was dead, and here I had proof that it was a lie. So I destroyed the letter."

"So why was he not executed?"

"Why execute free labor?"

The teacher Pozdnina later confirmed that Danila had not been executed "for the great help [he had] rendered to Soviet power." Instead, he was given a life sentence to a labor camp in the lumber industry. His last name was changed to Kniga (a very common last name in Belorussian villages). The teacher was told this story by prisoners who had obtained their freedom.

Notes

1. Shklovsky (1973: 237).
2. Musatov (September 1962).

3. *Pioner* (May/June 1933); *Pavlik Morozov* (1968).
4. Antonov (30 November 1932).
5. Smirnov (9 January 1933); Solomein (1933: 8).
6. *Tavdinsky Rabochy* (28 November 1932).
7. Smirnov (9 January 1933).
8. Gubarev (January 1940: 7).
9. *Tavdinsky Rabochy* (30 November 1932).
10. Antonov (28 November 1932).
11. Solomein (eyewitness testimony).
12. Rostovshchikova (27 August 1967).
13. Solomein (1979: 107); *Tavdinsky Rabochy* (28 November 1932); Yakovlev (1938: 120); Antonov (28 November 1932).
14. Aleksin (20 December 1952).
15. Antonov (28 November 1932).

7

Who was the Real Murderer?

In the course of my private inquiry time and again I encountered obstacles that impeded the search. Chekist agents were involved in both the investigation and the show trial, but the OGPU is mentioned in neither the trial nor the press in connection with the murder of the Morozov children. Observers and readers can only guess at who conducted the investigation, as well as how and where. It is curious that this very organization, acting in secret, strove to make the trial as noisily public as possible.

When did the OGPU begin to investigate the murder? From the Special Note on the Terror Problem included in the File of Investigation No. 374, it is obvious that OGPU District Commissioner Bykov "took over the case from the militia" and began the interrogation of Sergei and Danila Morozov on September 16, 1932, ten days after the bodies were discovered. The following day Bykov reported to Sverdlovsk by special courier that the district apparatus was preparing for a trial.

Bykov was inaccurate. His subordinate, Special Branch Assistant Commissioner Kartashov, took up the case for the OGPU on September 13, as is obvious from another document. But even Kartashov had drafted the Minutes of Meeting No. 4 after he had already begun working. As early as September 12, Kartashov spoke at a meeting he held in the village of Gerasimovka and sent his superior Bykov this document. The text reads that "the murder of the Morozov brothers was carried out according to the previously outlined plans of a group of foreign elements (kulaks and their yes-men)," and that "the group accomplished their plan to stab both the Morozov brothers several times with a knife." At the meeting it was determined to ask that a proletarian court come to the locale so that this "group of foreign elements [would] be brought to trial under the highest penalty of social defense, execution." At the same time, the illiterate peasants, knowing that there were no Young Pioneers or Komsomols in the village, reported to the higher authorities that in honor of the dead Pioneer Pavel, Chukhontsev, Yudov, Ivan Potupchik, and four others of the twenty-two people present enrolled in the Komsomol. At the bottom of the Minutes of Meeting No. 4 there is an interesting signature: "Copy verified by OGPU Dist. Com. Bykov." The document, also concerning the timely organization of a kolkhoz there, was sent on to the higher authorities awaiting it.

This means that on September 12 the OGPU initiated a kolkhoz and that Kartashov addressed the meeting, demanding the execution of the murderers in the name of the community. In the document, he formulated all of the political phrases that went into the prosecution's findings and the press lexicon for years to come. But that isn't all. Bykov himself conducted the first interrogation of Tatyana Morozova the day before the meeting, on September 11.

Now let us examine more fully the enigmatic document that I un-earthed, "Interrogation Record for the File No. —." The case number is not included, since it had not yet been formally established, but a place for the number is set aside. The interrogator indicated his name and rank, "Asst. Commissioner Kartashov." For Ivan Potupchik, "education: el-ementary; candidate of the All-Union Communist Party...relation to the suspect, and/or victim: none." Potupchik is also "the party questioned in the capacity of witness." Actually, the party questioned was the grand-son of Sergei Morozov and the cousin of Pavlik Morozov.

In the report, Ivan Potupchik intimated that the murder was commit-ted "for political reasons, being that Pavel Morozov was a Young Pio-neer and activist. He frequently appeared at town meetings and spoke in favor of Soviet power, as well as against the Gerasimovka kulaks." Fur-ther, it lists the heroic exploits of the Young Pioneer and activist in hav-ing unmasked anti-Soviet activities and perpetrators.

The strangest thing about the secret document, however, is the date: September 4, 1932. This detail stands out because neither the village residents nor the police knew about the murder before September 6. It seems odd that two men, OGPU Special Branch Assistant Commissioner Kartashov and his informant, a twenty-year-old country boy who only had just acquired Party candidacy, Ivan Potupchik, knew all the details of the case as much as two days earlier.

On September 4, the bodies are still lying in the woods. For the next forty-eight hours, villagers searched for the children. By some coincidence, they "just happened" to be found by Potupchik. "I was the first to find them," Potupchik proudly spoke of his heroism a half century later, not suspecting that I knew about the secret document. Of course he was first: he knew exactly where to look. It seems the villagers were trying to secure the arrival of an investigator in Gerasimovka, not knowing that one was already in their midst. Forty-eight hours before the discovery of the bodies, Kartashov had already questioned the witness Potupchik, and the paper was ready, down to the perpetrators' names. The murderers named were the very persons of anti-Soviet persuasion later to be executed; for the time being they were unaware they had killed two children. Potupchik would actively participate in their arrest. Although not a word in the document suggests when or how the murder was committed, it is definite in stating that the murder was political and of a class nature, "inspired by kulak agitation." The murder victim is declared a Young Pioneer and activist, that is, a representative of a revolutionary organization. Everything was in readiness for the show trial.

A serious accusation thus falls upon the witness Ivan Potupchik, policeman Yakov Titov, and two OGPU investigators, Kartashov and Bykov. I was able to locate two of the four, Potupchik and Kartashov.

What is known about Ivan Potupchik? "Ivan was already an adult when he went to school," Korolkova remembers. "He was in Kabina's class with Pavel and me. And later he married her. He lived with her a year or two and left her." In the aforementioned protocol of the interrogation, Potupchik is called "single," meaning he married the teacher after the murder. "Vanka in his whole life never ate his fill at home, so he goes digging up pits in other people's yards," his grandfather Sergei Morozov said of him in Solomein's book, *Pavka the Communist*.[1] The teacher, Kabina, told me that "Ivan was often in Tavda on business, but he kept an eye on his neighbors in the village. He was strong and energetic, the first one in the village to become a Party member. He kept a rifle at home. He loved carrying out orders at night. He'd come by people's houses: 'Get dressed! Take the grain to Tavda!' The sleepy muzhiks were frightened and would do it." Before Arseny Kulukanov was arrested Potupchik personally threatened to send him to a camp. In the November 21, 1932 newspaper *Tavdinsky Rabochy* (The Tavda Worker), I found two denunciations of people from Gerasimovka. One is anonymous, signed, "I know"; the other is signed by Ivan Potupchik.

Ivan had his reasons for the anger he felt toward his grandfather. Ustinya, Ivan's mother, told Solomein that Sergei Morozov would come to her, demanding that his grandson stop the denunciations against their neighbors. Ustinya recounted one conversation to her son. According to Solomein, he did not take the news kindly: "You know what he needs?" Vanka shouted. "Does he need a grave? I'll dig it. I know what to do. Nobody orders me around!"

In Ivan Potupchik's apartment on Lenin Avenue in central Magnito- gorsk, when I called upon him a portrait of Stalin stood in a prominent place. By my next visit the portrait had been removed. Potupchik spoke slowly (he had recently suffered a stroke). He complained of how inci- dental people grabbed the glory from the true heroes of collectivization. He carefully recounted details, trying to clarify what I already knew. I could not be sure, but it seemed to me that he was on the lookout and trying to avoid suspicion.

Potupchik gladly told how the policeman Titov and he organized the search of the woods, and how it was he who first found the bodies of the children: "Only the murder sites, where there are two obelisks to Pavlik and Fedya, are false. The real site of the incident was about a kilometer deeper in the woods. It was there in the tall grass where the old man and Danila stabbed them to death. No murderer would try to kill someone any closer to the village."

I asked him the date when the murdered children were found, as well as the date when the first protocol was written. Potupchik was ready with an answer. "You can forget a lot in fifty years," he said. "The dates in the newspapers aren't exact. The children were killed on September 3, that's correct, but they weren't found right away. Then a group of inves- tigators from Sverdlovsk came and immediately announced that 'a ter- rorist act took place here.' They interrogated half the village. Well, I, of course, took part and helped out. They took those I pointed out. No sort of experts were needed, it was that clear."

Potupchik said that he was soon promoted from candidacy to full Party membership, and then, shortly after the trial, he was sent to serve in a punitive OGPU division. "It was done for my service in collectiviza- tion," he added.

Much has been written about Ivan Potupchik. He was a honorary citizen of Gerasimovka as well as a honorary Pioneer. The newspapers even referred to him as the investigator who broke the Pavlik Morozov murder case. In 1961, the respected Pioneer disappeared from public view because he was convicted of the rape of a teenage girl. Through an act of special amnesty, Potupchik returned to freedom without having served his full sentence. After camp he was again well provided for, with a position in the personnel department. Such cadre work is often connected with the KGB. The newspapers renewed their praise of his heroism, but his criminal record followed him and eventually they dropped him. Magnitogorsk Criminal Department Investigator Yakovenko, whom I questioned regarding Potupchik, knew him well: "A respected Pioneer raped a Young Pioneer. As a rule, such people commit crimes repeatedly without getting caught." I was finishing work on this book when I learned that Ivan Potupchik had died.

I now come to the second figure on the list of officials: the policeman, or more precisely, District Inspector Yakov Titov.

> I, district inspector of the 8th District of the Police Directorate Titov, have taken the report-statement of citizen Pavel Morozov, under oath against perjury in accordance with Article 95 of the 1932 Criminal Code. On the 27th of August at nine O'clock in the morning, I, Pavel Morozov, went to Sergei Morozov's for my saddle girth. There, Danila Morozov beat me and said, that I'm going to kill you in the forest. I've nothing more to say. The words of this report, which I am signing, were correctly recorded and read to me out loud—Morozov. The report was taken by the district inspector of the 8th District—Titov.

This statement is included in the File of Investigation No. 374, although Pavlik's mother at first confirmed that he did go to the police but later that he did not. Titov knew that he had an OGPU case on his hands. He also understood that if he did not find the guilty parties he could instantly find himself on the bench of the accused along with those who finished off Pavel, and Titov certainly wanted to protect himself. This concern was understandable; not long before the trial the reporter V. Mor wrote in *Uralsky Rabochy* (The Ural Worker), "Either out of political shortsightedness or for other reasons, the district policeman did not look into the matter sooner."[2] What could these "other reasons" have been? Did they involve Yakov Titov's negligence, his reluctance to get involved in a "dirty" case, his complicity in the murder of a teenager who did not give his village room to breathe?

In the beginning the policeman took part in the investigation, but later he was quickly pushed aside. Then he was put on trial by the investigators. Subsequently the court found Titov criminally responsible for failing to defend Pavlik from the kulaks. Thus, he was incriminated not for negligence in the line of duty but for political shortsightedness. District

Inspector Yakov Titov was arrested shortly after the show trial. According to Ivan Potupchik, OGPU Special Branch Assistant Commissioner Kartashov took a special interest in the business: "Kartashov didn't like Titov because he stuck his nose in Kartashov's case," Potupchik said. It's not to be ruled out that Titov suspected or knew something about the murder and that Kartashov wished to dispose of him. Titov was tried by the Ural military tribunal. He got seven years, served his time, and returned to live in Tavda. He died long before my arrival. Titov was not a participant in the death of the Morozov brothers.

The reader may recall that the first secret documents from the investigation into the case of the children's murder are signed by OGPU workers Kartashov and Bykov. No matter how hard I searched, I never managed to find these names in the press from that time. Nor did any of the eyewitnesses, including Ivan Potupchik, substantiate these names. Once, a middle-aged librarian in Sverdlovsk took a newspaper clipping from a folder and gave it to me. She was keeping the clipping for the next exhibit dedicated to the Young Pioneer hero. Beneath the article entitled "His Song Will Not Die," and published in the small Ural city (not far from Tavda) of Irbit's newspaper *Voskhod* (Sunrise), was the signature "S. Kartashov."

Thirty-one years after the murder, on September 3, 1963, the OGPU investigator suddenly began to talk about himself in the newspaper. Putting aside the grandiose verbosity of the article, let us take note of some important new details expressed therein. The investigator reported that Fyodor was killed by the butt of an axe and that the bodies were laid "side by side." He wrote that Danila found the murdered boys and started to yell, having decided that it would remove any suspicion from himself. And most importantly, the article contends that Pavlik and his brother went into the woods and were killed, not on September 3, as was always assumed, but twenty-four hours earlier. Kartashov is the only person who gave this date.

Why at that time did Kartashov, having painstakingly avoided the limelight, suddenly speak up about his service, and not on the occasion of a more conspicuous anniversary, but thirty-one years later? Had he decided that over time articles about the case had grown stale? Or had Khrushchev's thaw set his memories free? Doubtful. The main reason was that Kartashov had just turned sixty, and he was trying to apply for a special pension. To do this, the aging invalid who had long since been dismissed from the security apparatus needed to prove his distinguished service to the Party, but he had little documentation at hand to do so. Here, the calculations of the experienced Chekist proved to be accurate; a special pension was granted to him.

In the welter of fiftieth anniversary articles about the exploits of the Young Pioneer hero, Kartashov's name appeared a second time. The Sverdlovsk writer in the magazine honored Spiridon Kartashov as the old Chekist "to whom we are indebted for having made the case of Pavlik Morozov's murder known throughout Soviet Russia."[3] For the first time in an interview, then, it was openly said that the Morozov case had been taken up by the OGPU. Kartashov recalled that he learned of the Morozov murder while he was in the neighboring village of Gorodishcha on another matter. Curious as to whether Titov had started an investigation, and learning he had not, Kartashov went to Gerasimovka. He arrested everyone involved, and overnight they all confessed.

In 1982 I went to visit Spiridon Kartashov in Irbit. Sitting with me in his cluttered, squalid room, which resembled a flophouse, and recalling his life, the special pensioner Kartashov declared, "I was full of hatred, but at first I didn't know how to kill. I learned. During the Civil War I served in a Special Action Squad. We used to catch Red Army deserters in the woods and execute them on the spot. Once we caught two White officers, and after shooting them I was ordered to trample them with my horse to see whether they were dead. One was alive and I finished him off." Another time, Kartashov was serving in Odessa on a border unit, and with a group of Chekists he detained a ship full of people trying to escape the Bolsheviks. They were all lined up along the shore and shot. Then came collectivization, and Kartashov, having risen from a common soldier to an OGPU special branch assistant commissioner, was sent to Tavda. He was given a duty quota of how many people to dekulakize. Kartashov recalled how he and some soldiers from a punitive battalion herded well-to-do peasants from all over the district into a church under guard. From there they were sent without trial into exile. "Collectivization was being carried out any way possible," he recalled. "Once I rounded up some self-sustaining peasants, took them into a large room, and whoever didn't want to go into a kolkhoz had to sit in on the meeting under the muzzle of my carbine until they agreed." Kartashov always carried two revolvers, one in his holster and a spare in his bag.

In 1932, the OGPU district apparatus received secret orders to find out who in the villages were anti-Soviet and who were against collectivization. Next to their names on a list was put the letter "T" for "terror." Kartashov began to visit Gerasimovka frequently because no one there wanted to join the kolkhoz. Ivan Potupchik and two others were his informants there.

"On the night of September 11 (a new date, but not September 13, as in the magazine), I went to Gerasimovka and stayed at Potupchik's apartment," Kartashov said. "The children were already buried and all that was left was to try the murderers. Potupchik himself didn't arrest anyone. He acted as my informant. He only found the bodies. Persons of an anti-Soviet persuasion already on the lists with the letter T, it was they who killed the children. I never went to the murder site because everything was already clear. There wasn't any autopsy. The perpetrators had confessed, so why bother checking?"

Kartashov ordered a guard from Tavda for the prisoners. Five soldiers arrived and then transported the arrested peasants to Tavda. "The transfer of the enemies of Soviet power to the town went quite well," Kartashov said. "And then a meeting was also called to register peasants for the kolkhoz."

I asked the assistant commissioner about his boss.

"Bykov as a rule didn't ever go to Gerasimovka," Kartashov answered. "He ran things from the district center. Without me, Bykov couldn't have handled this case. Instead, he commanded us from Sverdlovsk and Nizhny Tagil. After that, Bykov didn't work much longer and disappeared."

"Where did he disappear to?"

"Where everyone else did. That's the kind of job we had."

Following this exchange, Spiridon Kartashov showed me his OGPU citation. It expressed thanks for his "devotion, discipline, and steadfastness in the fulfillment of his service obligations."

Much has been erased from Kartashov's memory over the last half century, but let's forgive the district OGPU assistant commissioner for his desire to take all the credit in the murder investigation. The authors of books about Pavel Morozov forgot him entirely, and Kartashov's work in those years was not easy: "I figure," he said modestly, "that thirty-seven people were shot dead by me personally, and I sent even more to the camps. I can kill people so that the shot won't be heard."

"How?" I asked, taken aback.

"The secret's this: I make them open their mouth and I shoot down their throat. I'd only be splashed by warm blood, like *eau de cologne*, and it doesn't make a sound. That I can do—kill. If I didn't have seizures, I wouldn't have taken my pension so soon. I had seizures even before the war, but I didn't pay them any mind. And then during the war I went into the hospital."

His medical records state that Kartashov's epilepsy is aggravated by nervous exhaustion.

I asked about the Interrogation Record of 4 September.

"I don't remember any such thing," Kartashov answered. "Potupchik is lying. I was in Tavda during those days, with Bykov. I went to Gerasimovka on September 11."

Our conversation came to an end after midnight and Kartashov, despite my objections, insisted on seeing me to my hotel. He rummaged through some old rags and tucked an army knife in his belt under his jacket. "It's German," he said. "Fine steel. Around here it happens that we sometimes have mischief-makers on the streets. You walk ahead of me and I'll be behind you." We walked about twenty minutes in pitch darkness. I felt better when a streetlight near the hotel was within sight. Through the stairwell I caught sight of Kartashov as he went up to the night clerk and wrote something down on a scrap of paper. It was probably information about me.

Let's go back again to the meetings in Gerasimovka in the fall of 1932, when the theoretical base of the terror conducted against the peasants was put into law. Political murder was sanctioned from above. "In the struggle against the enemies of Soviet power," *Pravda* read, "we do not shy away from viciousness."[4] Four months before the Morozovs' murder, in Moscow an attempt was made on the German ambassador's life. The assassins were being held by the OGPU, and it was announced that they were acting on orders from Poland. In reality, however, they were secret OGPU agents providing kindling for igniting the conflict between Germany and Poland. The very same method, murder according to OGPU orders, was later used to kill Party leader Sergei Kirov. There are too many similar incidents to count.

Ten days before Pavlik and Fedya's murder, a decision made by the Soviet government came out resolving to deal with kulaks, their underlings, and speculators on the spot—without a trial or the possibility of amnesty. Appealing the illegality of this was forbidden; in many places,

OGPU tyranny was the only law. A show trial in the Urals called for a show murder. But in Gerasimovka, where the secret-political district apparatus had to organize a trial, there really was no crime. The peasants living there were peaceful; they didn't want to kill one another. So they needed help.

Let's try to imagine how the murder was carried out.

The investigation, the court, and the press did such a considerable amount of work that the murder weapons (one knife, two knives, a club, the butt of an axe, etc.) and the assortment of murderers tend to obscure more material details. Criminologists and medical pathologists (for their own safety, they cannot be identified) whom I familiarized with all the facts at my disposal, contend that, judging from the array of direct and circumstantial evidence (murder weapon, actions following the crime, etc.), there could be only one killer. This conclusion is all the more curious in that it contradicts the logic of the entire investigation, which strove to convict not an individual but a group. The question remains: who was that lone murderer?

An official functionary of the OGPU Special Branch makes his way from Tavda to Gerasimovka to perform a special task. For simplicity's sake I shall call him the executor of the deed. In order that no one in Gerasimovka see him, the executor stays in a neighboring village, one hour to the north, under the pretense of investigating a criminal case there. Although in theory the executor is aware that the Morozov family will be going through the future trial (as in the Special Note on the Terror Problem, "the aforementioned came off repeatedly in workers' summaries as persons of an anti-Soviet persuasion"), he collects supplementary information from an informant personally or through a third party. In particular, he learns that Sergei Morozov threatened his grandson Pavel for having denounced his own father; that Pavel's mother Tatyana asked Danila to slaughter the calf she later took to Tavda; and that Pavel and his brother went into the woods around Krugly Moshok, a cranberry bog outside of the village, where they also might spend the night.

These pieces of intelligence were received by the executor on September 2 or 3. Theoretically, the executor cares less about whom he is to kill than that the murder is savage. On that day, he goes into the woods, finds the children without any difficulty, and kills them as quickly as possible, having run them through with his carbine's bayonet so as not to get down from his horse and leave footprints. The executor strikes the younger boy, who ran up to him, with his rifle butt. He later recalled this blow to the body and the deep wounds, obviously from a bayonet.

Having waited a while in the neighboring village, the executor summons his informant from Gerasimovka on September 4, informing him that the OGPU has received word of a political murder in Gerasimovka. The executor and the informant go to the site of the murder, where they draw up the "Interrogation Record for File No. —." Because of the crime's special importance the executor orders the informant to keep quiet about what was taking place until further instructions.

Over the next three days it rains in the taiga, washing away the concrete traces of the crime.

On September 7, Potupchik, having received orders, organizes a noisy search for the children, and the peasants (from seven to fifteen people by various accounts) find their bodies. The village starts to panic. There is general mourning. The women weep, frightened for their own children, and prepare to give away their grain, to give away anything possible in order to spare their young lives. Fear paralyzes the area. A rumor spreads that the whole village will be tried for not joining the kolkhoz.

The policeman, Titov, draws up his semiliterate "Crime Scene Report." He and the village Soviet try to summon an investigator from Tavda, but instead a crew arrives unexpectedly and buries the children without observing any formalities. After this, the executor appears openly in the village and, together with Titov and his informant, conducts a search of the unsuspecting Morozov, Silin, and Kulukanov households. Zoya Kabina recalled, "There wasn't any warrant. They went into the hut and told the old man, 'Give us the knife which killed the children.' And they themselves took it out from behind the icon." It just so happened that a knife used to slaughter animals was kept there and that Danila put the knife back in its place after having slaughtered the calf; the informant knew this. Later in the press this household knife was transformed into a Finnish knife, a professional murder weapon. During the search they take as evidence the clothes splattered with calf's blood that Danila's grandmother hadn't washed. (The knife and the bloodstained pants and shirt were added to the prosecution's findings, later drawn up by the OGPU. As mentioned earlier, there was never a forensic examination of them.)

After the arrests and official submission of the reports on the first interrogations, the executor's mission in Gerasimovka draws successfully to a close. The "kulak-terrorist band" is transferred to Tavda, where the commissioner of the district OGPU apparatus takes the investigation into his own hands. Over the next two weeks, the press's complete silence regarding the events in Gerasimovka continues. The Ural newspapers report on the Moscow civil servants executed for embezzlement; on how the American Communist newspaper *The Daily Worker* promises to make America a Soviet republic; about the preparations of the world's working class for the sixty-fifth birthday of the "stormy patrol of the revolution," Maxim Gorky; about the theft of some Party membership cards with invalid serial numbers; about the derring-do under the big top of the Flying Giovanni Brothers. But there is not one word about the murder. The case was well-coordinated and watertight. Cleared of unnecessary evidence and superfluous witnesses, it is perfectly suited to its purpose as propaganda in dramatizing "the murder of a Young Pioneer, a representative of Soviet power, by kulaks and their agents."

Within two weeks, all of the accused have "confessed." On September 17, District Commissioner Bykov reports to the chief of the Ural OGPU secret-political section that the special task had reached completion. On that day, the newspapers announce that the investigation has concluded.

Now Pavel Morozov becomes the darling of the mass media. The show investigation begins. In Sverdlovsk, inhabitants become roused with indignation toward the very district authorities who "didn't take steps in organizing a political protest against the onslaught of a class enemy," that is, to put it bluntly, toward those who are still being quiet. "Show no mercy to the class enemy," *Pionerskaya Pravda* declares on October 2, at once formulating the grist for the present and future verdicts "The Young Pioneer-activists Pavel and Fyodor exposed and unmasked a kulak gang that was carrying out its sabotage in the village Soviet."

The newspaper correspondents work "in conjunction with the investigating authorities," *Pionerskaya Pravda* informs its readers on October 15, "and they have managed to stop a wide array of criminal activity." In actuality, the journalists were far ahead of not only the investigation, but even the court. In their articles, they proved the guilt of everyone who was arrested without waiting for the trial, and demanded one punishment for all—execution. Here are some of the titles of newspaper articles from October 1932:

"Concentration Camp for Speculation."

"Find and Convict the Guilty for the Loss of Thirteen Calves and One Cow."

"Quickly and Severely Condemn Embezzlers."

"Ten Years Behind Bars for Theft of Kolkhoz Property."

Newspapers printed lists of those sentenced to be executed in other districts of the country. A "wave of the people's indignation" had begun. Not just letters, but lists of organizations that held meetings demanding "the sternest measures" were printed. Thousands of boys and girls called upon by the authorities to execute the adults. The trial, scheduled to start in October, was postponed in order for the political campaign to envelop the entire country. Finally, this general conclusion appeared in the newspaper *Kolkhoznye Rebyata* on October 29: "Young Pioneers and USSR schoolchildren demand, 'Execute the kulak-murderers!'"

The trial was held up a bit by the inconceivable steadfastness of the accused, who stubbornly refused to take the blame on themselves. But it would be naive to suggest that the confusion, lies, and dirty deals were the result of a frivolously conducted investigation. Traces of the crime were all fully obliterated from the very beginning. Tyranny was deliberately enhanced in order to create an atmosphere of defenselessness and fear. In general, that is in political terms, there wasn't any opposition. The organization of a kolkhoz in Gerasimovka, the enrollment of peasants in the Party (Potupchik was among them), mass meetings throughout the country with resolutions condemning the accused, demonstrations—all this attest to the fact that the propaganda machine was humming like a top. Three weeks after the show trial, "the unsleeping eye of the dictatorship of the proletariat," the OGPU, celebrated its fifth anniversary. Stalin solemnly greeted the secret police as "an unsheathed sword."[5]

After the show trial, the possibilities for a subsequent investigation of the murder of Pavlik Morozov mysteriously disappeared; the house in which he lived burned down, and Danila's father as well as Pavlik's mother's relative, Lazar Baidakov, turned up in labor camps. The informant Ivan Potupchik and Special Branch Assistant Commissioner Spiridon Kartashov were sent to opposite ends of the country to serve in punitive OGPU detachments charged with the cruel suppression of dissent.

The purge also touched the apex of the Party in the Urals. Secretary of the regional Committee Kabakov, leader of the terror in the Urals and one of the initiators of the show trial against the kulak-murderers of Pavlik Morozov, was arrested in 1937. Alongside his name, Chairman of the Soviet of People's Commissars Molotov placed the abbreviation HOP, indicating his fate as the "highest order of punishment," execution. The Ural city of Nadezhdinsk on the river Kakva, renamed Kabakovsk during the reign of Kabakov, was nameless for two years. The city was later named for the pilot-hero, Serov.

After Stalin's death an order came to Tavda to relocate the grave of the Morozov brothers from the cemetery to a new site under the windows of the kolkhoz offices in Gerasimovka. A retiring district executive committee worker who had taken part in the reinternment told me that the customary solemn transference of heroes' remains was strangely ignored in this instance.

They began the operation secretly at night, since they were afraid of stirring up the neighborhood. By the light of automobile headlights, the men pounded together a box into which KGB men shoveled whatever was found in the old grave, where the two coffins had lain. They broke up the skeletons with shovels, mixing the bones of both children together in the one box. The box was then moved in darkness under a reinforced guard. (Another eyewitness told me that they lost one of the skulls, and that afterward scoolchildren played football with it.) Lowered into the fresh, deep grave, the remains of the Young Pioneer-hero and his brother were covered with a two-meter slab of concrete, on which was placed a statue of the boy wearing a Young Pioneer scarf. The transfer of the remains in such a manner was sanctioned by those who had begun to fear a real investigation of the case. Today, an inspection of the grave and its contents is impossible.

I have already discussed the removal or secret classification of the Morozov case archives. Even local newspapers with very important materials connected to the show trial were missing from libraries in Moscow and the Urals. Volunteers, however, assisted me in getting hold of them. With them, I can openly review the matter of who really committed the murders in Gerasimovka.

As the reader may have already noticed, in the picture of the murder sketched out above, the real names of the informant, the OGPU commissioner, and the executor (or professional killer) are omitted because this identification is only a hypothesis in which there is a significant degree of likelihood but no definitive solution. I don't have enough proof to give the names of the murderers.

Potupchik and Kartashov denied all questions that compromised them. I didn't find Titov and Bykov alive. These four carried the secret to their graves. Nor can it be ruled out that only one of the four knew everything. I will only add the following, which several witnesses confirmed. The schoolteacher Pozdnina: "Kartashov was a dreadful man, but I won't say any more." The doctor at the psychiatric hospital where Kartashov was treated: "He slandered himself, saying how he ran the children through with a bayonet and trampled them on a horse." But this hardly constitutes proof.

I do have a final condemnation, however, that should be heeded by those who are able to dig deeper into the Pavlik Morozov murder case than I. One thing is certain: whoever the executor was, the murder could only have been committed, or at the very least provoked, by the hands of the OGPU. The criminal actions of the OGPU remain incontestable even if it is proven that the murder of the two boys was committed by their relatives out of vengeance. Agents of the Soviet secret police were fully responsible for the murder.

While I may not have had all the secret documents in the Pavlik Morozov murder case at my disposal, I do know every one of the parties involved. In addition to the aforementioned investigators, I can name five more responsible for the organization of Dossier No. 374. They are Commissioner of the Second Local Militia Office, Secret-Political Department, Plenipotentiary OGPU Representative Shepelev; Temporary Chief of the same department Voskresensky; Chief of the Secret-Political Department Prokhorenko; and Deputy Chief of the Ural OGPU Tuchkov. The reward for a guilty verdict in the Morozov case, and for all the OGPU labor connected with it, motivated their signatures. To them we need only add then Chief of the Ural OGPU Reshetov. During the Thirties, each of the men lived in Sverdlovsk and Nizhny Tagil. Which of them survived, I don't know. They are the real heroes of the system that had come into being, the authentic participants in an actual, not fabricated, government terrorist organization. It is doubtful they will ever turn up alive or be sentenced to die, but the world should know their names.

Notes

1. Solomein (1979: 79).
2. *Mor* (19 November 1932).
3. Balashov (September 1982).
4. In E. Zamyatin's "Elizaveta Angliiskaya," quoted in *Strana i Mir* (May 1984).
5. *Pravda* (20 December 1932).

In the center of Moscow stood a bronze monument to the Pioneer-hero Pavlik Morozov—quite possibly the only monument in the world to an informer (removed in August, 1991). Behind the trees, the Council of Ministers of the Russian Federation, now called the White House, is visible. (Unless otherwise noted, all contemporary photographs in this book were taken by the author.)

The meeting hall at the time of the Tavda trial. The judges sit on a stage. (Photograph by Soyuzphoto)

On a bench sit the accused (from left to right): Sergei Morozov, Danila Morozov, Arseny Kulukanov, Arseny Silin, Ksenya Morozova. (Photograph from the journal *Pioner*)

Pavlik's first heroic deed—denouncing his father. (Artist: N. Moos, 1969)

The method of "socialist realism" exemplified. The hero announces to his grandfather and father that he has informed the authorities of their activites. ("Pavlik Morozov" by N. Chebrakov. Oil. Moscow State Tretyakov Gallery: The All-Union Artist's Exhibition, 1952)

Hallowed ground in Gerasimovka. The obelisk marks the site of the house where Pavlik Morozov was born. To the right, in bold, the words of Maxim Gorky: "His memory must never vanish." In the background, the forest where Pavlik and Fedya were stabbed.

Former investigator, soldier of the punitive division of the OGPU, personnel clerk, criminal, and pensioner, Ivan Potupchik. Magnitogorsk, 1981.

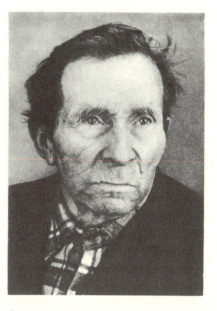

Former assistant to the representative of the Special Department of the Tavda district branch of the Ural OGPU, merit pensioner Spiridon Kartashov. Irbit, 1982.

"GPU—the Unblinking Eye of the Proletarian Dictatorship" (Poster, 1932) (Author's archives)

At his dacha near Moscow, Gorky meets with the Siberian Pioneers who had proposed to the Writers' Congress that a monument be erected to Pavlik Morozov.

I was fortunate to find this unique 1930 photograph of the Gerasimovka school's students. Pavlik is indicated by the arrow. To his left (holding the pole of a red flag) is Danila Morozov, who would be sentenced to death for the murder. To Pavlik's immediate left is Kuzma Silin, the son of defendant Arseny Silin. Below, in the center, is Matryona Korolkova. The picture was published for the first time in the Russian version of this book (London, 1988). This is a portion of the photograph, enlarged by the author.

A portrait of Pavlik in the seventies.

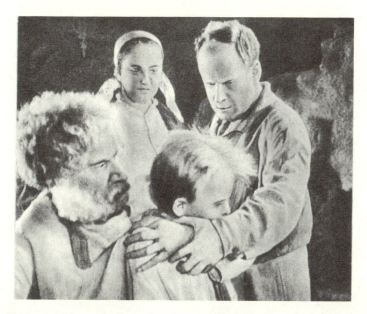

The filming of Eisenstein's movie about Pavlik Morozov. Here, the director demonstrates how to tear the Pioneer son from the murderous grip of his father. Playing Trofim Morozov is the famous actor Boris Zakhava. (Eisenstein museum, Moscow)

A ritualized meeting of Stalin with children. Moscow Aerodrome, 1936.

Pavlik's mother, Tatyana Morozova, in her house, the gift of Stalin. Alupka, the Crimea, 1981.

8

The Myth: An Example of the New Man

We should consider it a given that no one thought Pavlik Morozov a hero in his lifetime. Nothing was published about his deed; no one outside the village even knew of his existence. Nor can his death be called very heroic; the purpose of the murder was not to make a martyr-hero out of the boy but to intimidate the peasants and speed up collectivization. Morozov became a hero because such a hero was required. The propaganda machine was about to create the model of a new man, a man with all the traits necessary to set a standard of usefulness—one who would help to separate friends from foes.

On the same day that the show trial of Morozov's murderers began in Tavda, a general session of the Komsomol Central Committee opened in Moscow. It concerned instilling devotion in youth as well as preparing them ideologically to serve the Party. These intentions were pronounced in Stalin's name by a member of the Politburo, Pavel Postyshev. Vasily Arkhipov, assistant chairman of the Central Bureau of Pioneers, declared in a report published by *Pionerskaya Pravda* that "Pavlik must be a shining example to all the children of the Soviet Union."[1]

Morozov's name was invoked by speakers at various conferences. The Komsomol Central Committee developed a master plan for propagandizing Morozov's accomplishment. In December a special TASS agency bulletin appeared, addressed to "all Komsomol and Pioneer newspapers of the Union." Orders were issued from the top to "prepare a film script and plays for children's theaters," as well as to publish books and posters of the Pioneer-Hero Morozov.[2] This meant that through a collective effort of the Party bosses, one of the two children murdered in Gerasimovka was resurrected from the dead to begin a new life.

Pionerskaya Pravda announced that tens of thousands of rubles were collected for the construction of a plane to be christened "The Pavlik

Morozov." There was also an idea floating around to organize the collection of funds in order to build a tank named after the hero.

Young people's publications devoted the better part of 1933 to fostering devotion to Party leadership in the so-called "third generation." The struggle against the kulaks was largely at an end.

According to Lenin, communism had to be created from "human material spoiled by thousands of years of slavery."[3] Stalin simplified the problem by eliminating this "spoiled material," at first, mainly those who stood in the way of his path to absolute power. He began the liquidation with the first generation of the "old Bolsheviks" serving in government positions. The second generation, who had also grown up before the revolution, equally bore the burden of dead moral principles. It was the new generation, born like Pavlik Morozov in the years after the revolution, who were meant to obey their leader without question.

These youths were unfamiliar with the old moral criteria. They had no model for comparison, and therefore always followed the Party line. According to a popular song of the time, they were always ready to "sing and laugh, like children, amidst hard work and struggle." The propaganda slogans were hypnotic. The famous writer Ilya Ehrenburg wrote: "We have borrowed the plans for a tractor from the United States. But the drivers who man those tractors [here] are advanced models of the new people, unknown to the old world."[4]

Lenin's widow, Nadezhda Krupskaya, who was at the time an assistant to People's Commissioner of Education, proclaimed the "need for a certain type of man."[5] Before that People's Commissioner Anatoly Lunacharsky himself explained the essence of Bolshevik education at an All-Russian Conference of Teachers: "Since the state is a military dictatorship, it is impossible to act upon the humanitarian ideals that are a basis of our beliefs. To practice kindness and humanity is treason; first we must uproot our enemies."[6] Two things became the basis of this new educational system: the propaganda of hatred directed toward "class enemies," or relatives and neighbors; and the development of "vigilance," in reality hypertrophied suspicion toward everyone, including one's own parents.

Half a year before Morozov's murder, the newspaper *Druzhnye Rebyata* (Friendly Children) suddenly decided to change its name. Here is the explanation given by the editorial office: "'It is a bad name,' declared the children. 'We are not friendly with the kulaks. And one could look at the name and conclude that we are friendly with everybody.'" A few days later the newspaper appeared under a new title, *Kolkhoznye Rebyata* (Children of the Collective Farm).

According to an explanation given by the assistant chairman of the Central Bureau of Pioneers in *Pionerskaya Pravda*, the main goal of the Pioneer organization was to "cultivate hatred."[7] Morozov became a model for this hatred against the Party's enemies. The first poem written about Morozov, by Mikhail Doroshin, was titled "The Poem of Hatred."[8] And this new generation was being conditioned to think of itself as living in a nest of enemies; children learned from kindergarten on to unmask Trotskyites, kulaks, and spies. Even in the most recent edition of his book about Morozov, Solomein's first chapter title very unambiguously reads, "Not every brother is a brother."[9]

Alexander Kosarev, a young Komsomol leader, concurred in one of his speeches: "We do not have an all-embracing human morality. Morality is class-related. Our morality is the kind that undermines capitalism, explodes its remains, strengthens the proletarian dictatorship, and promotes the building of socialism."[10] Thus, a new class-conscious morality was to replace ordinary human morality; it was to abolish shame, conscience, pity, generosity, empathy, tolerance—every trait that distinguishes us from the animals. But the new man was not even an animal—an ordinary beast never betrays, never informs. What was this new man like?

In its coverage of the show trial of Pavlik Morozov's murderers, the press often used a famous quotation from Maxim Gorky: "If the enemy does not surrender, he is liquidated." Hence, from the very beginning the name of Pavlik Morozov became associated with the founder of "socialist realism," the man who in the beginning of the thirties was appointed the head "engineer of souls" (a common Sovietism of the decade) of the third generation of Soviet citizens. In his article "About the Old and the New Man" Gorky wrote: "A new breed of man is developing in the Soviet Union, and already one can unmistakably see his main distinguishing trait. He has an unlimited trust in the organizing power of intellect [in the organizing power of the dictatorship—Y.D.], a trust that has been lost by the European intellectuals, exhausted by the useless work of trying to appease the masses in their class struggle.[11]

Gorky wrote about the process of "the heroization of the masses."[12] And his theory had to be supported by "facts." *Pionerskaya Pravda* and other newspapers appealed to writers to turn to the feats of Pavlik

Morozov. With the help of the provincial journalist Solomein, Gorky found a hero worthy of contemplation. For it was Solomein who created the first version of the myth of Pavlik Morozov.

In his unpublished autobiography, which I obtained from his daughter, Solomein wrote that he came from a medium-income family. Even so, his father owned two horses, and such people were considered kulaks. His mother remarried, the second time to a kulak who beat him cruelly and later murdered her. Solomein became a runaway, then lived in children's labor colonies. He had three years of elementary school; later he worked as a carpenter's apprentice, at a slaughterhouse, a tobacco factory, as a trench digger, and as a delivery boy until he became in 1930 a probationary Party member and joined 25,000 other agents sent to the countryside to enforce collectivization. All of this gave him a start in his literary career.

But he did begin to write, and soon was hired by the newspaper *Vskhody Kommuny*, where he became an assistant editor. After that Solomein held at least sixteen different jobs in local Ural newspapers. He died of chronic heart trouble in 1962. One can best judge Solomein's worldview by his comparison between capitalism and socialism: "In the West they beat children, while here we beat drums." A special order from Ural Regional Party Committee to write a book about Pavlik Morozov became a stepping stone to his vocation. The deadline was ten days.

Solomein arrived in Gerasimovka approximately one month after the murder. He was not only a newspaper reporter, but also an agent of the regional Party committee reponsible for de-kulakization. In the Gerasimovka museum he is named as "Chairman of the Kolkhoz," but even though his photograph hangs with the corroborating signature, his status in this regard is pure fiction. Less fictitious are the copious notes he took during his first days in the village. In collecting the material for his book, Solomein did not rely on his memory; thankfully, he recorded nearly everything he saw in Gerasimovka immediately.

Solomein undoubtedly merits respect for his energy, hard work, and modesty. Unlike most authors of similar works, he conscientiously took down the testimony of witnesses and contemporaries. Nevertheless, he was without doubt a functionary of the propaganda machine with a clearly defined task. An honest interviewer, he wrote down even things that worked against the appreciation of his hero. But as a Party journalist he reported only the praiseworthy acts of the Pioneer-informer.[13]

In Solomein's memoirs pertaining to life in Gerasimovka we encounter a second hero-informer, and his story is no less interesting than that of the official hero. Solomein frankly tells us that after Pavlik Morozov's death it became increasingly difficult to fulfill the grain supply plans because there were no informers to encourage production. Then he started looking for a replacement for Pavlik. Vaska Karlovich was suitable enough, even though he was slightly retarded and a drunkard:

> Only after a week of serious talks did Vaska agree to help the village Soviet look for the kulaks' crops. In the morning we met in my apartment or in the village Soviet, and he drew maps in my notebooks, with the buildings marked: "A stable. Ten steps towards the bath." Or, "The bathhouse. Eight steps towards the large pine." I copied these plans onto small sheets of paper and gave them to the people from the grain requisitioning commission of the village Soviet. They came into the kulak's house, looked in every corner, and in the end "accidentally discovered" a pit full of buried grain. We sent Red show-transports filled with grain to Tavda once or twice a week. They were all dedicated to Pavlik Morozov. Many a load came from holes discovered in the kulaks' backyards.[14]

Solomein tells us ingenuously that Vaska did not inform out of love for Soviet power, but for a bottle of vodka. The writer concealed the name of his personal informer, but said that there were forty Pioneers helping him, thus saving one but putting a number of other children in danger of sharing Pavlik Morozov's fate.

After the grain was confiscated came the trials, in which the peasants discovered concealing it were convicted to five to ten years of labor camps. Solomein himself acted as public prosecutor. He walked around the village with a gun in his pocket, and once, when somebody threatened him, he shot and wounded the man. He also arrested anyone who peeked in the windows of the village Soviet on suspicion of an attempted assassination of himself—concurrently journalist and plenipotentiary agent for the Regional Party Committee and thus a possible target.

One can easily see that the first biographer of Pavlik Morozov did more than merely create the radiant image of the informer-hero for literature; he had a lot of firsthand experience in successful denunciation himself. Less successful was Solomein's first book, *In the Kulaks' Nest*, which seemed jinxed from the start. He wrote it in twenty days (instead of ten, as originally commissioned), and for this received an official reprimand from the Party. The book was hurriedly published—note the multitude of typographic errors and other proofreading mistakes. Despite these flaws, it was soon translated into the languages of other Soviet ethnic groups, and parts of the book were serialized in the French Communist Party journal *Mon Camarade*. Encouraged, Solomein sent the book to Maxim Gorky, "leader of the proletarian writers," as well as to some other authors. Gorky was the only one who responded, and he did so at once.

It is a well-known fact that the founder of "socialist realism" was always ready to praise weak and semiliterate books if the authors were proletarians. It would seem, then, that *In the Kulaks' Nest* would be, no matter how unrefined the writing, a prime candidate for his approval—the book was timely in the way that it illustrated the tasks of Soviet literature, corresponding to the very appeals made by Gorky himself. And suddenly, the answer came:

> It is a bad little book; it is written—artlessly, superficially, unthoughtfully. If the heroic feat of the Pioneer Pavlik Morozov had been described more skillfully and with the strength displayed by Morozov himself, the book would have had much more import socially, and its educational value for the Pioneers would have been much greater. Many of them would probably have understood that if a blood relative is an enemy of the people, he is no longer a relative, but simply an enemy; thus there is no reason to have mercy on him.[15]

Later on in the letter the criticism of the book becomes caustic: "Having read the book the reader would say, 'This is all made up, and made up badly!' The material is original and new, even clever, and it's all ruined. It is as if you took a piece of gold and made a latch for the barn with it, or built a barn from precious cedar."

This disastrous review from the founder of Soviet literature was issued and reissued, effectively closing the doors of publishing houses to Solomein; for decades he would think how to rewrite the book so as to measure up to its hero. The main obstacle to remaking the book was Solomein's terrible lack of education. Well into middle age he countinued to study Russian grammar, but still the publishers rejected his manuscripts on the basis of their lack of polish. Not long before his death, with the help of his journalist daughter and a crafty colleague, he rewrote the book once more. The rejuvenated legend was published under the title *Pavka the Communist*.

Gorky scolded Solomein for not generalizing the traits of the new hero. But what interfered with Solomein's doing so was too much knowledge of the real facts and no knack for twisting them. The authors who followed Gorky's precept preferred to deal with the facts as little as possible, simply creating the image of Morozov as they went along. Belatedly, Solomein learned to do that too.

One month after the letter to Solomein, all the central newspapers published an article by Gorky full of the very generalizations the lesser writer and the provincial journalist had been unable to make: "The struggle against small saboteurs—weeds and rodents—taught the children to counteract the large two-legged ones. Here it is appropriate to remember the feat of the Pioneer Pavel Morozov, a boy who understood that a man who is close to you by blood can easily be an enemy in spirit; for such a man we can have no mercy."[16] Through Gorky the Party declared that the most important thing now was to find the two-legged pests, the spiritual enemies, from among one's relatives and and friends: to suspect, to observe, and to inform. It was declared that from now on the new hero was not the "little fighter for collectivization" but the "little informer."

Human fate is ironic. Gorky's article appeared at exactly the time when rumors were spreading in Moscow that his own son Maxim Peshkov had been recruited by Gorky's personal secretary, OGPU agent Pyotr Kryuchkov, to provide information concerning what his father talked about at home in his secretary's absence. The tenor of these conversations was reported to the head of the OGPU, Genrikh Yagoda, who then related the general content personally to Stalin. A short time later the younger Maxim was murdered—by the Party's enemies, according to the official version. Two years later the same fate befell Gorky. Afterwards, following public trials both Kryuchkov and Yagoda were convicted and shot.

After Gorky's article the myth was enriched; a provincial boy informer was proclaimed a "tireless fighter for the cause of the proletariat." "His memory must not disappear," declared Gorky. "This little hero deserves a monument, and I am sure that a monument will be erected." Gorky's faith in that monument could not have originated with himself; that is, he personally could not have decided to build a statue in the center of Moscow. Soon a collection was started to provide funds for a Pavlik Morozov memorial. Near the central street of Moscow, the Tverskaya (by that time renamed Gorky Street), a monument was to be erected to the Pioneer-informer who became the focus of attention of the First Congress of Soviet Writers, which opened with pomp in August, 1934.

The question of Morozov's monument was raised immediately after the formal greeting the writers addressed to Stalin. Gorky directed the writers' attention to the fact that the growth of the new kind of man was especially clear in children. After Samuil Marshak's report on children's literature, the young Pioneers completed the ritual of greeting the participants. The published stenographic account differs markedly from the newspaper reports, but I will attempt to combine them here. Alla Kanshina appeared on behalf of the Siberian Pioneers:

> Alexei Maximovich [Gorky] was right in saying that it is necessary to build a monument to Pavlik Morozov. This must be done, and we Pioneers won't rest till this is accomplished. We are sure that the whole country will support us. Where else in the world will you find a country that builds monuments to children? We heard that somewhere abroad there is a single monument: A naked little boy stands by a fountain. During the war somebody put a general's uniform on him. What can this monument tell us? Nothing. But our monument will call all of us kids to heroism. [applause] Comrade conference, let's organize this matter! Let's build the monument! [more applause]

One can easily see that children were well prompted to "initiate" projects for such performances.

Komsomolskaya Pravda reported that the girl enthused from the podium, "'We have thousands of Pavliks!'" The article proceeded: "A proposal then followed to organize an immediate collection of funds for a monument to the valiant Pioneer Pavlik Morozov. Alexei Maximovich takes a sheet of paper, and pledges 500 rubles for the monument to the Pioneer-Hero Pavlik Morozov. People crowd around waiting their turn. Soon the list is covered with a long line of names."

Pionerskaya Pravda describes the affair somewhat differently; after the girl's address Nikolai Tikhonov, not Gorky, "immediately proposes to start a collection. Maxim Gorky is the first to pledge five hundred rubles; he is followed by Demyan Bedny, then by the Persian poet Lakhuti. Tikhonov and other delegates of the convention follow suit."

In his closing address Gorky did not forget the boy adopted by the Writers' Union; he again asked the government for permission for the writers to erect a monument to the Pioneer-Hero.[17]

In the beginning of the thirties it became the main task of Soviet literature to instill in the public consciousness stereotypes of behavior the authorities considered appropriate at any given moment. As soon as the matter of Pavlik Morozov arose, the writers rushed to show their dedication, readiness, and efficiency by taking it up as eagerly as possible. They thought it a more compelling display to propose a monument than to write books; additionally a mounument has a more impressive appearance. In this manner a traitor, the kind of person Dante placed in the ninth circle of Hell, was proclaimed to be the model of the new man and a principal hero of the socialist era.

After the First Congress of Soviet Writers the process of creating model citizens became industrial in scale. The phrases "children's literature" and "school of hatred" grew to be synonymous in the press. Closeness in following political directives became the main measure of quality in literature. And Pavlik Morozov became the primary model for the image of a complete hero. The poet Alexander Yashin later explained the essence of the matter in *Komsomolskaya Pravda*: "The authors are trying to write a book about Pavlik Morozov that would show the best, most typical traits of our children. They are trying to create the image of a Pioneer who could be imitated by generations of Soviet children."

In 1936, right before his death, Gorky remembered Morozov: "It is one of the little wonders of our era." There used to be only seven wonders of the world. Gorky managed to find the eighth—a little informer. But there were periods in the great writer's life when he had a different attitude toward denunciation. In his diary he described one episode that occurred after the February Revolution of 1917. He was then an editor of the Petrograd newspaper *Novaya Zhizn* (New Life):

A nice-looking, slightly embarrassed woman came to see him.

"You see, I used to be an agent of the Secret Police.... Is that really evil?" The woman explained that she had an affair with an officer, who then became a police adjutant. People gathered in her apartment, and through her lover she informed on their conversations.

"Did you betray many people?"

"I never counted. But I only told him about the ones I especially disliked."

"Do you know what the police did to them?"

"No, it never interested me. Of course, I heard that some of them were imprisoned or exiled somewhere, but the politics never interested me...."

The great proletarian writer was appalled. He quietly listened to the confession of the informer, "concealing a dreary wrath with a great effort of will." He then thought, "I used to know many traitors. When one after another their names were discovered, I had a feeling that someone of great, merciless evil sarcastically spat in my heart."

Gorky described the abominable depths of this woman's fall at length; she denounced her own father to the police out of revenge, because he had divorced her mother.

"Am I not responsible for all the vileness of the life going on around me," pondered Gorky. "Am I not responsible for this life, so loathsomely soiled at dawn by the dirt of betrayal?"[18]

A decade and a half later, in accordance with the new morality, this same man urged that the hero Pavlik Morozov be glorified. A betrayer of his father had become a national Soviet hero.

Notes

1. *Pionerskaya Pravda* (17 December 1932).
2. *Ibid* (23 December 1932).
3. Lenin (1963, vol. 37: 409).
4. Ehrenburg (22 August 1934).
5. Krupskaya (1958, vol. 2: 83).
6. *Detskaya...* (1920: 11).
7. Arkhipov (17 December 1932).
8. Doroshin (29 March 1933).
9. Solomein (1979: 9).
10. Kosarev (7 July 1932).
11. Gorky (1949: 21).
12. Gorky (1957: 497).
13. Solomein ("My Autobiography" in Manscripts...); Savitskaya (Questions...: 1–2).
14. Solomein (5 and 7 Septebmer 1967).
15. Gorky (1955, vol. 30: 328–29).
16. *Pravda* (29 October 1933).
17. Pervy... (1934: 1, 4, 15, 38, 680–81); *Komsomolskaya Pravda* (20 August 1934); *Pionerskaya Pravda* (24 August 1934).
18. Gorky (3 May 1917).

9

Authors and Victims of Heroization

The political directive was being fulfilled from the moment it was formulated. In addition to the already mentioned Sverdlovsk journalist Solomein, two of his competitors from Moscow, Vitaly Gubarev and Elizar Smirnov, also witnessed the Morozov brothers' murder trial. These three dedicated their entire lives to the creation and perpetuation of the myth of Hero-Informer 001.

The *Literary Encyclopedia* states that Vitaly Gubarev participated in the investigation of Morozov's murder and published the first book about it. As it turns out, it was not a book but just a short-story.[1] After a term of service in the Red Army, Gubarev arrived in Moscow and embarked on a career involving the Komsomol and journalism. A telegram from Gerasimovka was published in *Pionerskaya Pravda* with Gubarev's signature, and that made him the "discoverer of the Pioneer-Hero." Gubarev's first article was published on October 15, one week after Solomein's; his first book came out some years later. The encyclopedia also tells us that in 1933 Gubarev published a book entitled *One of the Eleven* (the name derives from the fabrication that there were eleven Pioneers in the village). In reality the book was only a newspaper article.

Not long before his death Gubarev told me that Gorky, whom he met in the office of the *Krestyanskaya Gazeta* (The Peasants' Gazette) charged him with writing a book about the boy-hero. The first version, entitled *Son: A Story about the Renowned Pioneer Pavlik Morozov*, appeared in the magazine *Pioner*.[2] For his popularization of Pavlik Morozov's exploits, Gubarev was made editor of *Pionerskaya Pravda* and decorated with the Order of the Medal of Honor. During the latter decades of his life he published didactic books about children's devotion to the cause of the Party. He died in 1981 of a heart attack brought on by chronic alcoholism.

The third creator of the Morozov myth, after Solomein and Gubarev, was Elizar Smirnov. I had difficulty finding his surviving colleagues because at work he was known under another name. Apparently, he had grown up in an orphanage, where he was called "Vil" (an abbreviation of Vladimir Ilych Lenin), later changed to William. Only as an adult did he find out his real name. A schoolteacher's son, Smirnov graduated from the Leningrad School of Journalism and, after that, worked for several different newspapers, some of them military. He also held the rank of colonel and had been decorated. In 1962, he was found in his Moscow apartment two days after his death. Solomein died the same year.[3]

As public prosecutor at the trial in Tavda, Smirnov participated in editing the text of the official record of the proceedings. He wrote a number of articles about Morozov, the book *Pavlik Morozov*, and other works about the Pioneer movement. However, he never claimed precedence in the creation of the myth. Moreover, in an article published a year before his death he denied his priority; neither did he mention his active role in the show trial.[4] There is a possible explanation for this. Late in life he became acquainted with the dissident writer Yevgenya Ginzburg, who for eighteen years during Stalin's rule had suffered imprisonment, forced labor, and exile; perhaps this widened his perspective. During the thirties, however, Smirnov was not just the main "mythmaker" but also the chief source of information for other authors, in particular the well-known Alexander Yakovlev, who was commissioned by a children's publishing house to write a book about Morozov.

Yakovlev took up the theme later than the others—in the beginning of 1937. In the words of the writer V. Lidin, who wrote the foreword to one of Yakovlev's books, he "hungrily sought the best in people." One can only guess at the reasons why the man who "sought the best" came to extol denunciations.[5] An active member of the Socialist Revolutionary Party before the Revolution, Yakovlev had been arrested twice and spent five years in exile. Once a deeply religious man, he later renounced his faith. In 1929, a seven-volume collection of the writer's works was published. The son of an illiterate painter, he wrote a novel, *October*, one of the first books about the Bolshevik revolution; it was later removed from the libraries because certain aspects were too realistic.

Then, suddenly, the times changed; Yakovlev fell into disfavor and had to become a reporter for *Pravda*. By the middle of the 1930s he was no longer being published. For long months he lived alone at his country house, talking to the birds. Lidin mentions in passing that the writer was indignant about the injustice done to him, but "only in private conversations." Yakovlev's decision to take up the book *Pioneer Pavel Morozov* was spurred on by mass arrests in the Writers' Union.

Yakovlev never went to Gerasimovka; neither did he hide the fact that the book he was writing was a compilation of others' work. Smirnov's son told me in an interview that his father used to laugh about his work with Yakovlev: "He is an artist, and we are laborers." Later, Yakovlev wrote books with such inspiring titles as *Great Communist Building Projects*. The writer died the same year as Stalin; his grave is now lost.

Dozens of top creative people in all fields were drafted to work on the project of describing Pavlik Morozov's feats. The majority of authors used as sources the works of these four mythmakers. But from time to time quarrels arose among them.

In Solomein's archives I found the draft of an article entitled "The Artistic Method of the Writer Yakovlev." "It is strange," he writes, "that not one of the authors bothered to go to the location, talk to the heroes, find out about the daily life and customs of Gerasimovka inhabitants. Reading the short stories, novels, and plays about Pavlik, we are forced to conclude that they contain more fiction than historical truth." Solomein gives examples, listing the Gerasimovka peasants who were invented by Yakovlev, then quotes from his work: "As usual, April in the Urals was sunny. Flocks of geese were migrating north. Swans settled in Satokovo Lake." Solomein adds that these lines would have made any villager laugh; in April temperatures often reach thirty below zero. Solomein ridicules Yakovlev's description of Pavlik Morozov, concluding, "This is a mannequin who only talks about the kolkhoz and the world revolution. He does not have a single negative trait." Comparing certain paragraphs from his book, *In the Kulaks' Nest*, to Yakovlev's book, Solomein also accuses the other writer of plagiarism.

Solomein's friends pressured him to refrain from creating a scandal. There was a reason for this: Solomein himself borrowed whole paragraphs from colleagues, and his Pavlik Morozov resembled a mannequin to a considerable degree as well. Most important, though, such conflict would necessarily involve the official hero in a scandal, and the participants could be dealt with severely. The article remained unpublished—it is unlikely anybody would have been permitted to publish it in any case. But one can understand Solomein's grievance; forced to keep quiet after Gorky's devastating response, he had to watch in silence from his country home as enterprising authors in the capital made a living from "his" hero.

Yakovlev published more than one edition of his book about Morozov and later wrote a play. Smirnov published a book, *Pavlik Morozov: The Life and Struggle of the Brave Pioneer*. On the other hand, Gubarev's position as editor of a large newspaper enabled him to publish endless versions of the same narrative about Morozov: for preschools, for elementary schools, for seven-year schools, and for non-Russian language schools. Gubarev's book was published in tens of different Soviet cities; soon many editions appeared in Prague, Bratislava, Bucharest, and Sofia. A play of his was produced in a number of theaters.

Using his connections, Gubarev made it impossible for Solomein to be published in Moscow and obstructed the publication of new editions of Yakovlev's and Smirnov's books, thus acquiring a monopoly to enforce his conveyor belt method of hero production. A list of the editions of Gubarev's *Pavlik Morozov* (under various titles) takes up several pages. In later books, Gubarev pictures himself as a detective—in reality he more closely resembled Baron Munchausen. Gubarev proclaimed, "The life, struggle, and death of Pavlik Morozov will occupy a glorious page in history."[6] As it was, he started with one page and ended up with millions.

Later, a new book of Solomein's was printed, one edition after another. In a small town in the Urals I once walked into a bookstore. Although the store was selling only one book, the room was filled with copies floor to ceiling. It was Solomein's *Pavka the Communist*. Pavlik thus provided a living for the writer until his death.

Let us now compare the information we have about the real Morozov to the stuff that appeared in books so that we can better understand how the myth came into being.

When the news arrived about Pioneer Morozov's death, a photograph of the hero was urgently needed. His mother didn't have one, but a group picture was found, one made by an itinerant photographer two years before the children's murder. Surprisingly, this single authentic portrait has never been published. There is nothing at all heroic in Pavlik's image. He looks like a small child, even though by the time the picture was taken he was already eleven. At that time his father had not yet been arrested. Pavlik has large, sad eyes. To the boy's right is his cousin and future alleged murderer, Danila, holding a red flag in his hand.

Pavlik's image was cut from this group picture and brought to the newspaper's editorial office. According to a woman who was then an employee of *Pionerskaya Pravda*, the staff determined that it was a photograph of the corpse. To make this more realistic, the shirt's collar was retouched and a bare neck drawn in. When it appeared in the October 15, 1932 edition of the newspaper, the caption under the photograph read, "Pioneer Pavlusha Morozov, murdered by the kulaks."

Morozov's head, cut out from the school picture began a separate life. A T-shirt was added to it, an overcoat collar, curly hair; then a hand was drawn holding a prophetically titled book, *The New Way*. In the second edition of the *Great Soviet Encyclopedia* Pavlik is wearing a different cap, crisp white shirt and Pioneer tie—the uniform introduced in schools according to Stalin's order only at the end of the Second World War. His facial expression is improved, in keeping with the mythical status of the First Pioneer of the Country.

One interesting counterfeit is on exhibit at the Tavda museum. At first it seems to be a fragment of the known photograph. But Morozov is older, and his expression is optimistic and purposeful instead of grim. A Pioneer tie adorns his neck. It is a complete hoax.

The real Morozov was not fit to be a myth. This is why the editors chose pictures that seemed to fit the hero's image better than his own did. For example, thirty-five years later, on August 27, 1967, *Tavdinskaya Pravda* made its contribution to the myth. Under the headline "Published For The First Time" it declared, "Before us we see a genuine photograph of Pavlik Morozov. This snapshot of the Pioneer-Hero was discovered in Sverdlovsk archives...." But it isn't him.

The schoolteacher Zoya Kabina had even seen manufactured photographs of the trial of the father, Trofim Morozov: "They sent me a picture of a trial. There was a teacher sitting there—fake, and Pavlik denouncing his father—fake. They asked me to write who was who. But it was all phony."

What did Pioneer 001 look like? He had "grey, shining eyes" (Kabina, interview with Solomein, 1932), "dark eyes" (my interview with Kabina, 1981), "black eyes" (Gubarev, *Pionerskaya Pravda*, October 15, 1932), "blue eyes" (Gubarev, *Pionerskaya Pravda*, September 3), "blue eyes or black eyes" (Solomein in newspapers and personal notes), and "brown eyes" (the writer Koryakov, preface to Solomein's book *Pavka the Communist*). There are also vaguer descriptions: "Bright," "very honest," "very brave eyes."[7]

All the Morozovs were tall, big people. What about Pavel? He was "small and thin from hunger" (Tatyana Morozova), "tall" (Solomein), "bony and long-legged, the best runner in the village" (Gubarev). "Pavlik had a birthmark the size of a fingernail on his right cheek," remembers Tatyana. To add masculinity to his looks Gubarev pictured a scar over his right eyebrow.[8]

Books and articles disagree concerning the color of the hero's hair, his voice, dress. When the authors lost themselves in fictional details, they turned to such generically euphemistic descriptions as "a very nice, ordinary kid" (Koryakov), or "Every schoolboy has something of Pavlik in him" (Doroshin).[9]

As the years passed there were fewer and fewer sources from which to verify the myth. Isakova, a schoolteacher, writes in *Tavdinskaya Pravda*: "Pavlik was a good student. He took his lessons seriously, was very disciplined. He loved his brothers very much, took care of Fedya, made sure the boy was warmly dressed."[10] Zoya Kabina, who knew him better than others, says just the opposite: "He couldn't help others with their studies. He rarely came to school himself."

"He liked to misbehave, fight, quarrel, sing bawdy songs, smoke," wrote Solomein in his notebooks. The following shows how the matter of Pavlik's smoking was dealt with in the published text: "Sometimes when we got together, one of the guys would take a cigarette, and Pavlik would grab him by the sleeve, saying, 'Cut that out! Smoking is bad for your health.'"[11]

"What did Pavlik do in his free time?" I asked Kabina. "He liked to play cards for money." And in response to "What kind of songs did he sing?": "All kinds. With other boys they sang vulgar songs." He enjoyed teasing, harassing people: "Talk to him all you want, and he will still do it his way. He often fought out of anger, simply because of his quarrelsome character." Lazar Baidakov, a relative of the Morozovs put it in a nutshell: "Pavlik was simply a hooligan. He walked around the village, an overgrown adolescent in rags, always hungry, and because of it always in a bad mood, looking for trouble. That's why everybody hated him."

The Pioneer uniform, the tie, shoes—it's all a myth. Morozov walked around in bast shoes. "His coat was ragged, old, a hand-me-down from Trofim," said Kabina. "People in the village called him a 'ragged asshole' and a 'bum,'" remembered Tatyana. "To tell you the truth, Pavlik was the dirtiest of all the kids in the school, never washed," recalled his classmate Matryona Korolkova. "The children in their family, when they quarrelled, would urinate on each other, then go to school covered with it.

Pavlik always stank unbearably of urine. Gubarev made it up that Pavlik and I wanted to get married. What a thought!"

Because of the textbook Pavlik holds in the photograph, the authors could present him as an insatiable reader, a scholar, an intellectual leader of both children and adults—the representative of new power in his native village. Newspapers mentioned some of his favorite revolutionary songs and poems, thanks to which, according to a *Komsomolskaya Pravda* article by poet Alexander Yashin, he felt "with all his pure heart the great truth and nobility of the ideas of the Lenin-Stalin Party."[12]

The usual adolescent traits—self-assuredness, stubbornness in his opinions, excessiveness in his judgments—were elevated by the authors to the realm of politics; they spoke about Morozov's beliefs, his dedication to the Party, his ideological maturity. The writer Koryakov solemnly pronounces, "He was a vehement, fervent lover-of-truth."

Much has been written about the boy's selfless courage. When the tracks were still fresh, however, Solomein wrote in *Vskhody Kommuny* that Pavel abandoned his brother Fyodor to flee the killers: "'Save yourself!' And Pavel rushed into the little aspen wood, intending to run straight to the fields. He did not go far, only a few meters. A kulak's knife penetrated his neck. Before he screamed Pavel heard Fedya's dying cry."[13] In the following editions the Pioneer's behavior is corrected. No longer afraid of the killers, Morozov tries to save his little brother by taking on the assailants; he gives Fedya a chance to run, but the younger boy is caught despite his brother's courage. Sometimes the authors lied on purpose. In his speech during the trial, *Pionerskaya Pravda* correspondent Smirnov suddenly asserted that Morozov was fifteen, even though earlier he had indicated a younger age. Why? Because of the famous quotation of Lenin's: "The generation that is now fifteen will live to see a communist society." For stronger effect Smirnov simply adjusted Pavlik's age to match Lenin's figures: "A fifteen-year-old hero.... was murdered."[14]

The newspapers demanded new material about the hero, but where could the reporters get it? It became necessary to make up new details. Gubarev told *Pionerskaya Pravda* readers that Pavlik, so merciless toward the enemy, was "comradely towards people, [that he] carefully explained to adults and children their mistakes." Smirnov wrote that Morozov had "unmasked the propaganda of the class enemy with all the fury of class hatred...[so that] almost every day he gathered a circle of schoolchildren and explained to them at length the nature of the enemy's propaganda, appealed to the struggle against kulakdom, taught the children how to enlighten their own families."[15] The child pontificated on the Party's goals and the task of building socialism, read newspapers to the peasant women, recommended that people accept the new agricultural code, and criticized the leftist extremes of local agents. If we are to believe the myth, the main representatives of new authority—the Tavda Party Committee and the Sverdlovsk Regional Committee—together accomplished less than Pavlik Morozov did alone.

Today it sounds ridiculous, but back then, when the political myth was being created, authors solemnly competed in inventing new merits for the murdered boy. Meanwhile, Morozov's real life bore little resemblance to the one invented by the writers.

In the real Gerasimovka and the neighboring villages the peasants were all related to one another. Many marriages were between blood relatives, and as a result children were often born with defects. Pavel's own mother was mentally ill; this information sometimes slipped through the censorship barriers and appeared in the Soviet press.[16] There are clues that Pavlik was jittery and unbalanced: "His chin twitched nervously, he had seizures, shook, could not say anything" (Gubarev).[17] In a letter to Solomein, Zoya Kabina wrote that "the boy talked slowly, with interruptions, barking out the words in a dialect composed partly of Russian, partly of Belorussian."[18] Kabina also told me, "He was a weak, sickly child. What can I tell you about his development? What can you expect?" "Other children's games rarely interested him, more often he just sat at the side and watched them," according to his teacher Elena Pozdnina.[19] Matryona Korolkova, his classmate, remembered, "He was weak, often fell sick. If the conditions of life had been better and if his mother had been normal, he would have been normal too." Baidakov described him as "an underdeveloped boy."

Confused articulation and a poor vocabulary are often evidence of late and slow development, retarded cognitive development, and lack of motivation.[20] Such children are more interested in what is happening on the other side of their neighbor's fence than in their own studies. A year before his death Pavlik entered the first grade for the third time—by then he was almost thirteen. In the middle of the year the teacher moved him up to the second grade because he had learned to read, although poorly.

In the beginning of the thirties the prevailing opinion in Soviet educational science was that if both parents were uncultured, the child's mental development would necessarily be retarded. Later, the consideration of social factors as a cause of mental retardation was officially prohibited; it could only be caused by disorders of the nervous system. Contemporary psychologists, however, have returned to considering such environmental factors as lack of paternal and pedagogical attention and bad social surroundings to be among the causes of mental retardation. There is frequently a correspondence between underdevelopment and mental retardation.

A mentally retarded child does not give sufficient consideration to his or her actions and does not foresee their consequences. Such a child is easily influenced; he is late in developing such moral qualities as a sense of duty, conscience, responsibility. He is easily manipulated to give offense and to commit antisocial actions.[21]

According to the people who knew him, Pavlik had spells of depression, annoyance, and anger; they alternated with periods of euphoria during which he would act happy and excited. Then a period of apathy would set in, and he would lose childish interests and become cold. This explains why different people ascribe such diametrically opposed traits to him. Pavlik's stubbornness is mentioned by many authors, although its manifestations differ. He also exhibited hostility and extreme sensitivity.

Pavlik Morozov, when he was alive, had never been seen by a neuropathologist; in fact, according to his mother, the boy had never been to a doctor at all. One would like to consider him psychologically healthy, but, to use contemporary terminology, he was a child from a dysfunctional family who displayed signs of mental retardation. Pavlik Morozov's behavior was a result of the conditions of his upbringing, a single-parent family with an unhealthy psychological climate, disorganized parent-child relations, lack of attention, and a generally low cultural level.

The three main values involved in a child's moral upbringing include respect for the individual, for the law, and for property; any lack thereof creates a potential criminal. There are characters for whom the hardships of others are a source of pleasure. For such a person denunciation is the shortest route to gratification.

And just such a boy, who in the process of heroization was transformed into an idealist and a fanatic, was accepted by the Soviet psychologists as a standard for impressing children with a sense of moral duty. The research of one contemporary psychologist states that Pavlik

Morozov had risen, despite the most difficult of circumstances, to become the embodiment of true, conscious self-sacrifice.[22]

To the authors whose task it was to create an image of the hero-informer, none of this mattered at all. Painters and composers followed the lead of the theater, where productions about Pavlik Morozov were a major theme well into the sixties. Dramatic moments from the boy's life appeared on canvas in various exhibitions. From there they migrated into symphonic music. A Moscow composer, V. Vitlin, created a cantata for chorus and orchestra about the boy. A Leningrad composer, Y. Balashkin, wrote the symphonic poem *Pavlik Morozov*. Here is how the journal *Sovetskaya Muzyka* (Soviet Music) describes it: "The poem is written in a flexible form bearing some particular features of a sonata allegro." In the final movement, when "the high flute registers sound the theme of the Pioneer march, it sounds as a reminder of Pavlik Morozov. The listener carries away in his heart a bright and elevated image of the young hero."[23]

In the fifties an opera by Mikhail Krasev entitled *Pavlik Morozov* was produced in Moscow. It contained lyric songs that turned into merry folkdances, arias for the teacher and the OGPU agent, and Pioneer choruses. The boy's father, a despicable character, sings, "Why did I ever let him become a Pioneer?" In the course of the opera Pavlik stands guard over the kolkhoz wheat, saving it from arsonists. (This plot twist about saving the collective's wheat was borrowed by the librettists from publicity releases about a motion picture dealing with Pavlik's life; the film was never released.) He is accompanied by a choir of peasants who sing,

> Hail to Pavlik!
> He is brave and honest!
> Not afraid of the enemies,
> Not afraid of his father.
> Hail to Pavlik,
> Humble and smart![24]

Little girls dance in a ring around him, tuck him into bed, and sing him a lullaby. In the course of the opera Pavlik finds in the bushes a counterfeit document of his father's, dropped by the gossip Akulina (a fictional character). Pavlik gives it to the teacher, and she turns it over to the OGPU agent. The opera was critically acclaimed for its music; its plot, however, was a different matter. According to the critics, even a seven-year-old could have found a piece of paper and taken it in to the schoolteacher. The correct move would have been to go directly to the OGPU.

At this point we should stop to consider another one of the creators of the myth of Pavlik Morozov, Alexander Rzheshevsky. In his youth he was noted for bravery; he later became a special agent of the Cheka division responsible for elimination of so-called political banditism. During this time he served directly under the famous associate of Felix Dzerzhinsky, Yan Peters. In his memoirs, carefully edited by Soviet censors, he proudly describes how as a child he used to taunt his Bible teacher, and how disappointed he was when later in life his friends stopped talking to him after they found out what he did for a living. People who used to know him remember that as a result of working for the Cheka he developed a peculiar outlook, separating everyone he knew into two categories: our people (those who would cooperate), and the rest (those who wouldn't—traitors). He wrote his books the same way; they were full of false enthusiasm and political pep talk.

Rzheshevsky claims that he was so taken with the heroic life of Morozov that he went to the Komsomol Central Committee and proposed writing a screenplay about the boy.[25] In reality he was simply appointed to immortalize Hero 001 because of his own appropriate background.

The fledgling author did not go to Gerasimovka to research the life and death of his hero; instead, he traveled to the Orel region in Central Russia, to the estate that used to belong to the famous nineteenth-century Russian author Ivan Turgenev. The secretary of the local Party committee showed him an exemplary collective farm; from this the author was supposed to extrapolate the other, real-life setting. The title of his screenplay, *Bezhin Lug* (Bezhin Meadow), he borrowed from the former owner of the estate, the Russian classical writer Ivan Turgenev.[26]

The film intended to show the clash between two orders: the old peasant misery and the new Soviet enthusiasm, atheism, and modern technology. A brief summary of the screenplay follows:

The Pioneer takes the body of his mother, who has been beaten to death by his father, to the cemetery. Then he informs the authorities that the kulaks want to burn the fields of wheat belonging to the collective. The kulaks hide in the church. The new authorities want to turn the church into a village club, and in order to do this they massacre the kulaks who have taken refuge there. They replace the icon of the Virgin Mary with a picture of a peasant woman. The kulaks are arrested, but they kill the guards and escape. The father kills Pavlik to punish him for the denunciation.

All of the above is set far from Tavda, amidst the idyllic Central Russian landscape so well described by Turgenev. One might say that, similarly, in this screenplay the myth of Pavlik Morozov finally achieved independence from any real-life events. The lie had become absolute.

By the time a famed film director came back from visiting the United States, the screenplay was ready. He returned, eager to make a film about the new Soviet man, the youth of the twentieth century. The director was Sergei Eisenstein, who saw in Pavlik Morozov just such a hero.

At that time, the American film scholar Jay Leyda was in Moscow studying at the Institute of Cinematic Art under Eisenstein. He also participated during the filming of *Bezhin Lug*. In highly expurgated form, his book about history of the Russian and Soviet cinema was published in Russian. In it Leyda remembers how during the International Film Festival in Moscow, Eisenstein announced he was making a movie to be set in a collective farm.[27]

Two thousand children auditioned for the role of Pavlik Morozov. The boy who was chosen to play the part was the son of a driver at the Mosfilm studios. He charmingly and doggedly persisted in rehearsing the scene in which he is mortally wounded and finally dies (to the accompaniment of Mozart's *Requiem*). The adolescent delighted everyone with his innocence and good nature.

The beginning of the film was photographed on location in the ancient village of Kolominskoe near Moscow; according to Leyda, that helped to establish a connection with the era of Ivan the Terrible. No one had any intention of going to the Urals. "Real life" was found in the south, near the Azov Sea, in an exemplary collective farm; for "socialist realism," as Leida saw it, consisted of idealizing all characters and events. In order to achieve the effect of spring, under the personal supervision of Eisenstein the autumn fields were plowed up again for the shooting.

Many noted actors had been cast in the film, and the photography was done by a well-known cameraman, Edward Tisse. Eisenstein demonstrated his directing method during the filming to many domestic and foreign guests, but the release of the film was held up because he fell ill.

There was not one shred of originality in either the writer's or the director's approach. The only difference between them was that Rzheshevsky depicted the boy as a little hero of our time, and Eisenstein, as a precursor of the future communist society. Later, in a book about Eisenstein, the noted critic Victor Shklovsky called the film a great and truthful work of art, one that reflected the triumph of life and literature.[28]

In reality the only triumph the film's creators reflected was the victory of the Soviet power in the countryside.

But in showing the cruelty and violence of collectivization the authors went too far. It became clear that there was really no justification for the brutality, despite their efforts to explain that it was due, not to the new order, but to the cultural backwardness of the peasants. The authors' desire to find a moral justification for the events only exposed their basic inhumanity.

Eisenstein himself was, of course, not opposed to class struggle, but his reflections about the right to murder, and the necessity to kill in the name of higher ideals could hardly appeal to those who were doing it and preferred to keep the matter quiet.

Authorities took a dim view of the previewed raw footage; they deemed the film inappropriate for displaying formalistic tendencies and being infected with mysticism. Its makers were ordered to provide motivation for the father's turn to sabotage and to create a more optimistic ending: the father should be arrested and the son remain alive. Though he rejected the happy ending, Eisenstein was forced to rewrite the screenplay. He explained his previous mistake by saying vaguely that the abstractness of the characters had come into conflict with the concreteness of the facts.

Eisenstein was so caught up in his work on the film that he overlooked an announcement just issued. At that time the Government and the Central Party Committee had passed a statute establishing a new order in matters of class education in a classless society. The statute, in part, demanded a strengthened "control over the literature and films for children, [and would] prohibit books and films that could have a detrimental effect on children."[29] As a result, the bureaucrats approached each new children's film with exaggerated caution.

Another former Chekist, the famous writer Isaak Babel, was involved by Rzheshevsky in the project of rewriting the screenplay. Babel took up the revising of the text, changing about 60 percent of it, according to Leyda. He also changed some of the characters' names, replacing them with the names of actors and the studio personnel. Philosophical generalizations became even more rigid, especially those pertaining to the denunciation and the murder.

Meanwhile, the times changed. The approaching wave of arrests threatened those officials in charge of cinema production, who now saw violations of Party line everywhere. Ironically, the team working under

Eisenstein-Tisse had its own Pavlik, an adult informer. Soon, the head of the State Cinematography Committee Boris Shumyatsky, also a vice chairman of the State Committee on the Arts, prohibited the crew from continuing the filming, hinting that the film was a piece of sabotage. Shumyatsky, of course, needed an important enough scapegoat to protect himself, but it was to no avail; Shumyatsky was soon eliminated.

As usual for the time, it was demanded that the creators of the film *Bezhin Lug* repent publicly. Eisenstein announced that he was ready to do so at once. But that was not enough—a noisy public trial was deemed necessary. Newspapers and magazines began persecuting the director. The press also reported the results of a conference on this matter at the top level of the government, and claimed that anyone who did not criticize was guilty himself.

Eisenstein repented privately in the bureaucrats' offices and publicly from the podiums and in the press, calling his creation deeply flawed and ideologically unsound. Cursing himself for his blindness, laxness, lack of vigilance, and absence of the connection with the masses, he begged for a chance to make films about 1917 and 1937—heroic, politically sound, and full of martial enthusiasm and love for Stalin.[30] He had a feeling (not entirely without foundation) that he was a hair's breath from arrest; again and again he swore his faithfulness to Stalin. But at this moment he was generously permitted to reform and serve as an example of the victory of Lenin-Stalinist human resource policy. This persecution, lasting many years, subsequently caused Eisenstein to suffer a heart attack.

Rzheshevsky made excuses, professing that he tried to present Morozov as well as possible using the tools of the Bolshevik cinema. But being removed from work on the project and replaced by Babel saved him. The new co-author was the one to take the brunt of the storm, becoming yet another casualty of repression.

Today, foreign guests are told that the unfinished footage from the first sound movie Eisenstein made was damaged beyond repair by water that flooded the cellars where it was kept. Another story is that during the World War II the building was hit by a bomb. One wonders what really happened to it.

Those responsible for the film had no intention of becoming dissidents. Paradoxically, they became the victims of the very myth they created. Their mistake lay in not realizing that what was permissible in 1933, when they began making the film, would become heresy in 1937, when the work was completed. By that time there was no longer any need for philosophical justifications for denunciation. Self-justification is a result of reflection, and there simply wasn't anything left to reflect upon. The Kremlin had declared that denunciation was good, and only the class enemies could debate that.

The fabrication of this myth reveals the essential method of "socialist realism." According to the statement of Chinese communist leaders, the hero is "a united production of party leadership, the intense support of the masses, and the writer's labor."[31] Throughout the process of creating the mythical Pavlik Morozov the real boy disappeared more and more into fictional images. The hero was invented at the top and then embodied. Art was turned inside out; matter was being changed by will, and all in the spirit of pure, one-party idealism.

A half-century's works about Pavlik Morozov are designated as documentary fiction, semi-documentary, or "almost documentary," as Yevgeny Permyak, a writer from the Urals called them.[32] One might just as well call them semi-art. The newspapers' image of a boy became the prototype of a literary hero. A hero made of paper had become the subject of monuments of bronze.

Notes

1. *Kratkaya Literaturnaya Entsiklopedia* (Moscow, 1964, vol. 2: 428); Gubarev (3 September 1993).
2. Later Stanislav Furin, the editor of *Pioner* (the magazine that published so much about Morozov), jumped from the window and died. He did it because his colleague informed the KGB that Furin criticized the authorities.
3. *Krasnaya Zvezda* (26 July 1962).
4. Smirnov (1961: 64–72).
5. Lidin (1957: 3).
6. Gubarev (15 October 1932).
7. Pavlik Morozov (1962: 3).
8. Solomein (1979: 10); Gubarev (1940: 6).
9. Koryakov (1979: 5); Doroshin (29 March 1933).
10. Isakova (17 August 1967).
11. Solomein (1979: 84).
12. Yashin (26 July 1950). After Stalin's death Yashin wrote a candid short story called "Levers" about more realistic life in a village. The story was forbidden.
13. Solomein (27 October 1932b).
14. *Pionerskaya Pravda* (5 December 1932).
15. All these details are in *Pionerskaya Pravda* (17, 18 October; 5, 23 December 1932).
16. Korshunov (23 September 1962); Balashov (September 1982).

17. Gubarev (1948b: 14, 32–34).
18. Solomein (Materials...).
19. Pozdnina (Memoirs).
20. *Pionerskaya...* (1963: 38).
21. Rubenshtein (1979: 98, 117, 158, 165).
22. Zosimovsky (1982: 31).
23. Orlov (December 1954).
24. Polyakova (July 1958).
25. Rzheshevsky (1982: 17, 33, 68–69).
26. Vishnevsky (1936).
27. Leyda (1960: 327–40).
28. Shklovsky (1973: 237–38).
29. *Pravda* (1 June 1935).
30. Vaisfeld (*Iskusstvo Kino*, May 1937); Eisenstein (17 April 1937).
31. Zhelokhovtsev (1973: 138).
32. Permyak (22 March 1963).

10

Hail to the Informers!

On March 16, 1934, *Pionerskaya Pravda* published a denunciation. Occupying almost all of the third page, it began as follows: "To the city of Spask. To the OGPU. I inform the organs of the OGPU that in the Otrada village outrages are taking place..."

The pretty face of a girl from the Tatar Republic, Pioneer Olya Balykina, looks at us from the accompanying portrait. In her letter, forgetting no detail of name or date, she lists everybody—including her own father, who from her point of view was guilty of various offenses. The letter ends: "I am pulling all the skeletons out of the closet. Afterwards, let the authorities do what they want with them." In its commentary on the letter, the newspaper compares Olya with Pavlik Morozov, adding: "A medical examination revealed that as a result of severe beatings Olya's health was undermined. Olya was sent to a resort for two months to relax and recuperate." During World War II, the now grown-up Olga Balykina was captured by the Nazis. Following her liberation someone denounced her as having been a prisoner of war, a charge that led automatically to ten years in Soviet labor camps. After Stalin's death she was released and exonerated. Later, the pensioner Olga Balykina was remembered in the press as a sort of Pavlik Morozov in skirts.

This publication of an exemplary denunciation in a central newspaper showed that the crusade was entering a new stage. No other campaign in the country was conducted with as much pathos and enthusiasm as these mass condemnations. Denunciations became a popular genre in the periodicals, accessible to amateurs, even to children. Pavlik Morozov became the hero of the new era, and this era demanded that children develop new qualities. Poet Alexander Yashin called for vigilance training and noted that two characteristics helped Pioneers: quick wits and sharp eyes.[1] The causes of heroism were simple and readily understood: "Why wasn't

Pavlik afraid to denounce his father and uncle Kulukanov?" questioned
Pionerskaya Pravda, answering: "Because he was a real Pioneer. He
knew how to tell friends from foes."[2]

Major Party figures in the 1930s shared their thoughts about how
children should conduct their lives, among them Lenin's widow, Nadezhda
Krupskaya, who was considered a leader at the time. She cautioned:
"Look around. You will see how many vestiges of individualism there
still are. It would be good if you discussed them among yourselves and
wrote them down. I am afraid you would get a whole thick notebook."[3]
Leaders of the international communist movement visiting from abroad
hailed the vigilant youths. Radio, newspapers, books, and speeches sang
hosannahs to every new denunciation and gave instruction in the fine art
of informing the secret police. *Pionerskaya Pravda* printed an article
about a Pioneer-Hero Kolya Yuryev, who was sitting in a field of wheat
with a pair of binoculars one day. He saw a girl tearing off ears of wheat
and grabbed her; she tried to get away, but couldn't.[4] The newspapers of
the time used the phrase "barbers of the kolkhoz bread" to designate
hungry people who stole ears of wheat. It was no wonder, though, that
the peasants tried to steal grain; after the creation of kolkhozes, starvation spread across the country.

"'Stop! Who are you? Where are you from?'—thus, the village Pioneers hail every stranger walking through the field, and if he turns out to
be a thief they detain him," commented *Pionerskaya Pravda*.[5] The newspaper cheerfully went on, describing how the children, in the absence of
adults, searched people's houses themselves. A true Pioneer, Pronya
Kolybin bravely unmasked his own mother when she went into the field
to gather fallen grain to feed him. The mother was imprisoned, while the
hero-son was sent to vacation in the Crimea at the Pioneer camp "Artek."
(This Black Sea resort, formerly visited by the rich and powerful, was
transformed into a vacation area for young volunteer-informers.) This
information about the hero Kolybin is kept in the card catalog of the
History Cabinet of the All-Union Pioneer Organization.

One school student from the Rostov-on-Don region, Mitya Gordienko,
apprehended several hungry people. Appearing as a witness at their trial
he proclaimed, "Having exposed the thieves of kolkhoz grain I swear to
organize thirty children of our commune to guard the crops, and to be the
head of this Pioneer group." Once, Mitya denounced two adults, a married couple; the husband was condemned to death, his wife sentenced to

ten years of hard labor in high-security camps. For this disclosure Mitya received a personally inscribed watch, a new Pioneer uniform, boots, and a year's subscription to a local newspaper, *Leninskie Vnuchata* (Lenin's Grandchildren).[6] Nikolay Aseev, a famous poet at the time, composed the *Song of Pioneers Guarding the Crops*:

> Caught in the field
> Grabbed by the hand
> Caught the enemy
>> in the
>>> act.[7]

During the same period, Aseev wrote to the OGPU that the poet Vladimir Mayakovsky, who had shot himself three years earlier, was in fact killed by the Trotskyites, and began writing a poem intended to glorify the OGPU for ages to come.

Even small-scale informers were being praised to the heavens. Child correspondents informed against those who came late to school, skipped classes, received bad grades, or did not want to subscribe to *Pionerskaya Pravda*. The newspaper instructed its readers to watch their friends during religious holidays. Children responded, "The Pioneer such and such, instead of coming to school, went to church." Some children stopped studying, dedicating themselves instead to the surveillance of other truants.

In 1934, Commissioner of Public Education Andrey Bubnov published an order to prosecute those undependable parents who were remiss in caring for their children. This was the idea: a child informs the teacher that he is unhappy with his mother or father, upon which the school files a lawsuit against them.[8]

"Newspapers must increase the political awareness of the child-correspondents," A. Gusev, editor of *Pionerskaya Pravda*, argued in response to the directives of the Politburo in his book *Child Correspondents in Schools*. "It means watching the teacher, keeping your eyes peeled in the struggle for quality teaching in the classroom." Children were expected to unmask class enemies from among the teachers. And the children eagerly complied. One boy wrote to the newspaper that his school's headmaster had given the following arithmetic problem in class: "The village had a total of 15 horses. When people entered the kolkhoz, 13 horses died. How many were left afterwards?" As a class enemy the headmaster faced "severe prosecution." Children willingly gave the names of teachers and counselors whom they considered lazy or professionally unfit. The Pioneers were also interested in the private lives of adults. The newspaper *Na Smenu!* printed an anonymous letter from a boy who said that his neighbor lived with a young Komsomol woman for a while, kicked her out, then took a new one. It became a Pioneer's duty to eavesdrop on every sound, every murmur, every sigh. Leafing through *Pionerskaya Pravda*, at the end of the year 1933, one finds the following:

7 November. "Lenya caught two thieves." Lenya saw two suspicious people and informed the powers that be.

29 November. "Child-correspondent exposes the kulaks." A Pioneer informs the newspaper, and from there the matter goes directly to the OGPU. The same public prosecutor from the paper, Smirnov, goes to the scene, where he himself organizes the judicial inquiry.

3 December. "Pioneer-Guards in Transportation." A Pioneer-guard catches a woman stevedore with stolen fish.

11 December. A Pioneer "confidently told the judges about kulak swindles in the village."

17 December. Smirnov again speaks at the trial. He "went into the details of class struggle in our country." Those whom the Pioneers informed against are sentenced to ten years of confinement in maximum security concentration camps."

17 December. In a paper quoting Stalin: The enemies "are not to be sought far from the kolkhoz, they are embedded in the kolkhoz itself..."

As the campaign was starting, Sverdlovsk newspaper *Vskhody Kommuny* warned those Pioneers who for some reason had not yet informed on their relatives; the ones who do not speak up are no longer Pioneers. The ones who do not inform are enemies, and should themselves be denounced at once. A year later Valentin Zolotukhin, chairman of the Central Bureau of Pioneers, promised informers protection by the State: "The whole country watches over every corner of the Union, over every Pioneer. And a Pioneer has nothing to fear."[9] Thus, the country watched over the informers, and the informers watched over the country. Soon a book came out by the journalist Smirnov. Entitled *The Young Guards*, it was an instruction manual for Pioneer vigilance. The author told how to look for the enemies of the people, where to find them, and whom to go to with the information. Smirnov explained how to send letters so that enemies of the people wouldn't intercept the mail at the local post office; a Pioneer should carry them to the train station and put them directly into the postal wagon of a passing train. *Pionerskaya Pravda* became the center for collecting denunciations from the readers all over the country. Here they were registered, organized, and passed on to those authorities concerned with the liquidation of the enemies of the people. The Pioneer organization becomes a branch of the secret police, a national school of informers. Of additional note, Soviet psychologist S. Rubenshtein observed, "Criminal organizations using children and cripples for their own purposes have been described by C. Dickens and B. Brecht."[10] Through all of this the plagiarized Pioneer motto, "Be Prepared," acquires a sinister resonance.

The child reader-agents were called "fighters," "guards," and "scouts." In calling for more denunciations, the newspaper nicknamed them the *Detkor*, "The Sharp Eyes." Their real names were kept secret. One newspaper praised an adolescent who went to the village Soviet to denounce without stopping to think about it. This is very important—not to stop to think. In order to lessen the amateurish nature of local denunciations, it was proposed that Pioneer vigilante groups be created. The newspaper advised, "Do not trust anyone whom you doubt in the least." It demanded, "One must immediately inform the village Soviet authorities about all strangers and suspicious characters."[11] All it takes to become a hero is to notice a suspicious person and give the authorities his whereabouts. See and inform. For that, a young person could expect a reward.

It became necessary to legislate denunciations. In 1935, the USSR Office of Public Prosecutor issued an order to involve the representatives of the press and the village correspondents (the informants) in the investigations. In practice, the informers participated in prosecution as well. An article in the newspaper was practically equivalent in power to an article of the Criminal Code. Then special commissions were created, the so-called "OSO," to replace trials by due process; these formed the administrative base for the mass repressions. The newspapers printed lists of the executed enemies of the people next to the lists of the informers. Courts of appeal were abolished—no pardons granted. In his book Solomein renames, and politicizes, the popular children's game of hide-and-seek "see-and-inform." Stalin made an appeal to keep a watchful eye out not only for Trotskyites, but also for those who follow the same path.[12] *Sotsialisticheskaya Zakonnost* (Socialist Law) explained in its August 1938 issue the true meaning of the phrase "freedom of speech";

in essence, keeping the authorities informed embodied the very liberty promised by Stalin's Constitution.[13]

This particular order from the Leader provided work for the Pioneers in the city where there were no kulaks, but where Trotskyites still walked the streets. Informers were needed in industry, in transportation, in government organizations, and in schools. A boy named Mikhas Chachnovsky unmasked sugar thieves at a food factory, and was rewarded for the denunciation with a trip to the Artek camp. Another Pioneer, Shishkin, wrote, "Please send a commission to inventory the grain warehouses." Chairman of the Supplies Commission Comrade Kleiner noted the alertness of Pioneer Shishkin and rewarded him with a bicycle.[14]

It's common knowledge that Lenin had branded internal passports a shameful heritage of tsarist Russia. But in 1932 internal passports were reintroduced in the USSR. Even so, they were only given to the city dwellers; indeed, it became impossible to live in the city without a passport. Peasants were not given passports in order to prevent them from deserting the starving villages for the generally better supplied towns. The newspapers, however, had a different explanation for the institution of the passport system; kulaks and other parasites move into large cities where it is easier to go unnoticed. They steal food from our stores, and start living at the expense of the workers. The purpose of passportization is to purge the kulak elements from society. The new duty of a Pioneer is to be as alert as possible for violators of the passport law and to help the police unmask the parasitic elements. An attempt was even made to entrust children with checking adults' passports in the streets, but the idea was not approved at the top. Alexander Khrabrovitsky, a literary critic who worked as a reporter during the 1930s, told me that Chairman of the Council of Ministers (and second in command to Stalin) Molotov read the February 3, 1933, issue of *Pionerskaya Pravda* urging that children monitor adults' passports. Molotov's response? He wrote on the front page, "What kind of an idiot edits this paper?" Here, apparently, *Pionerskaya Pravda* went too far; editor Georgi Soldatov was fired.

At school children took an oath, "I promise...to be on the alert for safety of the school property." Taken by itself this is not a bad idea; but Smirnov's *The Young Guards* tells students to watch their schoolmates to see who steals or breaks what. One newspaper ecstatically conveyed an account of a Pioneer Camp bearing the name of Pavlik Morozov where children carefully watched each other from dawn to dusk and dusk to dawn, reporting to the paper what they have seen. It was a good training ground before going on to more serious tasks. Now that it was especially important to have sharp eyes, nerves of steel, and muscles of iron, children were supposed to keep in shape. Youth leader Nadezhda Krupskaya, in her article "Be Well Armed," corroborates this necessity; a new purge of the Party was in the making.[15]

According to directives from the top, many kinds of people were being removed from the Party: class aliens, opportunists, hypocrites, transgressors of iron discipline, various corrupt bureaucrats, morally disintegrated personalities, as well as simple liars. Everyone was subject to the purge, with the exception of members of the Central Committee and the Central Control Commission. Krupskaya, the Deputy Commissar of Education, called on children to expose enemy elements that had managed to sneak into the Party in order to sabotage it. The idea of children keeping an eye on Party members was no more inspired than that of children checking adults' passports; nonetheless, it did not meet with objections. Lenin's widow urged, "We need more alertness—it is necessary to notice the enemy in time, to reveal him obstructing our common cause, and to stop him."[16] The new task was taken up by the papers. *Pionerskaya Pravda* wrote, "A Pioneer should not hesitate when he sees someone, even his father, sabotaging the working class. Pioneer Rumyantsev went back and forth for two days, unable to decide whether to inform or not. Two feelings struggled in him—filial love and his sense of Pioneer duty. Pioneer duty won—Rumyantsev went to the city bureau and told everything he knew about his father. The police immediately made a search." Having received an official note of gratitude the Pioneer next informed against his brother. The hero left what remained of his family and went to rest in a Pioneer camp.

Every region of the country promoted its own young informers. An All-Union Red Honor List was created for Pioneer-Guards; here appear only the names of the best. *Pravda* put every North Caucasus school organization on the list for their protection of kolkhoz crops. This so-called "light cavalry" acted in accordance with the formula "See—Hurry—Inform." Forty-four activist-informers are listed in the paper. On January 6, 1934, *Pravda* and other newspapers printed a letter to Stalin from the Pioneers of Siberian village of Novaya Uda. From the region to which Stalin had been exiled before the Revolution, the Pioneers reported who informed against whom in the village; self-criticism followed as they told the Leader about their own sins and those of others.[17] The newspaper used large print for the names of the young informers. Their noble accomplishments? One nabbed a shepherd; another turned his father over to the OGPU; yet another exposed a saboteur, unveiled a ring of thieves of the kolkhoz property, and caught a kulak woman. Two hundred guards, or "watchmen," were sent to the privileged Artek camp. Child-informers from different regions of the country challenged each other to a peculiarly socialist competition: who can inform the most. Delegations of Pioneer-watchmen traveled from one area of the country to another to exchange their know-how—that is, know to snoop and how to inform. In the Ukraine a Republican Conference of the "watchmen" was assembled, with Politburo member Postyshev as its guest of honor.

It seemed as if the campaign had reached its climax, that everyone had been denounced. But this was not enough to demonstrate the devotion of the "third generation" to the cause of the Communist Party. The powers that be demanded self-criticism and self-denunciations from those who had not yet started to inform; now executives, writers, actors, engineers, bureaucrats, workers, kolkhozniks, and schoolchildren started repenting and promising to reform. One week before the First Writers' Congress a poet was punished for not informing against himself. The poet, Alexander Oislender, was expelled from Komsomol for concealing his ancestry— he was a son of a lumber manufacturer. Later he was pardoned, getting away with only a severe reprimand in return for his sincere admission of guilt. Writer and Komsomol member P. Panchenko, who had known about Oislender's father, was given a light reprimand due to an absence of prior offenses.[18]

Meanwhile, news of the child-informers penetrated to the West in the form of vague rumors. The true builders of the bright future were only encouraged by this. "Let the emigré White Army officers sputter madly the lies that...the Red Pioneers are an eye of the Cheka in their own families and in school," wrote Komsomol leaders in the book *The Children's Communist Movement*. "Our enemies' anger is the best praise for us, the younger generation of Bolsheviks."[19]

Of course, children didn't have the monopoly on informing, nor were they solely informers. One girl-hero, Mamlakat Nakhangova, became famous and was decorated because she picked cotton with both hands, while adult women only used one. (Although machinery for that purpose was certainly available at that time, this helped reduce the labor surplus.) The little girl helped double the productivity of women's manual labor in Central Asia, thus increasing production of gunpowder in the country. Newspapers extolled Pioneers who bred horses and guard dogs for the Red Army. In the Kremlin receptions were held in honor of young winners of musical competitions between major conservatories.

All this went on. Even so, the poems and plays glorified not the cotton-pickers, nor the dog-breeders, nor the young Paganinis, but the informers. And all of these heroes were now measured against Pioneer 001, the most important hero of the country, Pavlik Morozov. Pavlik became, as the newspaper called him, "a founder and a young revolutionary."[20] His feat was glorified in songs sung by choirs all over the country. Sergei Mikhalkov turned out to be the most enterprising of his generation of young poets in that he wrote the first song about Pavlik, leaving a score of other denunciation lyricists in the dust. The song's music was composed by Ferents Sabo, a Hungarian then living in the USSR. Mikhalkov began by glorifying the informer's deed and wound up as a Secretary of the Writers' Union of the USSR. He also composed poems whose themes involved denunciation and the demand for executing enemies of the people. In this, however, he was not alone. The genre quickly acquired its own classics, many written by a number of prestigious authors. Mikhalkov's *Song of Pavlik Morozov* has been performed countless times since its publication.[21] The author of this book was compelled to sing it in a choir when he was ten years old, in the Center for Children's Artistic Development. Considering that the reader is already familiar with its source of inspiration, I will simply provide a translation of the song's end-rhymes:

> Grey—side—example—Pioneer.
> Not in vain—ardently—in the barns—kulaks.
> Pavel—taught—come forward—unmasked.
> Grasses—ringing—reprisal—relatives.
> Summer—leaf—young—communist.
> Clouds—straight—best—home.
> Banner—at the side—kulaks—Pioneer.
> Manage—in the lines—hero—never.

Notes

1. Yashin (26 July 1950).
2. Solomein (27 December 1932).

3. *Pionerskaya Pravda* (23 October 1932).
4. Shvartsman (7 and 9 August 1933).
5. *Pionerskaya Pravda* (11 August 1933).
6. Smirnov (1934: 45–48); *Pionerskaya Pravda* (17 July 1933).
7. *Pionerskaya Pravda* (27 August 1933).
8. *Prikaz...* (1934).
9. *Vskhody Kommuny* (19 December 1932); *Pionerskaya Pravda* (10 January 1934).
10. Rubenshtein (1979: 150).
11. *Pionerskaya Pravda* (27 January and 17 July 1933).
12. Stalin (1 April 1937).
13. Belyaev (August 1938).
14. *Pionerskaya Pravda* (6 March 1935). Kleiner himself was denounced, arrested, and liquidated in 1937.
15. Krupskaya (5 July 1933).
16. *Ibid.*
17. V. Z. (25 July 1933).
18. *Komsomolskaya Pravda* (12 August 1934).
19. *Detskoe...* (1932: 74).
20. *Pionerskaya Pravda* (5 December 1932).
21. *Vozhaty* (April 1934).

11

How Many Pavliks were There?

The preparations for the show trial of the case of Pavlik Morozov's murder were going full speed when in village of Kolesnikovo in the Kurgan region another boy was killed; his name was Kolya Myagotin. The official version of the event goes as follows. A Red Army soldier's widow turned her son over to the local orphanage because she had nothing to feed him. There, the boy became a Pioneer. When he later returned to his mother's house, the rich peasants were already exiled from the village, but the drunkards and hooligans remained. A real Leninist, the boy listened to the adults' conversations: "Kolya told the village Soviet about everything he heard or learned." But Kolya's friend Petya Vakhrushev informed the class enemies of his activities; in other words, Petya told his relatives who the informer was. *Pionerskaya Pravda* described Kolya's murder in detail:

> Ivan shot him in the leg.
>
> "Still alive?" He came closer. Kolka, pale, was crying. His legs were bleeding.
>
> "Alive..."
>
> "We ought to finish him, or we'll be in trouble."
>
> A shot sounded point blank...

The irony is obvious; one Pioneer informed the authorities, and another informed those who were informed on. During the interrogation, Petya reformed and denounced his older brothers. Judging by the papers, a new wave of violence was approaching: "The hand of proletarian dictatorship will smash the vermin." According to the rules of the time, the big show trial was followed by a series of a smaller local ones. Shooting no longer seemed enough, and children demanded "the most cruel punishment for the murderers," but could not agree just what that should be. The same journalists—Solomein and Smirnov—came to participate in the new trial. This time there were not one but three public prosecutors from different newspapers, speaking "in the name of millions of Pioneers and students." During the trial a leaflet entitled "Be on Guard" was handed out to the audience. It called for new denunciations. Myagotin was killed by one man; five people were sentenced to death. In addition, a large group of "thieves, drunkards and saboteurs" were sentenced to ten years in labor camps. The name of the murdered Pioneer-Hero was entered into the Book of Honor of the Pioneer Organization of the Central Committee of the Komsomol beside that of Pavlik Morozov, as Hero Number 002.[1]

We may never really know who killed Kolya Myagotin, or why. We have already noted the reliability of the press coverage of the time. Undoubtedly, however, the struggle on behalf of the informers has long been matched by the struggle against them.

The question arises: Why was it necessary to turn somebody who was not even a Pioneer, and whose denunciation had nothing to do with political fanaticism, into the best Pioneer of the country? Perhaps because in the line of hero-informers Pavlik Morozov was the first? Not so. I have collected evidence of at least eight other cases involving children murdered for denunciations before Pavlik Morozov. The first was another Pavlik, last name Teslya, a Ukrainian boy from the ancient village of Sorochintsy, who informed against his father five years before Morozov. Seven denunciations are connected with collectivization efforts in the countryside; one, Vitya Gurin from Donetsk, with the enemies of the people in the city. The best known of the eight is Grisha Akopyan, who was stabbed to death in Azerbaijan two years before Morozov. The official publication *The Children's Communist Movement* announced even before Pavlik Morozov's death that "tens of our best comrades [perished] in battle." These children, who fought valiantly against the leftist extremists and the rightist appeasers, were ostensibly murdered for their denunciations.[2]

But the glory of all these informers is meager compared to that of Pavlik Morozov. Why all the pomp and praise if it was largely undeserved? The official Hero-Informer 001 had to appear at the time when he became necessary to the political campaign. And we know that he did appear precisely when he was needed: on the eve of a monumental wave of mass repression. The campaign that started in a backwoods village of Gerasimovka began to take on vast significance.

October 1932, *Pionerskaya Pravda*: "Hundreds and thousands of children are taking his place today and will do so in the future."

November 1932, *Tavdinsky Rabochy*: "Pavel Morozov is not alone, there are legions like him. They disclose the hoarders of grain, thieves of socialist property; if necessary, they will put their own fathers on trial."

August 1933, *Pionerskaya Pravda*: "There are millions of Pavliks in the schools..."

A generalization regarding Pioneers, found in the preface to the book *In the Kulaks' Nest*, 1933: Morozov "exemplifies the intentions and actions of our army of Pioneers, six million strong."[3]

Stereotyping the consciences of adults in a *Pravda* editorial (December, 1937): "Every honest citizen of our country considers it his duty to help actively the organs of NKVD in their work."[4]

Politburo member Anastas Mikoyan, during an address at a meeting dedicated to the twentieth anniversary of the NKVD, declared from the stage of the Bolshoi Theater, "Every worker in our country is a member of NKVD!" He mentioned the ideal Soviet man—faithful Party watchdog Felix Dzerzhinsky—and called on the whole population to emulate Yezhov, head of the NKVD, in his Stalinist style of work. In essence the Stalinist style was not new. Lenin had declared the same ethos earlier: "A good communist is at the same time a good Chekist." Mikoyan merely explained this Leninist-Stalinist style of operation in popular terms: "Instead of discussions we use methods of uprooting and demolition." The anniversary of the secret police coincided with the end of the five-year period designated for the destruction of social classes in the country. The five-year plan was fulfilled with good measure, and the hostile classes destroyed, but Stalin declared that the class struggle had become more acute than ever.

Morozov's doubles matured. Some of them now worked in the NKVD, putting into practice the political education they received in school and in the Pioneer organization. Others simply volunteered their services.

According to newspaper reports, the multiplicity of Pavliks did more than just display personal enthusiasm. Their activity became an integral force in the construction of the new society. The country's leaders demanded new sacrifices and acts of heroism from trusting and inexperienced adolescents. Politburo member Lazar Kaganovich, addressing the Pioneers, announced, "Every one of you must ask himself, 'Am I ready to make sacrifices, to suffer for the cause of proletarian struggle, for commu-

nism?'"[5] Kaganovich thought that not everyone was worthy of becoming a
martyr, that only those who proved their readiness, should become Pioneers. And the best way to prove this readiness was denunciation.

But something unpredictable happened; the murder provoked more
hatred toward the Party itself than toward its enemies. The wave of violence coming from above encountered an equally violent response. Seeing no defense from the lawlessness of the state, the people took justice
into their own hands. The more powerful the pressure from above, the
more violent and desperate became the protest. Children, whom the system corrupted to the advantage of the people in power, often became
innocent victims of this conflict.

At a 1935 conference of writers, composers, and film directors, Maxim
Gorky declared, "Many Pioneers have already been killed."[6] The journalist Solomein wrote in his memoirs, "I took part in approximately ten
investigations of kulaks murdering Pioneers—that's just myself. And who
knows how many such victims there were. In the Urals? In the whole
country? Too many to count."[7]

The press presented the cases so that it seemed the children had been
killed simply for being Pioneers. The newspaper wrote that in killing
Pavlik Morozov the kulaks realized they "were causing great harm to the
Children's Communist Movement."[8] *Pionerskaya Pravda* graphically
commented on the deaths of two girl-informers, Nastya Razinkina and
Polya Skalkina: "A shot at Nastya and Polya is a shot at the body of the
Pioneer organization."[9] But why the Pioneers were killed and by whom
was seldom clear. *Pravda* openly called for vigilance: "It is the business
of every honest kolkhoznik to help the Party and Soviet power execute
the bastard who dares touch a child fulfilling his duty to the kolkhoz and
to the country as a whole."[10] The kolkhozniks, however, had their own
conception of duty, and the authorities reaped the fruit of the terror they
sowed. While the authorities glorified the murdered informers, the people
took their revenge, supplying the propaganda machine with ever more
victims.

Pionerskaya Pravda published an interview with public prosecutor
A. Vinogradov entitled "To Protect the Young Warriors More Vigilantly!"
In it he admits that the problem had become serious and promises to take
measures for the protection of young informers. The hypocrisy of these
declarations is especially clear now that we see how eagerly the propaganda machine used the child murders for its own purposes. According

to the press, however, the violence only increased. In the year 1932 (after Pavlik and Fedya Morozov were killed) there were three more murders of children for informing. I counted six murdered informers in 1933, in 1934 another six, and nine in 1935. The authorities acted crudely, arousing the base instincts of the mob. But in most cases it remains unknown who did the killing and why, whether for personal revenge or to rekindle the violence. I counted a total of fifty-seven murders of child-informers during the years of Stalin's terror. They all became Pioneer-heroes; books are written about them, and streets, parks, libraries, and Pioneer palaces bear their names.

The fate of the young spies who managed to remain alive constitutes a separate topic for consideration. Two authorized Bolshevik agents came to the Chukchei village of Anadyr in the Chukotsky district to oversee the dispossession of the kulaks and create a kolkhoz. They were killed. One day later a policeman showed up. A boy by name of Yatyrgin, son of Vuna, betrayed the killers, revealing their identities, and added that they had run away to Alaska. Some reindeer-breeding Chukchei decided to follow the others and take their deer along with them. Hearing about this plan, Yatyrgin stole a neighbor's dogsled in order to go and inform the authorities. His neighbors ambushed the boy, hit him with an axe, and threw him into a hole, but he managed to crawl out alive. In the *Pionerskaya Letopis* (Pioneer Annals) we learn of his reward; when Yatyrgin entered the Pioneers, the commissioners changed his name to Pavlik Morozov. The new name was later written in his passport. (In the 1970s Yatyrgin, under the name Pavel Morozov, was a schoolteacher and a Party member.)[11]

The promotion of denunciation was having its impact, as even the highest-ranked officials of the Soviet state took part in it. Not long before his mysterious death, Politburo member Sergo Ordzhonikidze in his address to the All-Union Conference of Stakhanovites praised the achievements of the Artemov family. The father, Alexei Artemov, his wife Ksenya, and their two sons and three daughters informed the secret police about 172 suspicious people—enemy spies, in their opinion. All the suspects were arrested, and this family of champion-informers was awarded medals and valuable gifts.

Results of the mass-denunciation campaign looked pitiful. Under the facade of the popular involvement of millions of Pavliks in building communism, the country was flooded with a wave of child delinquency. After millions of parents had been liquidated or had died from starvation, millions of children were left homeless, a waste of the "third generation of builders of socialism." In order to cope with this problem, the youth laws of 1935 established that children over the age of twelve would be "subject to criminal punishment."[12] The laws resulted in the rapid growth of regular orphanages, special orphanages, isolation wards, reform colonies, foster homes, and the introduction of children's forced labor camps. Now the system had reached a kind of equilibrium; as a result of children's denunciations the adults were sent to the camps, and the children, informed on by adults, were sent to reform colonies. The scale and pathos of the campaign leaves no doubt that it was sanctioned by the very highest levels of authority.

Notes

1. *Pionery-geroi* (1956: 5); Sukhachevsky (1972); *Pionerskaya Pravda* (27 and 29 December 1932, 3 January 1933).
2. Detskoe... (1932: 78–81).
3. *Pionerskaya Pravda* (15 October 1932; 1 August and 3 September 1933); *Tavdinsky Rabochy* (26 November 1932); Lomonosova (1933: 3).
4. *Pravda* (20 and 21 December 1937).
5. *Pionerskaya Pravda* (7 October 1933).
6. Gorky (1953, Vol. 27: 440).
7. Koryakov (1977: 276).
8. *Tavdinsky Rabochy* (30 November 1932).
9. *Pionerskaya Pravda* (14 December 1934).
10. Gusev (1948: 45).
11. Gusev (1970: 51); *Pionerskaya Pravda* (7 June 1955).
12. *Ugolovnoye...* (1957: 23); *Pravda* (1 June 1935).

12

Pavlik Morozov and Comrade Stalin

None of Stalin's written orders concerning Pavlik Morozov are available to us; Stalin's orders were often issued verbally—more than sufficient—although it is impossible to doubt that written orders existed as well. There is indirect evidence, however, that questions connected with the hero-informer were personally decided by the Great Leader, and that he returned repeatedly to these questions.

"Stalin, of course, played a role in Morozov's fate," I was told by Matryona Korolkova, Pavlik's classmate in Gerasimovka:

> In January of 1934, I was taken to Moscow together with a group of Pioneers. I was given to understand that we were about to be brought to a reception to meet Stalin, and that I was to speak about Pavlik. I was told what I should say and how I should say it. I waited for a long time. But then the meeting was canceled—they told us that Stalin was busy. I was sent away to the Pioneer camp, Artek. I received a gift of one hundred rubles at the camp, and after that two more gifts of twenty-five rubles apiece were sent to me in my own village.

Most probably, Stalin's interest in the murdered boy was promoted by one of the three apparatchiks closely connected with the Morozov case: Postyshev, Kosarev, and Poskryobyshev. Politburo member Pavel Postyshev was forty-five years old in 1932. He sported a moustache and went about in boots, a greatcoat, and a military peaked cap, in close imitation of Stalin's image. Then secretary of the Party Central Committee, he had previously directed its two most important departments, Organization and Agitation-Propaganda. His present responsibility was the political campaign for the liquidation of the kulaks. He also controlled the Komsomol. The press habitually referred to him as Stalin's comrade-in-arms, and as the Pioneers' best friend.[1] Pioneer detachments were named for him. Postyshev's importance at that time can be judged by a remark in the 1932 anthology *On Pioneers and the Pioneer Movement* to the effect that its contents included "the speeches of eminent Party activists from Lenin to Postyshev," omitting mention of Stalin.

It was Postyshev who successfully initiated the large-scale system of informing on one's fellow citizens to the OGPU, utilizing for this purpose the editorial and correspondence sections of newspapers. In a speech to the Sixteenth Party Congress, he concocted a fable to the effect that the kulaks had created their own network of counterrevolutionary agents within the Bolshevik Party. By his direct order, the Komsomol Central Committee and the People's Commissariat of Enlightenment released a barrage of propaganda about the heroic feat of the boy informer. This program was carried out by Alexander Kosarev, the twenty-year-old general secretary of the Komsomol, who was Stalin's favorite and Postyshev's right hand. Kosarev signed many of the authorizations for disseminating the Morozov story to schoolchildren. He received a delegation from Gerasimovka that reported to him on the success of the campaign of denunciation waged by the Pioneers of the Ural region. Kosarev's aides personally led the campaign: Sergei Saltanov, secretary of the Komsomol Central Committee; Valentin Zolotukhin, leader of the Young Pioneers; and Vasily Arkhipov, Zolotukhin's assistant.

Later, Postyshev himself was arrested after being denounced by a colleague who was officially cited as a heroine for her act.[2] The Postyshev Pioneer detachments were thereupon stripped of their name and renamed for Pavlik Morozov. Kosarev and Saltanov were also denounced and sent to labor camps, where they were executed. People's Commissar Bubnov was liquidated as well. According to one story, Kosarev disappeared after a letter to Stalin in which he denounced the denunciation system and the mass arrests. But both he and Bubnov had already dispatched untold numbers to their deaths. For resisting arrest on the front during World War II, Arkhipov was shot in the back.

Stalin's personal history left its imprint on his educational views and moral positions. It is said that before the Revolution Stalin worked in collaboration with the tsarist Secret Police. This allegation has never been refuted, nor has it been substantiated. It is known that as general secretary of the Communist Party he personally eavesdropped on his colleagues by means of a special listening apparatus.

But the universal informing system had begun in the Soviet Union as early as Lenin. Lenin's old comrades recall his commissioning them to write anonymous denunciations compromising his political adversaries.

Lenin personally directed the preparations for show trials, and Stalin followed his example. Stalin and Trotsky competed in denouncing one another to Lenin until Stalin gained the upper hand. Trotsky, incidentally, was murdered, in accordance with Stalin's personal order, by exactly the same brutal method as had been used on the Morozov children. It was Lenin who appointed Stalin head of the RKI, the Worker-Peasant Inspection, through which compromising information was collected on all the employees of the State. Under Stalin's leadership the RKI collected denunciations and busied itself with purges.

Even earlier, Stalin had begun to make use of the OGPU apparatus to rid himself of those not useful for his purposes. Stalin's secretaries would receive from the OGPU compromising information based on denunciations both genuine and concocted. And Stalin, in turn, transmitted through the same secretaries his verbal decisions. Back then the OGPU did not yet have the power to arrest members of the Party. This occurred only ten years later, at the time of Morozov's murder, when the Special Section was created and attached to Stalin's personal secretariat. The special sections of the District and Regional Party Committees, which maintained their own personnel in all factories and state institutions, were subordinate to Stalin's Special Section. Within the OGPU organization were the two subdivisions of Special Section: OO (Special Departments) and SPO (Secret-Political Sections). These were also under Stalin's direct orders, answerable to no one else.

The Special Section was headed by the forty-year-old Alexander Poskryobyshev, "Stalin's most faithful dog," in the phrase of Nikita Khrushchev.[3] The broad features of his coarse face, the shaven head, and the semi-military, Stalinesque style of dress—this was his image. Old Party workers who had known him in the thirties told me that Poskryobyshev, who was born in Ekaterinburg, later Sverdlovsk, still managed to retain his solid connections in the Ural region after becoming Stalin's right-hand man. All of the OGPU's actions in the Urals were carried out under his supervision. Documents from that part of the country, bypassing other means of transmission, were delivered directly to him. In this manner, the system of universal informing succeeded in creating a surveillance apparatus leading straight to the primary source of power, thereby rendering Stalin all-seeing. This office, the Special Section, headed by Stalin personally through Poskryobyshev, became during the thirties the power that ruled the nation. The rules were primitive.

Stalin killed not only his friends but also their wives. Postyshev's wife and son were shot. Kosarev's wife spent a third of her life in labor camps. When Poskryobyshev's wife was arrested, Poskryobyshev commented, "The NKVD is always right." Later, by order of Stalin, he was presented with a new wife, a pretty Cossack girl. The wedding was held in Stalin's country house—wile the first wife still languished in a labor camp. Poskryobyshev himself survived not only Stalin, but even the post-Stalin purge. He died in 1965 and was buried with honors in the elite Novodevichy Cemetery. He is said to have written his memoirs as a patient in the Kremlin hospital.

Another survivor was Kosarev's colleague Zolotukhin, who was made a general, headed a department of the Central Committee and then, under Khrushchev, worked at the official rehabilitation of prisoners discharged from the camps.

In the thirties the documents of the Morozov murder case flowed through the channels of the SPO. But the SPO by its very structure demanded millions of Morozovs. It would be an error to attribute the informer system to the evil will of Stalin alone. The agricultural crisis and resultant famine had led to widespread disaffection inside the Party, and its middle echelons sought a way out. Basic factors included the Party's fear of an outraged people and the Leader's fear of the Party. To these internal problems was added the instability of the nation's foreign relations.

The shakiness of his position drove Stalin inexorably to ever-increasing repression. It is known that during this critical year he absented himself from Politburo sessions from spring to fall. The Leader himself announced, "We have never been so driven into a corner as now."[4] Stalin required information in order to remain in power. The informer system became a practical instrument for destroying adversaries as well as a means of consolidating his own position. For his subordinates, too, informing was doubly expedient, both as a dramatic means of proving loyalty and as a way of smoothing over the most reliable career road— the one that led to their Leader's favor.

Thus was created and perfected the mechanism of universal political surveillance and mind control. Now the duty to inform on one's fellow citizens had become the distinguishing characteristic of the new Soviet man, signifying honesty and frankness. This criticism of others in furtherance of a better life, was an indispensable means in attaining the great goal in which many informers of all ages sincerely believed. And a portion of the population even welcomed the idea, took pleasure in the act of informing, and participated in the denunciation campaign not so much submissively as enthusiastically. A dark side of the human soul had emerged and adorned itself in red.

It is often thought that the heroes of the 1930s were discovered and popularized in accordance with Stalin's favorite adage, "Plucked from the dirt and set down among princes," or, in the words of a popular Soviet song of the period, "Here with us anyone can be a hero." But, in fact, heroes were hard to come by. A man selected for leadership had to meet many criteria, yet might become an idol in his circle of influence. The great cult of personality required subsidiary cults. Minor Stalins had gained footholds in science, art, law, even nutrition. Such cult figures included Maxim Gorky in literature, the clown Karandash in the circus, the antigeneticist Lysenko in science, People's Commissar Mikoyan in sausage production, and so on. It appeared that only children still lacked their own cult object, that is, until Morozov appeared to fill the void.

A statistical count shows that during the years 1932–34 the name of Pavlik Morozov appeared in *Pionerskaya Pravda* more often than did Stalin's. It should be understood, however, that the glorifiers of Morozov were actually exalting Stalin in the process, since the two names were ideologically hyphenated into a single unit.

The long poem "Pavlik Morozov," by Stepan Shchipachev, depicts the hero driving away with the grain seized from his relatives and neighbors, a red banner in his arms, and inspired by thoughts of the Leader: "Stalin is for it. Of whom shall I be afraid? And if they try to lay their hands on me, they won't get away with it!"[5] In betraying his biological father, Pavlik understands that henceforth he will have another:

> Father—a precious word:
> There is tenderness in it, there is also sternness.
> To Stalin, reaching
> The great turning point of all his life,
> The people express their love
> In this word: Father.

If there is a new father, Stalin in Shchipachev's view, then to what purpose is Pavlik's old father, the one who punished him? And so the boy chooses from the two fathers not the one who punished him, who made him carry dung from the fields, but the new father, the one who will lead

him to the radiant future. The old father can now be conveniently liquidated, inasmuch as Stalin has liberated the individual from prejudice and
taken all moral responsibility upon himself. And so Pavel:

> Stands erect as if beneath a banner,
> Concealing nothing from the Court.
> From the wall, from its slender frame
> Stalin gazes at him.

Pavel and the local OGPU agent think in unison. The agent has his own
program to develop: he must transmit Pavel's denunciation of his father
to Moscow: "The slender copper wire / Runs to Moscow, to the Kremlin." And the agent, a petty local official, has a dream of his own—if the
denunciation succeeds, his entire life will change:

> And, it may be, from the forest places,
> It will reach the Kremlin Tribunal.
> Perhaps it will be seen
> By Comrade Stalin.

The father has been replaced by the Leader, who has already prepared
a replacement for the mother as well. "Be worthy sons and daughters of
our mother, the All-Union Communist Party" wrote Stalin, summoning
these sons and daughters to arouse the fury of the masses in their millions.[6] At Stalin's initiative, a state institution for the collection of denunciations was activated—the Complaint Bureau, a distinctive new
nationwide ear. In fact, the information reaching the Complaint Bureau
was used by the public prosecutor's office and the OGPU.

The biographical chronology of Stalin's collected works states that
the laws of this period were written by the Great Leader himself.[7] It was
by those laws that local leaders began to carry out the plan for destroying the kulaks. In the heat of this campaign the name of Pavlik Morozov
was lauded to the skies.

Many of Stalin's biographers have taken note of his penchant for as-
cribing to his enemies his own criminal intentions. He was a master of
political intrigue, anticipating his opponents' every move. The NKVD
operated a special center for the fabrication of such cases as Pavel's.
While initiating the collectivization of agriculture, the Leader was already contemplating the mass actions that were to follow, for which a
system of mass denunciation was necessary. There, in the same offices,

were fashioned the details of the show trials of those political opponents of Stalin who would allegedly plot to murder him. Under this program, the Hero-Informer fulfilled a truly historic mission.

Within a year after the First Congress of Soviet Writers, Maxim Gorky wrote to the Department of Culture and Leninist Propaganda, "I call your attention the fact that up to the present time nothing has been done on the matter of a monument to Morozov."[8] At that same time, Gorky was pushing for a monument to Pushkin in Leningrad, but with less persistence. In a speech to the Conference of Authors, Composers, Artists and Film Directors, Gorky once again reminded his listeners that their works lacked young Pioneers unmasking the enemies of the Party. Shcherbakov, who had been appointed secretary of the Writers Union by Stalin and who was a member of the presidium, answered in a way that showed that the speech had been approved from above. Later, Shcherbakov was "destroyed by pernicious medical treatment," as central newspaper reported.[9] The phrase was automatically applied when victims were dispatched on Stalin's personal order.

In January of 1934 Valentin Zolotukhin, president of the Central Bureau of Young Pioneers, announced in *Pionerskaya Pravda* that the matter of the monument to Morozov in Moscow had been decided.[10] He did not say by *whom* it had been decided, but explained that the money was not to be requested from the Party or the government, but rather "collected on a voluntary basis." Nor did Nadezhda Krupskaya, who was unenthusiastic about the monument, know by *whom* the decision had been made. In a letter to Tatyana Naumova, editor of the newspaper *Kolkhoznye Rebyata*, she wrote: "Respected comrade, I am returning the album of children's projects for a monument to Pavlik Morozov. The entire campaign waged in connection with Pavlik's murder was very significant, sharpening as it did the problem of intensifying the political activity of young people. But I am not a specialist in monuments; I put greater emphasis on living monuments."[11] Naumova had been active in waging the campaign for child denunciations and had taken part in a pompous exhibition of projects for the monument to Hero 001. Later she herself was arrested on the basis of a denunciation, and perished in the camps.

In 1936, a book by the poet Valentin Borovin appeared, the preface to which stated, "It is not for nothing that thousands of [Pioneer] detachments, units, clubs, and communal houses bear the name of Morozov;

and not for nothing is a monument to him being erected at the entrance to Red Square in Moscow."[12] The monument was not yet built, but from office to bureaucratic office, scraps of paper were already proliferating.

The fact that the monument to the boy had been approved for erection at the Kremlin wall itself removes any doubt that the decision was made by Stalin personally, insofar as even the most prominent Party and State workers were buried in the wall without monuments. The placement might have consummated an ideal architectural trinity for the national center: the mausoleum for the Founder, the monument to the Informer, and the medieval execution site where, thanks to denunciations by the informers of their day, dissidents had their heads hacked off.

Elizar Smirnov, the correspondent for *Pionerskaya Pravda*, wrote the following in a book published in 1938:

> [Pavlik] is also remembered by the one who labors without rest for the happiness of the people, the beloved leader and father of all children, Comrade Stalin." [Stalin has now singly replaced all the fathers in the land.] A year ago, Comrade Stalin proposed to the Moscow Soviet that a monument to Pavlik Morozov be erected in Red Square. The finest sculptors and artists, and hundreds of Pioneers as well, have given thought to this project. Now it is confirmed. Soon in the Alexander Gardens, at the entrance to Red Square, a monument will be raised. On revolutionary festival days, thousands of joyous, merry children—Pioneers and schoolchildren—will march past the monument. They will salute Pavlik Morozov and sing songs of the happy life created for us by our own Bolshevik Party and our dear leader and teacher, Joseph Vissarionovich Stalin."[13]

Such words could not have been published without official approval; the censors vigilantly followed every mention of Stalin's name in print. And yet questions remain. The monument was not actually put up for another ten years, and then not at the entrance to Red Square. Neither was its location settled until the very last minute. It has been said that people were simply afraid of putting the question to Stalin directly. The Komsomol official and journalist Gusev stated in his book, *Young Pioneers*, that the unveiling was to take place not far from the city's House of Pioneers in downtown Moscow.[14] But the monument finally appeared in 1948, in a neglected square in one of the poorest and dirtiest sections of Moscow, on Krasnaya Presnya in Novovagankovsky Lane (renamed Pavlik Morozov Lane in the 1930s), not far from the old cemetery. Why was the bronze hero installed so belatedly? What caused Stalin to change his mind and dispatch Morozov from Red Square to the city's backyard?

At first it seemed that the delay was due to financial considerations, then to artistic ones, and finally, to the approaching war. More important, however, was the fact that the position of Stalin himself had altered; otherwise he might have requested that the author of the project, sculptor Joseph Rabinovitz, work overtime. It is not impossible that the aging Leader had already reserved the place beside Lenin for himself. But there was an even weightier reason.

The nature of the unveiling ceremony deepens suspicion that Stalin's attitude toward Morozov had undergone a change. For one thing, the audience consisted of second-raters. When the newspaper *Vechernaya Moskva* (Evening Moscow) announced the unveiling of the monument in December 1948, it failed even to mention the Great Leader of All Peoples in its news story, noting instead, "Gorky's dream has been fulfilled."[15] At the conclusion of the ceremony the participants sent a greeting to Stalin, but that was routine. A joke made the rounds of the city. It went, "We now have two monuments to Number One in our town: Printer Number One, and Informer Number One." (The first printer in Russia is considered to be the sixteenth-century figure Ivan Fedorov.)

A group of writers expressed their loyal sentiments in the pages of *Pionerskaya Pravda*, in the form of a summons to all the children of the land to continue Morozov's efforts. This collective appeal was signed by the most prominent writers, dramatists, and poets of the day. The signatories stated unequivocally that those children who followed in the path laid out by Pavlik Morozov would become heroes, scholars, and field marshals.[16] Strangely, this statement evoked little of the usual response from the press. Many newspapers failed to mention the monument at all. Such a lapse in press coverage does not occur accidentally in the U.S.S.R.

I viewed the monument shortly after the unveiling. The pedestal bore the inscription (later removed), "To Pavlik Morozov, from the writers of Moscow."

The old wave of denunciations had passed; a new wave dating from the forties and early fifties, associated with anti-Semitism and the so-called "Doctors' Plot," brought a new, educated heroine to prominence. This was the physician Lidya Timashuk, who denounced her colleagues, and whose name, as the journalist Olga Chechetkina wrote in *Pravda*, "has become a symbol of Soviet patriotism, high vigilance, and the courageous, implacable struggle against the enemies of our Motherland." Two weeks before Stalin's death, the paper called Timashuk "the daughter of our Motherland." She was awarded the Order of Lenin for assistance furnished to the government in unmasking the conspiratcy of the so-called "doctor-murderers."[17]

Reviewing the waves of denunciation from a historical perspective, we observe that the first surge, which flared up in 1932, was already subsiding by 1938. The second wave (1948–53) was less widespread, and the best-known informers of those years were, for the most part, adults.

The situation had altered, but Stalin did not forget our hero. Four years after the installation of the Moscow monument, Stalin authorized the construction of another monument to him in Siberia, at the informer's birthplace. Among the papers of Pavel Solomein, I found a letter from G. Fomin, chief of the Tavda Regional Department of Culture: "A resolution of the Council of Ministers of the USSR was passed and personally signed by Comrade Stalin, on the presentation of funds to the kolkhoz. Allotted for the year 1953: 220,000 rubles for the construction of the P. Morozov Village Club, and 80,000 rubles to erect a monument to P. Morozov."[18] Obviously, the collection of money on a voluntary basis had not met with much success.

Monuments to Morozov were still being raised, although the practice of denunciation was, for the time being, no longer commended. What forced Stalin to cut his campaign short?

The answer is simple; the epidemic had become uncontrollable, proliferating to the point where it hindered the normal activity of state security organs. It is also possible that still other factors were taken into consideration by the former Pavliks who were now the third generation of Party officials. By this time they occupied substantial positions and had no desire to raise a fourth generation to inform on them. To a certain degree, the mass denunciations touched the family of Stalin himself. His second wife, Nadezhda Alliluyeva, committed suicide at the very peak of the campaign calling for the execution of Morozov's family. There are theories that the suicide was precipitated by the wife's horror at the bloodbath loosed by her husband. When someone informed on Stalin's son Yakov to the effect that he had said something out of turn, Stalin imprisoned Yakov's wife as punishment. Another son, General Vasily Stalin, informed on his superior officer, Aviation Marshal Novikov. The latter was tried in court and not released until after Stalin's death.[19] But the chief reason for putting a halt to the practice of denunciation by children was the slackening of the repression that had been going on since 1938. The approaching war called for another kind of hero entirely, one ready to give his life in battle for Stalin on the front, and not spill his blood in feuds with his own relatives. The former type of hero, for the time being, withdrew into the background.

How, in the final analysis, did Stalin really feel about Pavlik Morozov? For Stalin, singling out and destroying human beings was an everyday, obligatory task. Obligatory, because he could not have remained long in power without it. Dossiers on thousands of Morozovs were prepared by the machinery of all Soviet institutions, first and foremost by the Party Central Committee, the OGPU, the Komsomol, as well as by their local counterparts. To the Leader were presented those proposals most advantageous at any given moment, not only to himself, but also to the chief of the presenting department. This is the key to the method which created and confirmed Pavlik Morozov as Informer 001 of the Union of Soviet Socialist Republics.

If one is to judge Stalin's attitude towards other human beings—regardless of their loyalty to him—whom he sent to their deaths, this misanthrope despised and distrusted all men without exception. But he did raise to prominence those useful to him at any given time. The Leader had such a need of Pavlik Morozov. It is a historical commonplace that Stalin ruthlessly converted living people to corpses. In this instance, he effected the conversion of a corpse into a living symbol. It must be acknowledged that Stalin and his cohorts succeeded in raising up an army of Morozov imitators; a myth had become the reality of Soviet life.

Notes

1. *Pionerskaya Pravda* (27 August 1933).
2. Maryagin (1965: 294).
3. *Khrushchev Remembers* (1974: 292).
4. *Strana i Mir* (August 1985).
5. Shchipachev (1950: 30, 36–37).
6. *Pravda* (9 July 1932).
7. Stalin (1952: 409).
8. Gorky (1955, Vol. 30: 383).
9. *Pravda* (3 January 1953).
10. *Pionerskaya Pravda* (10 January 1934).
11. Krupskaya (1963, vol. 11: 513).
12. "Predislovie Severnogo kraikoma VLKSM" (Introduction of North Komsomol District Committee), in Borovin (1936: 3).
13. Smirnov (1938: 78).
14. Gusev (1948: 41).
15. *Vechernaya Moskva* (18 and 20 December 1948).
16. *Pionerskaya Pravda* (21 December 1948).

17. Decree, *Pravda* (21 January 1953); Chechetkina (20 February 1953).
18. Fomin (Archive of Pavel Solomein).
19. Avtorkhanov (1975: 102).

13

Pilgrimage to Gerasimovka

After two court sessions, the execution, and the following arrests, the only people from the extended Morozov family left in the village were Pavlik's mother and her youngest son, Roman. Two of her children were killed; the fourth, Alexei, she turned over to an orphanage. In the newspapers Tatyana Morozova was "The Hero's Mother," a privileged position in the Soviet Union. However harshly *we* might evaluate Pavlik's actions, for Tatyana he remained a son. She lost two of them then, and she loved the dead ones as long as she lived. This was sacred.

Pavlik's mother had a good memory and readily told me about what had happened then in the village. The popular adulation of the Hero stressed in the media didn't appear quite so glowing in her account: "Pavlik had many enemies. People stomped on his grave, broke the star—half the village went to defecate there."

The death of her sons was only the beginning; the mother still had to ascend her own Golgotha. One month after the funeral, on the occasion of the fifteenth anniversary of the October revolution, the authorities organized a massive bolshevik wake for the murdered children. The production went well, in accordance with the special role of the children. The myth repeated at the top came to the village and started to displace reality: "The reading hut was alive with the cheerful laughter and songs of the children," wrote Pavel Solomein blissfully in a *Pionerskaya Pravda* article titled "On The Fresh Grave." "Two women accompanied Tatyana Morozova, Pavlik's mother, who looked thin and old from grief." A wreath lies on the table. Happy children sing, then stroll to the cemetery. There, near the grave, a podium is already erected. From there visiting representatives give speeches about Morozov's heroic deed and the kulak-murderers. The article proceeds:

151

A curious thing—a result of the cultural backwardness and illiteracy of Pavlik's mother—Tatyana Morozova. The bodies of Pavlik and Fedya Morozov were of course buried without a priest. On the grave there is a red star and a mourning banner with an inscription "The fraternal grave of the Morozov brothers." And on the other side of the grave...there is a cross.... Tatyana Morozova understands that a kulak is a "bad man," but the belief in god, supported by the advice of her pious neighbors, is firmly rooted in the conscience of the grief-torn mother.

The newspaper declared the necessity "Not to cry, but to form a tighter circle around the Party."[1]

Morozova was moved to a large house whose owners had recently been arrested. She received a part of the kulaks' property, but people in Gerasimovka hated and insulted her. The peasants blamed Tatyana for raising the child who brought so much grief to the village. The privileges accorded to her maddened the people even more. It was necessary for her to move from the village to the district's main town. "The NKVD took me under their protection," remembered Morozova. "They gave me a room, a bed, two pillows, food. As the Hero's Mother I didn't work."

The antipathy towards Pavlik Morozov's mother remains in Gerasimovka half a century later. I felt it, but now it is expressed with more reserve. Kabina, the teacher, offers her version: "They gave Tatyana an apartment on Stalin Street—it was freed after the enemies of the people moved out. The furniture, the lace curtains, underwear, clothes—everything that used to be somebody else's—all became hers. Before, she couldn't even dream about that. People were starving everywhere, but she got good food, sweets—all at the OGPU. They sent her son Alexei to the Artek summer camp every year." The newspapers wrote about that, too. The government took care of the Hero's mother, giving her a life-long personal pension, and the doctors advised that she move to a resort in Crimea. It was said that Stalin personally gave an order to take care of her. But she could be demanding. She would enter a place and declare, "I, mother of the Pioneer-hero," and people were afraid to refuse her.

In Crimea the Tatar, Greek, and German minorities were being shipped out. The luxurious nineteenth-century tsarist palace in Alupka became a resort for high-ranking Party officials. In the surrounding areas whole blocks were "cleaned up" (in the idiom of the time), and trusted people were rewarded with the emptied houses. Here, on the southern coast, Morozova lived till the end of her days.

Her third son, Roman, was wounded at the end of the World War II and died at home with her. After that she lived alone. Destiny was not kinder to her than to the others—rather the contrary. The only one of her sons who remained alive, Alexei, the one who testified along with her against his grandparents, demanding their execution, was in prison. The head of the cultural section of the District Executive Committee, Fomin, wrote to Solomein in the letter I quoted above: "Alexei Morozov spent the years 1941–1951 in prison. He was freed in the fall of 1951. He was imprisoned for treason (disobeyed the orders of his superior officers)." "Alexei was sentenced to death by court martial," remembers the peasant woman Berkina. "But his mother pleaded for him, and as a hero's brother he got ten years instead of execution."

The reasons for Alexei Morozov's arrest are not altogether clear. He graduated from an Air Force academy. In his military unit there were Pavlik Morozovs, ones who would willingly inform on an innocent person. A woman from Gerasimovka, Alexei's aunt Berkina, whom he visited with his wife and son after his release, said that her nephew got drunk before a battle flight. He told her that somebody had got him drunk, and that now he didn't drink any more. Alexei's relative, Baidakov, who was imprisoned on the same charge (Article 58), told me that he ran into Alexei in prison. According to him, Alexei was not liked by his comrades in the Air Force because he always demanded special treatment as the brother of a Pioneer-Hero. They got him drunk, and when he was asleep they put some film with pictures from the front lines inside one of his boots as incriminating evidence. After that they called SMERSH, the secret military police.

The Soviet press carefully conceals the fact that the brother of the Pioneer-Hero spent ten years in prison for espionage. Today, Alexei is a quiet, hard-working man. He does not want to remember the past. In order to get a better retirement pension he worked for two years as a freight loader at a toxic chemical plant. Alexei's son, Pavlik, was named in honor of the dead hero-uncle; he is the fifth generation of the Morozov family known to us. This Pavlik served in the army, then became a metalworker at a factory. When Pavlik Morozov Junior got married, the press announced it with due fanfare; of course, there was no publicity when he divorced. "This is the way the young people live now," Tatyana Morozova told me in judgment of the morals of the younger generation. Pavlik is a cheerful young man who lives as he chooses, likes to drink with his friends, does not want to study, prefers foreign movies to Soviet ones, and, unlike his famous uncle, has no intention of informing on his family and neighbors.

A white-haired old woman in a flowery bathrobe and a colorful shawl met me in a room that looked like the warehouse of a provincial museum. Portraits and busts of various sizes depicting her famous hero-son hung on the walls and stood on the cupboard, the table, and the dresser. Right next to them were busts of Lenin and Anton Chekhov, who had lived nearby in Yalta. And among the portraits of Pavlik—icons.

The remaining Morozovs live in a cozy house on a mountain on the coast of the Black Sea. All around, behind tall fences, are villas and resorts for the Soviet bureaucratic elite. Heirs of the Morozovs returned to the life of small enterprise, the life against which Pavlik's contemporaries fought half a century earlier. In the summer they lease the house and the small cabins around it to tourists. This gives them a decent income. During the disclosure campaign after Stalin's death, an article appeared in a Crimean newspaper. It reported that "old woman Morozikha" bought fruit cheaply, and then sold it in the market at a profit, that she engaged in speculation. The paper called upon its readers to "form their own conclusions," but the authorities hushed it up.[2]

"No one comes to visit me," complained Tatyana Morozova during our last visit. "Nobody needs me now. It used to be that five or eight letters came every day. Now there aren't many of them. Children write stupid things: 'Dear Tanya, what grade are you in? Let's write to each other.' And I am turning ninety soon!"

Until her final days (she died in 1983), the mother of Pioneer-Hero 001 sat on the stage during ideological meetings, a living example of dedication to the communist cause. Audiences applauded when Pioneers tied a red kerchief around her neck. The only difficulty arose when she had to speak. "Be like my Pavlik," pronounced the illiterate woman— and stopped, unable to read the text prepared by Komsomol officials. Now and then the local Gerasimovka authorities would invite the hero's mother, schoolmates, and relatives to various celebrations, rounding up the populace of the entire district to further enhance the event's public nature.

The local kolkhoz bore the name of Pavlik Morozov, since his example so well demonstrated the achievements of collectivization. After Morozov's murder five people enlisted in the kolkhoz. Two years later the kolkhoz was reorganized; seventeen peasants took part. By the year 1937 one more person entered. And in 1941 it had fifty members. Meanwhile, the long Gerasimovka street had 104 houses on it. It turns out that by the time Soviet power celebrated its twenty-fifth anniversary, half of Gerasimovka remained under private ownership.

"We didn't have any kulaks at all," the peasant woman Vera Berkina told me:

> But many activists showed up who wanted to live at other people's expense instead of working. They would remove somebody from the village by informing on him, then plunder his house. They would celebrate—drink and eat everything— then go home and become activists again. They'd have sent more people out, but in our village the poorest person had one cow, and the richest—two. The whole village had only nine samovars, and children and cattle stayed in the house together during the winter—they even ate from the same pan.

The desolation of the 1930s was worsened by the almost complete absence of men during the war and afterwards. The head of the regional Department of Culture told Solomein about it in a letter: "The kolkhoz is weak financially, and productivity is low. There has been little return on the crops. Livestock production is also low, and in addition the kolkhoz's plantings during a few years after the war rotted. This circumstance undermined the economy of the kolkhoz." No, it was not this circumstance that undermined the economy, and not just of one kolkhoz but of all of Russia.

Denouncing the kulaks who were ruining the village, Elizar Smirnov wrote about Siberia before the revolution in *Pionerskaya Pravda*: "The market was big and rich. From here the best grades of wheat, butter, cheese, furs, and leather were sold abroad."[3] In the year of Stalin's death the level of agriculture in the country was lower than before the revolution. Since the time when the struggle against the kulaks was won, there have been chronic shortages of meat and butter in Siberia and the Urals. Milk is only given to children, and one must stake a place in line at five in the morning. And, as everybody knows, most of the wheat comes to Russia from abroad.

The exploitation of the members of the kolkhoz in Gerasimovka occurs at a level the landowners of tsarist Russia could never have dreamt of. In return for working the kolkhoz land a peasant receives the right to have a small plot of land where he can grow something with which to nourish himself. Here he labors a second working day: according to the official statistics, five hours in addition to the nine for the kolkhoz. And still he lives on the edge of starvation. On the train I talked to a pediatric doctor from the local clinic. Because of chronic malnutrition, the adolescents here aren't as tall as children of their age in the cities, and the death rate as a result of psychiatric disorders is three times as great. Many babies are born sick and mentally retarded.

When Gerasimovka became the destination of a sacred political pilgrimage, Stalin, as we remember, personally allotted funds for the village. Today people close to the Hero and the kolkhoz named after him continue to reap the benefits of his glory. His former teacher told me proudly that once a month she gets an extra ration coupon for a half pound of butter. The road to the village is now paved, and electricity provided. Many houses are roofed with tile instead of straw, some even boasting television antennas. A brick elementary school was built in front of the grave of Informer 001. Pavlik's statue faces a faded placard calling upon the students to build communism, the bright future of humanity.

Everybody in the village was told to whitewash their fences. And here they are, all whitewashed alike, but darkly streaked from the rain. Along these fences, buses take tourists to the Pavlik Morozov museum. Party bosses continue to force the peasants to work. Now, however, they drive state cars instead of riding horseback. And even though all the churches were demolished, burned to their foundations, in the houses icons still dominate the portraits of Pavlik Morozov and the country's leaders.

Gerasimovka is situated amid the forced labor camps that dot the vast spaces of the Urals and Siberia. The train from Sverdlovsk to Tavda passes along barbed-wire fences for hours, and day and night one can hear the barking of guard dogs. Through the villages pass seatless buses with iron grids on the windows, filled to capacity with exhausted-looking prisoners, their heads shaved. And near the rear doors of those buses stand large, well-fed dogs held on leashes by the young soldiers of the Internal Forces. Wherever one looks there are military, police, and certain types in plain clothes who suspiciously look over every passerby. A terrible, inhuman land, populated, however, with people.

The fates of Pavlik's contemporaries worked themselves out in different ways. His classmate Yakov Yudov, who according to the newspapers carried the red flag of the young Pioneers in front of everybody with his head raised high, disappeared; apparently, hiding from his family and alimony claims, he became an alcoholic and was killed in a fight. Another classmate, Matryona Korolkova, worked in a special boarding school for children left orphaned by the arrest of their parents. I found her in Kharkov, in the Ukraine. There she worked as a police guard. She did not want to answer any Pioneers' letters; she said she was tired of that. I was able to find the teacher Zoya Kabina in a hospital. Although Gubarev never met her, he wrote confidently in the magazine *Molodoi Kommunist* (Young Communist), "Without exaggeration we can say that it was she who brought Pavlik up as a hero."[4] Now we know differently. Having divorced the informer Ivan Potupchik, Kabina married an exile, a kulak's son; for her marriage to a class enemy she was expelled from the Komsomol. It is said that she threw her Komsomol registration card into the face of the official. A teacher by profession, she was forced to work as a salesperson in a store. When she retired she lived contentedly in Leningrad, raising her grandchildren. She spoke about the past carefully, without enthusiasm or censure. The assistant OGPU representative Spiridon Kartashov and the informer, executioner, and careerist Ivan Potupchik lived on personal pensions until the middle of the 1980s. I was fortunate to find them both alive.

Much has been written about the people surrounding the Hero, and many words have been put into their mouths as needed by the authorities. "Many of the heroes are still alive," wrote Solomein with indignation in an unpublished article I found in his personal archives. "They read the books and frown about the lies that have been written." Many, however, are not frowning; on the contrary, they are quite content.

People other than his dying contemporaries assume places of honor, basking in the rays of the Hero's glory. Some call themselves his teachers even though they came to Gerasimovka after his death; others swear that they sat at the same desk with Pavlik. I counted; according to the various memoirs it turns out that approximately twenty people shared with the Hero a desk designed for two.

Gerasimovka leaves a baffling mixture of contradictory impressions. The ancient wilderness and modern sights mix here fantastically. While nature still bears a hint of its former beauty, the amazing lakes and fast rivers are being poisoned with chemicals, and the vast forests are being cut for lumber or firewood for thousands of miles. Because of the swamps there are swarms of mosquitoes that eat you alive. Just before my arrival a bear killed a cow in the forest. Not too long ago a peasant went fishing at a lake, got lost, walked around in the swamps for thirteen days, then barely crawled out to find human habitation. And these primeval forests are filled with soldiers carrying radios, searching for and shooting fugitives from the camps.

In the village students dressed in jeans listen to rock music on their tape recorders and laugh at the Hero-Informer, but at school they recite beautiful poems dedicated to him. The local papers say that the happy life Pavlik Morozov struggled for has finally arrived, but in a bus I saw blood shed as two young men fought for a free seat. At the bus station their wives fought too; they cursed and furiously threatened to take revenge on each other's family.

Elena Sakova, an old peasant woman, and one of the first to settle here, told me about the life of Pavlik Morozov's neighbors today:

> The worst thing in our village is the drinking: everybody drinks now, the whole Gerasimovka. They even let the children drink. If there is no vodka or moonshine, they drink cologne and insect repellant. A son of my neighbor (she is Pavlik Morozov's aunt) burned in a truck; he was drunk and drove it into a bus. So many deaths! His wife is now the director of the museum. Gets paid for Pavlik's heroism. She is specially trained how to talk about this heroism. Son, don't press the buttons on this box any more, and put away the notebook—don't write anything down. Don't you know what happens for that?"

And the old woman crossed the fingers of both hands on the table. This gesture, in Russia, symbolizes imprisonment. Now, after her death, this can finally be published.

Notes

1. *Pionerskaya Pravda* (27 November 1932).
2. *Kurortnaya Gazeta* (22 August 1956).
3. Smirnov (15 January 1933).
4. Gubarev (September 1962).

14

To Inform, or Not to Inform?

How should the story of Pavlik Morozov be told today? Does the hero-informer remain the government's standard of citizen conduct that he had been in the 1930s? During Stalin's rule the magazine *Ogonyok* (Small Fire) declared that Morozov exemplified "the history of the motherland during the Stalin epoch."[1] Has that epoch really come to an end?

The tyranny of the Stalinist era was officially condemned, along with the massive repressions it engendered. The 1965 *Soviet Encyclopedia of History* permits no interpretation other than a negative one to the role of such activists as Morozov; similarly, in the 1930s one could not avoid honoring such types.[2] In the 1960s there were attempts (not crowned, it's true, with success) to publicly condemn the informants of the 1930s. Nevertheless, three years after Stalin's death something peculiar occurred; the name of Pavlik Morozov was "forever" entered into the All-Union Pioneer Organization Book of Honor under the title Number 001.

Statues of Stalin have long been removed, while monuments to the hero-informer in different cities still stand. Identical monuments of the Pioneer with the red banner are erected in many towns, a dismal bequest of socialist realism. Modern Soviet historical analysis rewrote the period of collectivization. These more recent compositions generally do not mention the fundamental task of the Party at that time as the annihilation of kulakdom, although they did mention the "education" of the peasants in a suitably florid style. There are works in which the word "kulak" does not appear at all.[3] But what about informing?

Thomash Rzhezach, in his book *The Spiral of Solzhenitsyn's Treason*, released by the Soviet publishing house Progress in 1978, provides an epigraph taken from the words of Plutarch, "Traitors betray first and foremost themselves." Rzhezach believes that informing exists as a consequence of cowardice. He condemns Alexander Solzhenitsyn, whom the book holds in shame, as an informer since childhood. According to Rzhezach, Solzhenitsyn "has informed and informed about anti-Soviet activities…on his wife…on his friends…on the chance fellow traveller …on people near and far." He maintains that when the writer was incarcerated during the war his term was reduced in exchange for information, and for that reason he became a secret informer for the camp administration. Soviet security agencies used this prisoner "only on the lowest rung—in the role of a camp stool pigeon." "Moral death" would be his ultimate reward.

The book is an obvious attempt to compromise the world-famous writer. Its author's inspiration is transparent—he is simply performing the task assigned him. Soviet power believes it could find no better way to compromise Solzhenitsyn's reputation than by spreading, by massive circulation, the rumor that he had been an informer. The book unequivocally presents the image of a Soviet citizen-collaborator as human scum, beneath contempt. Rzhezach's portrait of an informer implies animalistic cunning and moral turpitude of the lowest order. The informer, in short, evinces dramatically the most vulgar psychological characteristics of a criminal.[4]

Revised official Soviet appraisal concerning the possible activities of contemporary Pavlik Morozovs suggests that it is, in principle, immoral to submit political accusations. I am prepared to embrace this point of view.

Throughout recent years propaganda concerning the heroic exploits of Pavlik Morozov was spread listlessly, hushed-up, even disparaged. It seems as if the powers that be are uncertain what to do with this boy. The second edition of *The Great Soviet Encyclopedia* maintained that Pavlik unmasked his father; the third, that Pioneers "exposed enemy activities of the kulaks." The third edition of *The Condensed Soviet Encyclopedia*, however, not only does not report that Pavlik informed on his father, but neglects his more generalized informing entirely. It turns out that "together with poor peasants [he] took part in the distribution of grain during the period of collectivization." In the preface to the first edition of *The Children's Encyclopedia* (1962) Nikita Khrushchev positively appraised Pavlik Morozov, referring to him as the "immortal of that age." In the second edition Morozov is moved aside in favor of a little-known hero, the child-correspondent of *Pioner*, Nikita Semin. By the third edition it vaguely states that Pavlik and other such children "accomplished feats of labor and civic duty."

The shell of the myth remains while the essence changes. It is written that Morozov was simply a hero, and that he was killed for being one. Significantly, he is also called a "tragic hero." His merits are extolled in such vague formulations as "of noble, moral make-up," and "an example of selfless service to the people."[5] The writer Gubarev published his memoirs in the magazine *Molodoi Kommunist*, generally revising the core of the matter. Indeed, it was not Morozov who betrayed his father, but the father who betrayed his son: "It was difficult to the point of tears for the boy to endure the treachery of the father."[6] Later histories seldom mention the boy at all.

Despite the boy's apparent decline in popularity, the press recently termed the Pioneer organization "the Morozov Guard."[7] Morozov has been ineradicably canonized as the well-tempered propaganda machine plays the same tune over and over. The anniversary of his death has entered into the government system of jubilees. Sacred oaths are sworn in his name, and in solemn ceremonies Pioneers take handfuls of earth from his grave. Sporting events in his honor, lessons of courage to the beat of a drum, and competitions for the right to light the bonfire on the day of the hero's death are organized. The name "Morozov" is adopted in the USSR and other socialist countries for a multitude of streets, schools, libraries, camps, parks, Pioneer troops, collective farms, cultural centers, Pioneer lodges, and even entire forests (doubtlessly in view of the fact that Pavlik and Fedya Morozov were murdered in the woods). A special resolution exists to establish a National Memorial Park in the village of Gerasimovka.

But how is he regarded in real life? People inwardly renounce the hero-informer—a practical consideration. By honoring the act of informing, the powers that be achieved results different from those they had intended. The government's complete lack of respect for individuals and individual property could not help but create reciprocal feelings in these same individuals toward the government and its property. Now, when every child knows where his mother secretly gets sausage, and his father nails and boards, it becomes even more difficult to find Pavliks in families. Is it necessary today to have child-betrayers as supervisors of the country? Soviet ideology demanded allegiance to an authoritative set of beliefs, but this very allegiance is inherently undermined by informants. Children of responsible workers of all ranks are eager to serve as Morozov had, and not for small change but for higher stakes, including the privilege of traveling abroad. When compelled to inform, it's understood that they will generally protect their families. Twofold morality becomes three-fold: for oneself, for family and friends, and for others. But this ethical elasticity may be additionally relative under any given equation of situa-tion, cultural standards, and internal taboos.

Recent circumstances dictate that the basic formula for informing is similarly obsolete; one must inform to a prescribed person, and against those deemed necessary. The very word "inform" today sounds unpleas-ant to the Russian ear; therefore newspapers employ the euphemism "warn." The system of recruiting informers became secret. Heroes are registered without publicity, but they receive real compensation. Surveillence equipment has been improved with the advent of Western computer technology. Technical advances have thus distanced the par-ticipants, incidentally making the activity less burdensome to the con-science of the informer.

In the eyes of the majority of citizens, the outmoded snitch-enthusiast has become a villain. In the company of an unfamiliar person they care-fully ask whether he isn't a Pavlik Morozov. It would be difficult today to find from among a group of famous writers one who would take it upon himself to extol the activities of Informer 001.

Given all this, is it possible to part with the myth, to rehabilitate the victims of the Morozov trial, and to name the real killers? More generally, is it possible that we no longer need either new or class morals, but can return to a simpler norm, to human morals? No. One responsible Party worker explained to me that destroying such a concept of heroism would be devastating in its effects. As he saw it, these days many celebrities fight and become drunkards. Therefore, giving the names of living heroes to institutions is forbidden. But old heroes are proven. Pavlik has gotten a little older, concluded the Party worker, but he still proves useful.

The powerful in this country strongly encourage that practical reason conform to history; denouncing one's predecessors implies an improved historical and ethical perspective. A generation of functionaries the same age as Morozov is departing. These contemporaries of October possessed many of Pavlik's main qualities and occupied the key positions in the Party for ages. All that they possessed (and they possessed all) was at-tained thanks to the official Morozovian morality. It seems as if their hero is dead. But many among this present generation of leaders have made their way to power using the very same methods. Even now it is much easier to enter the ruling ranks if one cooperates with various se-cret agencies. And if tomorrow the powerful were to renounce Pavlik Morozov, the day after tomorrow they would replace him with a differ-ent myth. Epochs and leaders change, but denunciation and betrayal live on as instruments of power. Is this sad fact a matter of chance?

In all utopian models of government an important role is assigned to informants for protecting the model from any encroachment that threat-ens to destroy it. But here the utopian scheme is realized with neither the premise of freedom nor the promise of prosperity.

The second stage is advancing, one of universal disappointment and dissatisfaction. For the powers who have legitimized violence, the pro-cess of suppression is not technically serious; however, it does have dis-tinct demographic implications. They can do away with undesirable ethnic groups, they can annihilate half the population, but they cannot destroy all the people, for then there would be no one over whom to rule. Further-more, widespread civil war would lead to hunger and economic collapse. Gradually the general suppression of discontent will be exchanged for selective suppression. And, to this end, those agencies concerned with suppression will need information about what, or who, more specifi-cally, remains defiantly unsuppressed.

The informant's social situation is unstable; whether out of fear or in accordance with natural inclination, he takes the bait in which he invari-ably finds a hook. The informer has built his happiness on others' misfor-tune. He fixes all of his devotion on his employers, but he is not his own man and the feeling is seldom reciprocated. Returning to the peace of a less complicated existence is impossible; his employers will not allow it. The legal status of informer is also hazardous. Within the agencies of coercion he is registered under a pseudonym, receiving compensation for his ser-vices under the table until a trade union for squealers is created to defend his interests. As a rule, he is compelled to use some other job as a cover for his informing; he may act the part of a maintenance man or a poet.

Democratic governments generally limit surveillance technology and monitor its use even when uncovering such highly illegal activites as terrorism. The legality of using such equipment for shadowing the favor-ite activities of an individual or other activities here is either lacking entirely or temporarily upheld. Unofficial intellectual life, underground economics, and other manifestations of daily life rouse the authorities to constantly expand their network of informants. Here, military administration, government management, and State security itself are literally set in motion by informants. In contrast to the selective nature of repression, participation under this system may theoretically reach one hundred percent. The grand finale: everyone in the country would be spying on each other.

Universal informing drives the remainder of the people into their individual shells. Society as a collection of human beings ceased to exist during the Stalinist era; the social fabric was destroyed, and people, forced to be deaf and dumb, were transformed into shadows—apathy became the only way to survive. It may be that, having reached its apogee, the protracted "heroism" campaign for informers quieted down at the end of the 1930s. Collaborators reached their maximum carrying capacity and began to receive more information than they could digest. They had almost attained the theoretical ideal.

Of course, at that time authority rested basically upon adult informers. Child informing was supplementary in terms of its practical use, but it was crucial for the education of future citizens. Children are much easier to persuade that this baseness in a new system is really a symbol of its greatness. It is not surprising that children's informing on adults was cultivated in Hitler's Germany and in the so-called sister socialist countries in Eastern Europe, in Cambodia, and in Communist China. A character in Soviet writer A. Prokhanov's book *A Tree in the Downtown of Kabul*, published when the Soviet army occupied Afganistan, reminds us of Pavlik Morozov.

The appearance of millions of Pavlik Morozovs is in conformity with the natural law of a system that, without its base of informers, would have toppled long ago. I know of no other hero who more accurately represents the essence of a system with one-party ideals.

In the 1920s the question of informing was discussed by leaders in the Soviet government. The director of the Marx-Engels-Lenin Institute, David Ryazanov, demanded as a goal of social enlightenment that "every citizen would know that informing to the court is not 'informing,' it is his duty. If you want to nurture a feeling of confidence, then develop an aptitude for informing and don't intimidate people to the point that they give a false report."[8] Ryazanov himself was also arrested on the word of an informant and died in a prison camp. It is doubtful whether today a responsible worker could be found in the apparatus of power who would publicly proclaim so harsh a position of guidance. But, in point of fact, informing will always be necessary, in periods of darkness and freeze as well as in times of brightening and thaw. It helps the old-timers tighten the screws, but it also helps the new group of leaders deal with their adversaries. Consider the implications of the following rhetorical question: Can one enter history without knocking? Note that in Russian the verb "to knock" is slang for "to inform."

During the Khrushchev thaw of the early 1960s, *Pionerskaya Pravda* openly searched for new Morozovs: "Where did my father get so much money?" wondered Pioneer Valery Zhelezny. "How does my father's friend live? Why, he doesn't work anywhere!" Valery came out against his father, and hid nothing from the court about his father's accomplices. The paper beamed, "We are proud of you, Valery."[9]

Twenty years later, in the period of the Brezhnev stagnation, a 1982 edition of *Pravda* told of a mother who informed the proper authorities that her son had received a letter from abroad and that he also listened to foreign radio transmissions. Security agencies, the newspaper assured, had been tracking the young man for a long time and knew all of this already. The son was shot for espionage.[10] The mother's informing was simply an expression of her moral duty. What has transpired here? While earlier Pavliks informed only on their parents, now they are grown and have become parents themselves, parents who inform on their children. The continuing tragedy of this generation persists as one of the most immoral in the history of humanity.

Glasnost (the "openness" to speak freely) has been proclaimed throughout the country, but for the KGB that word is understood to mean "glaznost" ("to see clearly"—people are using their freedom to speak out and inform on themselves as well as on others). Newspapers call on readers to report which of their neighbors are not living in the same style as everyone else, and secret police register every bit of information as evidence of the dissidence they must continue to stifle. Even now, they fatten up dossiers and revive the data cards of informants.

Riding this new wave of informing, which began with the Soviet press in the mid 1980s after Gorbachev came to power, Viktor Rozov's play *By the Sea* was performed in many theaters. The protagonist of the play is a tenth grader whose father seems to be a responsible V.I.P. but is tried for bribery, as was Pavlik Morozov's father. All of the author's sympathies are with the brave youth. The father is already in prison when the son composes not simply further incriminating information, but spends his whole summer reconstructing the minutiae of his father's activites in order to unmask him even more thoroughly than the authorities had, and thus lengthen his term of imprisonment. This otherwise completely normal and competent youth hysterically shouts to the entire audience that he will expose everyone who is like his father. The hero of *By the Sea* surpasses Pavlik, for he publicly denies not only his father but his mother as well, and leaves home to reeducate himself in the family of a simple proletarian laborer.

Is the conviction of the writer within the orthodoxy of Communist moral principles? Or is this evidence of the familiar aspiration to advance—only now on the pellucid wave of Glasnost?

Posssibly they are one and the same. One must understand that, first and foremost, in the Soviet Union ideological fetishes never die. Occasionally they are put on the shelf because they are not especially advantageous at the time. But this does not in any way mean that doctrine has become more humane.

Soviet ideology changed the rituals, but it was not capable of changing the postulates. This ideology corrupted, but it could not regenerate. "What might he have become?" pondered a newspaper about Pavlik on one of the previous anniversaries of the day of his death. "Today, would he raise unprecedented harvests in the Ural region or make super-strong steel?"[11] We can't know what he would have done regarding steel, but even without Morozov's help, harvests have always been "unprecedented"—that is, poor. And I doubt that, as has been suggested by other authors, if Pavlik had lived until our epoch he would have become a cosmonaut.[12]

Any doubt regarding Morozov's behavior always arouses hostility in the authorities. In V. Terentyev's 1964 article, "Don't Dirty an Honored Name!" (subtitled "Our Answer to the Gentlemen Across the Ocean"), the Ural newspaper printed that Americans had slandered Pavlik Morozov in their school textbooks.[13] The paper was disturbed by the statement, "A child must honor his father and his mother," found in the chapter titled "Political Arithmetic and Communist Morals" in the American textbook *The Meaning of Communism*:

Part of the efforts of the Soviet system of education is the affirmation in textbooks of "Communist morals." To the extent that Communism denies religion, it also denies Western moralistic criteria, which is founded mainly on religion. Consequently, Soviet children are taught to discern what is good and what is bad not on the basis of fundamental moral values as we understand them, but more on the basis of Soviet doctrine. So, to kill another person is bad, but it was entirely moral for Stalin to kill millions during the forced collectivization. A child must honor his mother and father, the Communists say, but in Moscow stands a monument in honor of eleven-year-old Pavlik Morozov, whose father was destroyed after young Pavlik informed...that he was concealing grain. A child must obey and respect his teacher, say the Communists, but is obliged to report if she is tolerant of expressions of religious views.[14]

This excerpt from the American textbook is not accessible to Soviet readers without special permission, especially in the Urals. While not fully citing the authors' ideas, the newspaper charged the American professors William Miller and others, with "playing the role of Judas toward the children." The paper also compared them to the Gerasimovka kulaks, concluding that the kulaks were better people even if they were illiterate. In the Soviet paper's opinion, the American historians committed as despicable an act as the murder of Pavlik Morozov at the hands of the kulaks: "This is a transgression," the article solemnly pronounced. "We charge you with transgression against the name of Pavlik Morozov, gentlemen professors, with transgression against his honored memory.... A criminal court sentenced the kulaks to the firing squad. William Miller, Henry Roberts, Marshall Shulman, Harry Savage; any court of honor would sentence these names to death. Shame!"[15]

Such militant defense of the morals of Morozov on an international scale showed that the boy remained at his post. "The foreign press lies that we raise our children according to the example of a betrayer of his father," contends the contemporary Soviet writer Balashov in a 1982 article published for the fiftieth anniversary of Pavlik Morozov's demise in the magazine *Uralski Sledopyt* (The Ural Pathfinder) under the title "The Boy with the Courage of a Man." In the article Balashov additionally maintains that Pavlik's life is yet awaiting its Shakespeare.[16] The question remains: do they now raise children on the example of the betrayer or not?

Undoubtedly, to a large number of quite loyal yet thinking Soviet people the costs of the lie in practical terms are completely clear; if nothing is sacred, then nothing is sacred—neither the authorities nor their leaders. The cynicism of children of the following generation was massive. How could it be otherwise when the Party cultivated honesty on the example of meanness, and devotion on the example of betrayal?

Soviet leaders loved to repeat that throughout history there is no return route, that the progress of society cannot be turned back. But in the thirties those very Soviet leaders succeeded in turning back history as Russia returned to a wholesale oppression similar to that of the Middle Ages. The damage to people's morals turned out to be so severe that even after the death of Stalin, rumors spread of a massive destruction of people in Stalin's torture chambers—all on the basis of fabricated charges. The writer Vitaly Gubarev boasted in his memoirs, "For thirty years we pulled a lot of weeds."[17] Where is the guarantee that tomorrow morning the next ruler of men's minds won't decide to occupy himself with weeding the garden he has managed to get his hands on? The Soviet poet Stepan Schipachev declared that Pavlik Morozov will be our contemporary "for all ages to come."[18] This is a pleasant thought.

"To inform, or not to inform? That is the question." So every Soviet Hamlet must have asked himself. And the answer to the question is not as simple as it seems. A hooligan strikes a woman, grabs her purse, jumps on a motorcycle, and takes off. You see the motorcycle's license number and there is a telephone nearby. Should you report this to the police or not? In this case the answer is simple; your sense of justice dictates that you must report it. But this does not bear any relation to the problem I am discussing. It concerns political informing, which is immoral in principle. Now, concerning informing inside the family, contemporary morals, like Biblical morals, do not distinguish between informing in political cases, in criminal cases, or in simple family matters. Within the family and from within the family, it is said, any aspect of informing is immoral. Although in certain instances this philosophy does not serve the interests of society as a whole, it can serve the interests of the family. But without the family there is no society. In countries where there is no absolute conformity of ideas, where political informing doesn't exist as a "sacred duty," where the family is inviolable, every person answers this question himself. Informers exist by vocation, but generally they are no more powerful than those of other vocations. They are often superfluous.

Soviet power always needed political informers. All was well until they begin to recruit individuals personally. Having selected a victim, they would call your home, offer to meet you "at the Square"; they would send you to the special department they have in every workplace and then lead you to "their" hotel room. They began with blackmail, threatening to damage your dissertation or to prevent your son's being accepted into the university. Peace in your family, career, and sense of the future would all be shaken. They would promise you a better job, the privilege of reading forbidden books. They would then ask you to explain some trifle: "What were the views of your neighbor?" Of course, it was better to remain quiet—but then they would make trouble for you. Could you talk and then go? Or should you take the middle road: "Yes, certainly I understand how this is important, but unfortunately I didn't hear anything..." But they don't believe you. And they summon you again and again because you, insignificant and lowly you, are "material," according to Lenin's expression. They are genuine Leninists, they are the government, they are the Party, they are the law, and there is no escape.

But what a misfortune for them as well. Heaven forbid that they would stumble from the little office of the regional police or the rooms of the General Secretary. Then they themselves would become "material," and this would be the end of them. They themselves clearly understood that in this country there existed but one real law—tyranny. There also existed but one real right—to inform.

Let me return to the starting point of this narrative. Who, ultimately, was guilty of what happened in Gerasimovka? Pavlik Morozov himself? His ancestors? Family? School? The system? Historical conditions? Are they all to blame? Correspondingly, is no one to blame? Morozov seems least guilty of all; after all, he was but a child. One's identity begins with the ability to choose, and Pavlik and the other village children of the 1930s had no choice. If adults in those years lacked a stable set of moral criteria, what can be said of an undeveloped boy? Neither should Pavlik bear any responsibility for what, after his death, was done in his name.

The innocence of the boy-informer raises little doubt; children, after all, are victims of circumstance. The guilt rebounds doubly on those who corrupt children in order to retain their power; these are the real criminals. As of late, the Party began an effort to disassociate itself from this matter, to shift the blame onto separate individuals, onto the criminal inclinations of Stalin, and onto the particular conditions that compelled them to destroy one part of society in order to stregthen the power of another part. In contrast to the national genocide that took place in Nazi Germany, the annihilation of "hostile classes" in the Soviet Union deserves its own term, which I would call "socialicide." And it is Pavlik Morozov who unwittingly became a symbol of Soviet socialicide, of the ideologically grounded terror organized and practiced by one party against an entire populace.

As the show trial concerning the matter of Pavlik Morozov's killers was in progress and the censorship battle directed against enemies of the people reached its peak, in 1932 in the newspaper *Uralsky Rabochy* an article appeared commemorating the three-hundredth birthday of Spinoza. I do not know whether it was the result of coincidence or intention, but this article notably quotes the great philosopher: "To what level will fear set people to folly?"[19] Folly out of fright—this state more accurately than any other defines the life of the country during the events herein described.

But the tempered objectivity of the historian is amazed by something else; how did it happen that, ground under by the mighty wheel of terror driven by the Party and the authorities, all did not succumb to the monstrous pressure of becoming informers? The very fact that appeals to enlist "as Pavlik Morozov [had]" continued in use for more than fifty years attests to the fact that all did not enlist. This very book, which I worked on for several years in Moscow, proves it. The manuscript went into *samizdat*, or underground, publication in 1984. Since then it has been scrutinized by many writers, and no one, as far as I know, has suffered for it.

The fundamental task of Soviet literature, as is well known, was to create positive heroes, idealized role models who existed solely to bolster Soviet authority. Despite this programmed effort, however, no enemies could cause as much harm to authority as it wrought on itself; it is compromised by the very myths it creates. Time goes on. Pavlik Morozov may be tinted, condemned, withdrawn, restored, or altogether withdrawn—all evidence of the myth's malleability, its fragility. They say that a Soviet man is trained to believe everything that he hears, sees, and reads. But this training doesn't insure that he will always act as he is ordered to act. Even in Stalin's and Hitler's prison camps unbroken people miraculously survived. In Soviet Russia the ordinary man demonstrated a front of unflagging solidarity. But what was he really thinking? He lied when they demanded lies; in his soul he yearned for truth. He gave way when, as in Dostoyevsky's expression, "they narrow[ed] him," but this pliancy was never complete. He confided little to the other narrowed people. And through all this, he constantly prayed that his children wouldn't inform on him.

Notes

1. Yunovich (1951).

2. *Istoria SSSR* (1967, vol. 8: 584, 589–90).
3. Abramov (August 1982).
4. Rzhezach (1978: 7, 72, 82–83, 104–19, 209, 211).
5. *Pavlik Morozov* (1962: 8–9).
6. Gubarev (September 1962).
7. Skorynina (19 May 1979).
8. *Sovetskaya Yustitsiya* (1925).
9. *Pionerskaya Pravda* (4 September 1962).
10. Stepichev (8 January 1982).
11. *Pionerskaya Pravda* (4 September 1962).
12. *Pavlik Morozov* (1962: 9).
13. Terentyev (12 January 1964).
14. Miller et al. (1963: 133).
15. Terentyev (12 January 1964).
16. Balashov (September 1982).
17. Gubarev (September 1962).
18. Shchipachev (1950).
19. Novik (27 November 1932).

Epilogue

What Has Happened to Informer 001
Now that the Soviet Union Has Collapsed

This book and its author have both had very unusual fates.

Work on the manuscript of *Informer 001* was completed in the early eighties, at a time when the Soviet Union was undertaking a momentous fiftieth anniversary celebration of the Pioneer-hero's death. Publishing the book inside the country was out of the question. The manuscript circulated in the *samizdat* network and the author's name was blacklisted by the very organization whose work was epitomized by Informer #001. The *glasnost* and *perestroika* which were under way at the time had no effect.

The book appeared as a London Overseas Publication at the end of 1987; anyone attempting to bring a copy into Russia found it confiscated by customs officials. Meanwhile, the Voice of America began to broadcast some of the material about Pavlik Morozov that I had uncovered. In the summer of the same year I read the whole book, chapter by chapter, before a microphone in the New York City studios of Radio Liberty; by then foreign broadcasting was no longer jammed in the Soviet Union. The broadcasts were repeated every four hours and reached millions of listeners in the expanse stretching from Eastern Europe to the Far East.

Letters flooded the editorial offices of Soviet newspapers and magazines. For example: "Recently I found out that Pavel Morozov bears no resemblance at all to the way we used to speak about him, he is not a Pioneer-hero, but a traitor," wrote a boy from Tsimliansk (near Rostov) to *Pionerskaya Pravda*. He continued: "We have these words in our troop song: 'Be like Pavlik Morozov!' Who should we be like? I was very proud that our troop bears his name. And now look what has happened."[1]

This boy asked a very good question, and *Pionerskaya Pravda* published his letter in order to respond to it. The propaganda organizations, it seems, did not anticipate that this issue would be quite so crucial. "We receive letters from Pioneers and their parents," wrote *Pionerskaya Pravda*, "letters from teachers, librarians, war veterans, and students. There are many questions in the letters, but they are substantially the same: 'We want to know the truth about Pavlik.'"[2] After many years of obeying the taboo, the Soviet press finally spoke about Morozov. This was an encouraging sign in itself. It became more difficult to remain silent.

In the spirit of the times the popular *Znanie* ("Knowledge") society organized a round table discussion entitled "Blank Spots in the History of the Communist Youth League." Historians were divided over the issue. Some tagged Morozov "the Pioneer-informer," sharply denouncing the symbol that was created out of him during the years of the "cult of Stalin." Others stated that "a civic stand should be valued more highly than family relations," affirming that denunciations of parents by their children are morally justified. One should note that the latter historians were employed by the Center for Research of the Upper Communist Youth School, a branch of the Central Committee of the Communist Youth League.

A boy of Morozov's age, living in the *glasnost* era, naïvely wrote to the newspaper to find out the truth. Educated men and women held a round table discussion, repeating rather than critically examining Morozov's mythical deeds, and arrived at a scientific conclusion published by *Pionerskaya Pravda*: "Having studied in detail all the circumstances surrounding the life and death of Pavlik Morozov, one cannot but respect him."[3]

Meanwhile, the distaste the intelligentsia felt toward the hero-informer made itself felt on the pages of the reformed press. In an article about the rehabilitation of Bolshevik leader Nikolai Bukharin printed in the magazine *Yunost*, writer V. Amlinsky said among other things that Morozov's deeds were "a symbol of romanticized and legitimized betrayal."[4] *Ogonyok*, a leading reform magazine, reported about fourth-graders in one of the Moscow schools who, at the peak of *perestroika*, were attempting to earn the right for their troop to bear the name of Pavlik Morozov. The magazine wrote fearlessly to the effect that under Stalin's rule the nation had managed to pervert "even the most basic ideas of morality."[5]

Those were controversial times, and *Yunost* plagiarized photographs and other materials from my book without citing their source. Suddenly the magazine's editors declared that "the time has come when we must once and for all deprive Western publishing houses of the prerogative of uncovering the blank spots of our history."[6] Why did these editors suddenly feel a need to take their livelihood away from historians in the West? Something similar had already happened in Soviet history, of course, and nothing good came of it.

There were voices in the Soviet press who called for eradicating the remnants of Stalinism from the moral climate. It is well-known that Lenin himself had proclaimed the rise of a communist class morality, distinct from normal morality, and Lenin was still untouchable. Some hints about Pavlik Morozov, at times very veiled, slipped into the press here and there, but even that was important.

Gradually, more serious declarations began appearing. V. Kondratiev, a writer who long ago became one of the first people to read the manuscript of *Informer 001*, stated his distaste for the informer morality.[7]

This sentiment was echoed by the writer I. Grekova in an article that appeared in *Moskovskie Novosti*.[8] "The passion for informing," wrote Feodor Burlatsky, a publicist in *Novy Mir*, "was imbibed by the older generation with their mothers' milk, it was taught and encouraged. I still shudder every time I drive up to my house on Pavlik Morozov street. The kid finked on his own father, yet became an object of emulation for millions of young people."[9] A Pavlik Morozov street did not exist in Moscow, it was just a lane, but the sentiment expressed by this active participant of *perestroika* sounded very decent.

One thing, though, was frightening. Although public appeals to topple the figure of the national informer-hero were passionate, his defenders had no intention of retreating. They repeatedly appeared on the pages of various publications disputing my book's arguments, and they were more than merely emotional. With the confidence of their powerful position they declared that Morozov was and remained a hero.

In the newspaper *Argumenty i Fakty*, there appeared an article by senior justice advisor I. Titov, officially representing the point of view of the Prosecutor's Office of the U.S.S.R. He told readers that he had researched "the archival materials of the investigation and trial of the murder of Pavlik Morozov."[10] What he retold was an old myth that he had adopted from Soviet newspapers and books. Even the wording of the indictment he quoted made it obvious that the justice advisor had only studied contemporary propaganda. He did not refer to a single archival document, cited neither sources nor names of witnesses, and thus complicated the truth even further.

The agenda of this article was clear: to neutralize *Informer 001*, with its eyewitness testimonies and documents that were published in London and publicized by radio stations abroad. But by repeating and renewing the old legend of a young Bolshevik fighter for socialism, Pavlik Morozov's defenders forced their audience to turn to non-Soviet sources for information. Avant-garde journalists and writers called for an increase in social conscience. Meanwhile, schools around the country kept teaching morality by using the example of treason whose epitome Pavlik Morozov had become. Metastases testified to the gravity of the disease. Curing it would require renouncing class-based ethics, acknowledging the correctness of Judeo-Christian morality, and admitting that the socialist experiment in Russia merely reinstated serfdom using methods that would have appalled Ivan the Terrible.

Meanwhile a certain strong hand began manifesting itself in the Soviet press, for *Informer 001* was undermining the foundations of socialism. The Central Committee of the Communist Youth League, the Prosecutor's Office of the USSR, and the editors of *Pionerskaya Pravda* and the magazines *Pioner* and *Chelovek i Zakon* created a joint commission to review Morozov's heroic feats. As a result, the Bureau of the Central Committee of the Pioneer Organization declared: "The decision of 1955 to enter Pavel Morozov's name into the Book of Honor should be considered sound. This conclusion is to be issued through the media to all Pioneers, their parents, and the public."[11]

At the height of *glasnost* it was widely announced that the well-known adolescent should remain Hero No. 001. Thus, after two previous incarnations, a real one and a mythical one, Pavlik Morozov began his third, surreal life: a desperate attempt by the forces of the past to turn the wheels of history back to the time of stagnation. Some journalists displayed an obsessive zeal in praising the informer (e.g., V. Kononenko in the magazines *Chelovek i Zakon* and *Sovetskaya Pedagogika*, V. Bushin in the newspaper *Sovetskaya Rossiya*).[12]

What was that boy from Tsimliansk supposed to do, along with millions of other boys and girls in the Soviet Union? Should they sing "be like Pavlik Morozov" or not? Should they inform the authorities when Daddy tells a joke about Gorbachev?

The denunciation of his own father, Pavlik's main feat, began to sound unsavory. And the Soviet newspapers assigned the task of informing the populace declared in unison: Pavlik's denunciations were not in the records! Therefore he was simply a young communist and a fighter for a better future. It became clear that the campaign to keep Pavlik a hero was being centrally directed. From where? Perhaps the Communist Youth League, recently deprived of its former power and glory, wanted to reestablish its reputation by finding merit in the past? But the youth League was merely a wheel in a larger mechanism. Who would benefit from the informer remaining an object of widespread imitation?

At that time there were already some insistent calls to publicize the lists of secret informers in a press recently freed form censorship. It soon became clear which organization was most concerned with preserving the glory of the hero-informer. The orders came from that establishment which detests any kind of openness, is threatened by the truth about history, but which could always use more informers. In an interview published in *Izvestia*, senior KGB official A. Burakov spoke of the necessity to strengthen the network of "part-time agents in every collective."[13] Whether it was a political winter or a political spring, the informer-hero was always useful. The lamentations of some audacious intellectuals about damaged morality did not change the facts of the matter. Stalin had first wanted to erect a monument to Morozov on Red Square, but later settled on a location in the Krasnaia Presnia. The true home for the betrayer of his father would have been the Lubyanka—the secret police headquarters. The organization occupying that square in the center of Moscow is surely convinced that the Pavlik Morozovs of that world serve it well now, and will continue to do so in the future.

Under pressure from above the press undertook a concerted attack against my book, published in London, an attack reminiscent of the darkest times of the past. The author was accused of libel, of creating an "anti-Soviet" forgery, and of insulting the dignity of a Soviet hero. *Chelovek i Zakon*, a magazine with a circulation of ten million, threatened to sue the book's author. Especially bitter were the articles whose authors had a hand in creating the myth of a Pioneer-Hero.

The book about Pavlik Morozov, published in London, was vocally debated by the press in the US, France, Israel, and Germany. Bit by bit copies kept trickling through the Iron Curtain into the socialist world. An abridged version of the book was translated into Estonian and published in Tallinn by the magazine *Pioner*; it was followed by a later translation into Hungarian. The book was published in Polish and became a bestseller in Warsaw. Chapters were printed in Riga in Latvian newspapers and magazines and in Russian by *Rodnik* magazine.

As a result of a weakening in censorship, fragments of the book began appearing in various publications in Moscow and on the periphery: *Semya i Shkola, Vek, Semya, Kurortnaya Gazeta.* However, when publishing houses tried to print the entire book in Moscow and in Novosibirsk, they were unsuccessful. Someone interfered. It was published in Moscow only in 1995.[14]

Meanwhile there was another, international aspect to the case of Pavlik Morozov. Earlier the *New York Times* had published a pessimistic article about the celebration of the fiftieth anniversary of Pavlik Morozov's feat.[15] As soon as the informer-hero was subjected to public criticism in the Soviet press, the same paper published an article from its Moscow correspondent, saying that "the times are changing the status of a saint of Stalin's era."[16] The *Times* reported that, according to certain publications in the Soviet press, Pavlik Morozov, the hero inscribed in the Book of Honor under the number 001, was a traitor.

Why did the West follow with such obvious curiosity the regime's attitude towards Pavlik Morozov? The child-informer mattered not at all; the issue at stake was the pervading moral code of the nation. If the official criteria for the state morality should remain political and communist, how could this state coexist with the rest of humanity? In other words, if the Kremlin uses a different set of ethics, Russia cannot be trusted either in global affairs or in details. For such a moral code justifies any prevarication and dishonesty directed at a class enemy.

Simply stated, in the eyes of the international community, economic aid to Russia depended on Pavlik Morozov. A country in a state of crisis will not be saved by KGB informers, but by multibillion dollar credits and trade and disarmament agreements with the West. That is why the *New York Times* and other Western publications noted with satisfaction the very first hints in the Soviet press that point to the denial of the morality symbolized by Pavlik Morozov. It was a question of the future of the Russian state; if Pavlik were glorified, this future would not exist.

One bronze version of Informer 001 stood next to the new American embassy in Moscow up to August 1991. One night in the trail of the August 1991 coup the crowd tied him up with a steel cable and pulled him down to the ground with a tractor, as was done with the monuments to Stalin. Yet stories arguing in his defense keep surfacing still.

Pavlik Morozov was a hero in the Soviet Union, and the first truthful book about him was written there, with an understanding of events particular to that time and place. But I decided that, apart from a few typos, nothing in this book should be changed. A new era has arrived in Russia. A secret statistical figure became known to public in August 1995; there were 11 million registered informers of the KGB in the former Soviet Union.[17] This means that among every eighteen citizens of the country at least one was an informer. The world has not heard of a state with a more sophisticated secret police!

Old myths die out, and new ones are created. But the informer-hero #001 remains a warning and a fearful reminder to all of us—those who inform, and those who become the victims of denunciations. And, as history has demonstrated, the informers themselves are also victims.

God forbid the past be repeated, but there still is such a danger.

Notes

1. "Yesli govorit..." (9 June 1988).
2. Ibid.
3. Ibid.
4. Amlinsky (March 1988).
5. Ivanova (June 1988).
6. Zerchaninov (May 1989).
7. Kondratyev (20 October 1988 and 24 May 1989).
8. Grekova (28 May 1989).
9. Burlatsky (October 1988).
10. Titov (1988).
11. *Komsomolskaya Pravda* (5 April 1989).
12. Kononenko (January 1989 and February 1990); Bushin (3 September 1992).
13. *Izvestia* (1 March 1989).
14. Yuri Druzhnikov, *Donoschik 001* (Moskovsky Rabochy, 1995).
15. Schmemann (16 September 1982).
16. Barringer (21 March 1988).
17. "Strana stukachei," *Panorama* (Los Angeles, 749, August 1995).

Russian Periodicals
Mentioned in the Book

Argumenty i Facty (Arguments and Facts), Moscow.
Arkhitekturnaya Gazeta (Architectural Gezette), Moscow.
Chelovek i Zakon (Man and the Law), Moscow
Druzhnye Rebyata (Friendly Children), later *Kolkhoznye Rebyata* (Children of the Collective Farm), Moscow.
Iskusstvo Kino (The Art of Moviemaking), Moscow.
Izvestia (News), Moscow.
Komsomolskaya Pravda (Komsomol Truth), Moscow.
Krasnaya Zvezda (The Red Star), Moscow.
Krestyanskaya Gazeta (Peasants' Gazette), Moscow.
Kurortnaya Gazeta (The Health Resort Gazette), the Crimea.
Leninskye Vnuchata (Lenin's Grandchildren), Rostov-on-Don.
Literaturnaya Gazeta (Literary Gazette), Moscow.
Molodoi Kommunist (Young Communist), Moscow.
Moskovskie Novosti (Moscow News), Moscow.
Na Smenu! (To the New Generation!), Sverdlovsk.
Novaya Zhizn (New Life), Petrograd.
Novy Mir (New World), Moscow.
Ogonyok (Small Fire), Moscow.
Omskaya Pravda (Omsk Truth), Omsk
Pioner (Pioneer), Moscow.
Pionerskaya Pravda (Pioneer Truth), Moscow.
Pravda (The Truth), Moscow.
Prosveshchenie Sibiri (Education in Siberia), Novosibirsk.
Semya i Shkola (Family and School), Moscow.
Smena (The New Generation), Tavda.
Sotsialisticheskaya Zakonnost (Socialist Law), Moscow.
Sovietskaya Muzyka (Soviet Music), Moscow.
Sovietskaya Pedagogika (Soviet Pedagogy), Moscow.
Sovietskaya Yustitsiya (Soviet Justice), Moscow.
Sovietskoye Iskusstvo (Soviet Art), Moscow.
Strana i Mir (Our Country and the World), Munich.

Tavdinsky Rabochy (The Tavda Worker), later *Tavdinskaya Pravda* (The Tavda Truth), Tavda.

Tyuremny Vestnik (Prison Herald), Petersburg.

Uralsky Rabochy (The Ural Worker), Sverdlovsk.

Uralsky Sledopyt (The Ural Pathfinder), Sverdlovsk.

Vechernaya Moskva (Evening Moscow), Moscow.

Vechernaya Perm' (Evening Perm'), Perm'.

Vek (Century), Moscow.

Voskhod (Sunrise), Irbit.

Vozhaty (Pioneer Leader), Moscow.

Vskhody Kommuny (Cornshoots of the Commune), Sverdlovsk.

Yunost (Youth), Moscow.

Bibliography

Books and Periodicals

Abramov, B. "K izucheniu istorii kollectivizatsii." *Voprosy Istorii KPSS*, 8, August 1982.

Agapova, M. and K. Shadskaya. *Pionery-geroi*. Moscow, 1981.

Alekseev, G. "Proletarsky orlienok." *Komsomolskaya Pravda*, 2 September 1962.

Alekseeva, N. and A. Balchugov. *Gerasimovka*. Sverdlovsk, 1969.

Aleksin, Anatoly. "Put k podvigu." *Literaturnaya Gazeta*, 20 December 1952.

Amlinsky, V. "Na zabroshennych grobnitsakh." *Yunost*, 3, March 1988.

Andreeva, A. and Y. Kutakov. *Pionerskie druzhiny, skoly, lageria, parki i drugie uchrezhdeniya, nosiashchie imia Pavlika Morozova*. Sverdlovsk, 1978.

Antonov, V. "Ubiitsy Pavlika Morozova prigovoreny k rasstrelu." *Komsomolskaya Pravda*, 30 November 1932.

———. "Trebovania trudiashchokhca mass udovletvoreny." *Na Smeny!*, 29 November 1932.

———. "3-e sentiabria v sele Gerasimovka." *Na Smenu!*, 28 November 1932.

Antonov-Ovseenko, A. *Portret tirana*. New York, 1980.

Arkhipov, Vasily. "Vyshe klassovuyu boesposobnost." *Pionerskaya Pravda*, 17 December 1932.

Avtorkhanov, A. *Zagadka smerti Stalina*. Possev, 1975.

Balashov, Vladimir. "Malchik s muzhestvom muzhchiny." *Uralsky Sledopyt*, 9, September 1982.

———. *Koster ryabinovy*. Moscow, 1969.

Balchugov, A. and N. Alekseeva. *Kolkhoz imeni Pavlika Morozova* (booklet). Sverdlovsk, 1969.

Barringer, Felicity. "Changing Times Turn Tables on a 'Saint' of Stalin Era." *The New York Times*, 21 March 1988.

Bazilevich, K. *Istoria SSSR*, part 3, 11th ed. Moscow, 1952.

Begin, M. *V belye nochi*. Tel-Aviv, 1978.

Belova, M. *Tvorchestvo Aleksandra Yakovleva*. Saratov, 1967.

Belyaev, I. "Rabselkory—neustrashimie bortsy za sotsialisticheskuyu zakonnost." *Sotsialisticheskaya Zakonnost*, 8, August 1938.

Borovin, V. *Morozov Pavel*. Vologda, 1936.

Bud' gotov! Obshchestvo "Russkii skaut." Moscow, 1916.

"Budte bditelny k vragu." *Kolkhoznye Rebyata*, 20 October 1932.

Burlatsky, Feyodor. "Posle Stalina: zametki o politicheskoy ottepeli." *Novy Mir*, 10, October 1988.

Bushin, V. "On gluboko opasen." *Sovetskaya Rossiya*, 3 September 1992.

Chechetkina, O. "Pochta Lydii Timashuk." *Pravda*, 20 February 1953.

Chernyshov, A. *Salyut, pioneriya!* Moscow, 1982.

"Decision of the Ural court." *Tavdinsky Rabochy*, 30 November 1932).

Deti-geroi. Moscow, 1961.

Deti-patrioty sovetskoy rodiny. Moscow, 1964.

Deti-psikhonevrotiki. Moscow-Leningrad, 1934.

Deti s otkloneniyami v povedenii. Moscow, 1968.

Detskaya defektivnost, prestupnost i besprizornost. Moscow, 1920.

Detskoe kommunisticheskoe dvizhenie. Moscow-Leningrad, 1932.

Detsky selskokhoziaistvenny trud. Moscow-Leningrad, 1930.

Doroshin, Mikhail. *Pavlik Morozov*. Volgograd, 1973.

———. "Pavlik Morozov." *Pionerskaya Pravda*, 29 March 1933.

Dulnev, G. and A. Luria. *Printsypy otbora detei vo vspomogatelnye shkoly*. Moscow, 1973.

Eisenstein v vospominaniyakh sovremennikov. Moscow, 1974.

Eisenstein, Sergei. "Oshibki 'Bezhina luga.'" *Sovetskoe Iskusstvo*, 17 April 1937.

———. *Izbrannye proizvedenia*, 6 vols. Moscow, 1971.

Ehrenburg, Ilya. "Rech na Pervom c'esde sovetskikh pisatelei." *Komsomolskaya Pravda*, 22 August 1934.

Gersimovka pomnit Pavlika Morozova (booklet). Sverdlovsk, 1969.

Gordin, I. and V. Lebedinsky. *Pionerskaya organizatsiya v usloviyakh pobedy sotsializma*. Moscow, 1973.

Gorky, Maksim. *Pisma o literature*. Moscow, 1957.

———. *Sobranie sochinenii*, in 30 Vols. Moscow, 1953–55.

———. *O molodezhi*. Moscow, 1949.

———. "Privetstvie Bolshevskoy kommune." *Pravda*, 11 June 1935.

———. "Vystuplenie pered pionerami." *Pionerskaya Pravda*, 23 September 1932.

———. "Pokazat eshcho bolshe geroicheskogo truda." *Pionerskaya Pravda*, 9 July 1932.

———. "Koshmar, iz dnevnika." *Novaya Zhizn*, 13, 3 May 1917.

Grekova, I. "Vera i vospitanie." *Moskovskie Novosti*, 28 May 1989.

Gubarev, Vitaly. "Podvig Pavlika Morozova." *Molodoi Kommunist*, 9, September 1962.

————. "Podvig russkogo malchika." *Komsomolskaya Pravda*, 3 September 1957.

————. *Pavlik Morozov* (drama). Moscow, 1953.

————. *Yuniye Pionery*. Moscow, 1948a.

————. *Pavlik Morozov*. Moscow, 1948b.

————. "Syn." *Pioner*, 1, January 1940.

————. "V lesnoi glushi." *Pionerskaya Pravda*, 3 September 1933.

————. "Gigantskie shagi Petra Knigi." *Pionerskaya Pravda*, 27 November 1932.

————. "Imia ego leninets." *Kolkhoznye Rebyata*, 20 October 1932.

————. "Kulatskaya rasprava." *Pionerskaya Pravda*, 15 October 1932.

Gusev, A. *God za godom: pionerskaya letopis*. Moscow, 1970.

————. *God za godom: pionerskaya letopis*. Moscow, 1964.

————. *Yunye pionery*. Moscow, 1948.

————. *Detkory v shkole*. Moscow, 1935.

Isakova, L. ("Dudina" was her maiden name at that time). "On uchilsa u menia." *Tavdinskaya Pravda*, 27 August 1967.

Istoria gosudarstva i prava SSSR, 2nd ed. Moscow, 1981.

Istoria KPSS. Moscow, 1960.

Istoria sovetskogo kino, 4 vols. Moscow, 1973.

Istoria SSSR, 12 vols. Moscow, 1967.

Istoria SSSR v dokumentakh i illustatsiyakh. Moscow, 1963.

Istoria VKP(b). Moscow, 1938.

Istoria VLKSM. Moscow, 1978.

Itogi Odinnadtsatoi Uralskoi konferentsii VKP(b). Moscow-Sverdlovsk, 1932.

Ivanova, T. "Kto chem riskuyet." *Ogonyek*, 24, June 1988.

Kabakov, Ivan. *Ocherednye zadachi Uralskoy partorganizatsii*. Moscow-Sverdlovsk, 1930.

Kareev, N. *Teoriya lichnosti P. L. Lavrova*. St. Petersburg, 1907.

Kartashov, Spiridon. "Pesnia o nem ne umriet." *Voskhod*, 3 September 1963.

Khorinskaya, E. *Yuny barabanshchik*. Sverdlovsk, 1954.

Khrushchev, N. *Khrushchev Remembers*. Boston: Little Brown, 1974.

Klassovaya borba na Urale. Sverdlovsk, 1974.

Kondratyev, V. "Pogovorim o Svobode." *Literaturnaya Gazeta*, 24 May 1989.

————. "My budem zhit po-drugomu." *Sovetskaya Kultura*, 20 October 1988.

Kononenko, Veronica. "Pravda o Pavlike Morozove." *Sovetskaya Pedagogika*, 2, February 1990.

————. "Posmertno...repressirovat." *Chelovek i Zakon*, 1, January 1989.

Korshunov, Mikhail. "Serdtse materi." *Pravda*, 23 September 1962.

Koryakov, Oleg. "Predislovie." In Solomein, *Pavka-kommunist*, Sverdlovsk, 1979.

————. *Doroga bez privala*. Sverdlovsk, 1977.

Kosarev, A. "Doklad na Sedmoi Vsesoyusnoi konferentsii VLKSM." *Pravda*, 7 July 1932.

Kosior, Stanislav. *Orgotchet CK XV s'ezdu VKP(b)*. Moscow-Leningrad, 1932.

Kratkaya istoria SSSR, 2nd ed. Moscow, 1972.

Krupskaya, Nadezhda. *Pedagogicheskie sochinenia*, 10 vols. Moscow, 1958 (vol. 11 added in 1963).

————. "Byt' khorosho vooruzhennymi!" *Pionerskaya Pravda*, 5 July 1933.

————. "O perezhitkakh." *Pionerskaya Pravda*, 23 October 1932.

Krushansky, M. "Litso anonima." *Sovetskaya Rossiya*, 31 August 1982.

"K zakonu ob otmene ssylki." *Tiuremny Vestnik*, 6–7, 1900.

Lavrov, K. *Ocherki voprosov kriticheskoy filosofii*. St. Petersburg, 1860.

Leyda, Jay. *Kino: A History of the Russian and Soviet Film*. London, 1960.

Lenin, Vladimir. *Polnoe sobranie sochinenii*, 5th ed. Moscow, 1963.

Lezinsky, M. *Ryadovye voennogo detstva*. Simferopol, 1985.

Lidin, V. "Predislovie." In A. Yakovlev, *Isbrannye proizvedenia*, Moscow, 1957.

Lomonosova, A. "Predislovie." In Solomein, *V kulatskom gnezde*, Sverdlovsk, 1933.

Makarova, A. "Trudnym putem." *Literaturnaya Gazeta*, 27 July 1950.

Maryagin, G. *Postyshev*. Moscow, 1965.

Mikhalkov, Sergei. "Pesnia o Pavlike Morozove." *Vozhaty*, 4, April 1934.

Miller, W., H. Roberts, and M. Shulman. *The Meaning of Communism*. Morristown, 1963.

Minaev, B. "Druzhina, smirno!" *Komsomolskaya Pravda*, 3 September 1982.

Mor, V. "Delo ob ubiistve pionera Morozova." *Uralsky Rabochy*, 19 November 1932.

Morozova, Tatyana. "Budte takimi kak Pavlik Morozov." In *Pavlik Morozov*, Sverdlovsk, 1962.

Musatov, Aleksei. "Bolshaya vesna." *Vozhaty*, 9, September 1962.

"My trebuem rasstrela kulakov-ubiits." *Vskhovy Kommuny*, 23 September 1932.

Nalbandyan, Dmitry. "Oblik otvazhnogo pionera." *Komsomolskaya Pravda*, 24 January 1953.

Nalobina, V. "Pavlik Morozov." *Na Smenu!*, 30 March 1972.

"Na pamiatnik Pavliku Morozovu." *Pionerskaya Pravda*, 24 August 1934.

Novik, P. "K trekhsotletiyu B. Spinozy." *Uralsky Rabochy*, 27 November 1932.

Novikova, Y. "Pavlik Morozov." *Pioner*, 8, August 1953.

Ocherki istorii kommunisticheskikh oganizatsii Urala. Sverdlovsk, 1974.

Odinnadtsataya Uralskaya konferentsiya VKP(b). Moscow-Sverdlovsk, 1932.

"O likvidatsii detskoi besprizornosti." *Pravda*, 1 June 1935.

Ordzhonikidze, Sergo. *Otchet CKK i RKI*. Moscow-Leningrad, 1928.

Orlov, G. "Proizvedenia molodykh leningradtsev." *Sovetskaya Muzyka*, 12, December 1954.

Ostroumov, C. *Prestupnost i ee prichiny v dorevolutsionnoi Rossii.* Moscow, 1980.

"Partia govorit." *Pionerskaya Pravda*, 7 October 1933.

Pavlik Morozov (booklet). Izdanie Gerasimovskogo muzeya. Sverdlovsk, 1968.

Pavlik Morozov. Sverdlovsk, 1962.

Permiak, Evgeny. "Pavka-kommunist." *Literaturnaya Rossia*, 22 March 1963.

Pervy Vsesoyuzny s'ezd sovetskikh pisatelei. Moscow, 1934.

"Pervy Vsesouzny s'ezd sovetskikh pisatelei." *Komsomolskaya Pravda*, 20 August 1934.

"Piat' dnei v Moskve." *Pionerskaya Pravda* , 10 January 1934.

Pionerskaya rabota v spetsialnykh shkolakh. Moscow, 1963.

Pionery-geroi. Moscow, 1956.

Podvigu zhit! Moscow, 1962.

Polyakova, L. "Opera dlya yunoshestva." *Sovetskaya Myzyka*, 7, July 1958: 12–15.

Postanovlenie Uralobkoma VKP(b) ot 9 fevralia 1933 goda. Sverdlovsk, Tipografia PP OGPU, 1933.

Postyshev, Pavel. "K novym boyam za pobedu sotsializma." *Krestyanskaya Gazeta*, 14 November 1932.

Prikaz Narkomprosa RSFSR o distsipline d shkole. Moscow, 1934.

"Proverka gotovnosti." *Pionerskaya Pravda*, 3 August 1933.

Roginsky, G. "Sotsialistichekaya sobstvennost sviashchenna." *Sotsialistichekaya Zakonnost*, 8, August 1938.

Rostovshchikova, E. "Pervaya shkola." *Tavdinskaya Pravda*, 27 August 1967.

Rubenshtein, S. *Psikhologiya umstvenno otstalogo shkolnika*, 2nd ed. Moscow, 1979.

Rumyantsev, L. *Pesnya o nem ne umret.* Sverdlovsk, 1953.

Rzheshevsky, Alexander. *Zhizn, kino.* Moscow, 1982.

———. *Bezhin lug. Kinostsenary.* Moscow, 1936.

Rzhezach, T. *Spiral izmeny Solzhenitsyna.* Moscow, 1978.

Sanatin, V. "Reportazh cherez gody." *Pionerskaya Pravda*, 2 September 1982.

Schmemann, Serge. "Soviet 'Hero' Informer, 13, Leaves a Bitter Legacy." *The New York Times*, 16 September 1982.

Semnadtsataya konferentsia VKP(b). Moscow, 1932.

Shardakov, V. "Pavlik Morozov" *Vechernaya Perm'*, 11 October 1980.

Shchipachev, Stepan. *Pavlik Morozov.* Moscow, 1950.

Shestakov, D. *Predotvratit semeinuyu dramu.* Leningrad, 1981.

Shestnadtsaty c'ezd BKP(b). Moscow-Leningrad, 1930.

Shklovsky, Victor. *Eizenshtein.* Moscow, 1973.

Shvarts, O. "Pavlik Morozov." *Pioner* 5–6, May-June 1933.

Shvartsman, Y. "Dozornye urozhaya." *Pionerskaya Pravda*, 7 and 9 August 1933.

Skorynina, A. "Gvardiya Pavki Morozova." *Na Smenu!*, 19 May 1979.

Smirnov, Elizar. "Pavlik Morozov." In *Deti-geroi*, Moscow, 1961.

———. *Pavlik Morozov*. Moscow, 1938.

———. *Yunie dozorniki*. Moscow, 1934.

———. "Na bolshom trakte." *Pionerskaya Pravda*, 15 January 1933).

———. "Kulak Kulukanov." *Pionerskaya Pravda*, 9 January 1933.

———. "Oblik yunogo lenintsa." *Pionerskaya Pravda*, 17 December 1932.

———. "Vyshe znamia klassovoi boesposobnosti!" *Pionerskaya Pravda*, 5 December 1932.

———. "Kulaki na skamye podsudimykh." *Pionerskaya Pravda*, 27 November 1932.

Snow, C. *Variety of Men: Stalin*. New York: Macmillan, 1967.

Sokolov. "Pavla ubili kulaki." *Na Smenu!*, 24 September 1932.

Solomein, Pavel. *Pavka-kommunist*. Sverdlovsk, 1979.

———. *Pavka-kommunist*. Sverdlovsk, 1969.

———. "Kak ya igral na garmoshke." *Tavdinskaya Pravda*, 5 and 7 September 1967.

———. *Pavka-kommunist*. Sverdlovsk, 1962.

———. *V kulatskom gnezde*. Sverdlovsk, 1933.

———. "Zhertva kulatskogo obreza." *Pionerskaya Pravda*, 27 December 1932.

———. "Sud nad ubiitsami nachalsa." *Kolkhoznye Rebyata*, 29 November 1932.

———. "Na svezhei mogile." *Pionerskaya Pravda*, 27 November 1932.

———. "Dvenadtsatiletnii kommunist." *Tavdinsky Rabochy*, 27 October 1932a.

———. "Kak pogib Pavlik." *Vskhody Kommuny*, 27 October 1932b.

———. "Pochemu raiorganizatsii pozdno uznali." *Vskhody Kommuny*, 8 October 1932.

Sovetskaya ictoricheskaya entsiklopedia. Moscow, 1967.

Ssylka i obshchestvenno-politicheskaya zhizn Sibiri. Novosibirsk, 1978.

Stalin, Josef. *Sochinenia*. Moscow, 1952.

———. "Zakluchitelnoe slovo na plenume CK VKP(b)." *Vechernaya Moskva*, 1 April 1937.

———. *Voprosy leninisma*. Moscow, 1933.

———. "Privetstvie Sedmoi Vsecoyuznoi konferentsii VLKSM." *Pravda*, 9 July 1932.

Stepichev, M. "S polichnym." *Pravda*, 8 January 1982.

"S tribuny slieta." *Pionerskaya Pravda*, 27 August 1933.

Sukhachevsky, S. *Seriozha-moriachok*. Cheliabinsk, 1975.

———. *Pioner iz sela Kolesnikovo*. Kurgan, 1972.

———. "Po sledam geroya." *Omskaya Pravda*, 5 February 1963.

Sverdlovskaya oblastnaya organizatsia KPSS. Sverdlovsk, 1974.

Terentyev, V. "Nash otvet gospodam za okeanom." *Na Smenu!*, 12 January 1964.

Titov, I. "Chelovek i simvol." *Argumenty i Fakty*, 22, 1988.

"Trudnym putiem." *Literaturnaya Gazeta*, 27 June 1950.

Tucker, Robert. *Stalin as Revolutionary*. New York: W.W. Norton, 1973.

"Ubiits rasstreliat!" *Pionerskaya Pravda*, 14 December 1934.

"U etikh pionerov uchites bditelnosti." *Pionerskaya Pravda*, 6 March 1935.

Ugolovnoe zakonodatelstvo SSSR. Moscow, 1957.

Urin. "Rech na sude." *Tavdinsky Rabochy*, 29 November 1932.

Vaisfeld, I. "Teoriya i praktika Eizenshteina." *Iskusstvo Kino*, 5, May 1937.

Veltman, V. *Yuniye geroi*, in 2 Vols. Rostov-on-Don, 1933.

Vishnevsky, Vsevolod. "Vstupitelny ocherk." In A. Rzheshevsky, *Bezhin lug*, Moscow, 1936.

Vorotov, M. "Vkluchaites v podgotovku k tretyei bolshevistskoi vesne." *Prosveshchenie Sibiri*, 1, January 1932.

Vtoroi detkorovsky. Leningrad, 1931.

Vyshinsky, Andrei. "Osnovnye zadachi nauki sotsialisticheskogo prava." *Sotsialisticheskaya Zakonnost*, 36, 1938.

Vzveites' kostrami. Ocherki istorii pionerii. Sverdlovsk, 1974.

Yakovlev, Alexander. *Pioner Pavel Morozov*. Moscow-Leningrad, 1938.

Yashin, A. "Kogda bessmertna smert na zemle." *Komsomolskaya Pravda*, 26 July 1950.

Yermakova, L. "Geroi v krasnom galstuke." *Uralsky Rabochy*, 3 September 1982.

Yermilov, V., ed. *Literatura i novy chelovek*. Moscow, 1963.

"Yesli govorit o Pavlike Morozove…" *Pionerskaya Pravda*, 9 June 1988.

Yunovich, M. "Poema o yunom geroe." *Ogonyek*, 21, 1951.

Z., V. "V bolshoi semye." *Pionerskaya Pravda*, 25 July 1933.

Zerchaninov, Y. "Kto prikhodil nochyu v khudom tulupe. K istorii odnogo mifa." *Yunost*, 5, May 1989.

Zhelokhovtsev, A. *Kulturnaya revolutsiya s blizkogo rasstoyaniya*. Moscow, 1973.

Zosimovsky, A. *Formirovanie lichnosti v shkolnom vozraste*. Moscow, 1982.

"Zverskoe ubiistvo pionerov Morozovykh." *Pionerskaya Pravda*, 15 October 1932.

Brochures, booklets, fliers, banners, guidebooks, bibliographical guides dedicated to Pavlik Morozov were produced by Soviet museums, libraries, and also by local culture and propaganda organizations. The complete list of works pertinent to the myth of Pavlik Morozov would constitute a small book in itself. A large part of this material is plagiarized from a small number of firsthand accounts and consequently is of little scholarly interest.

Archival Materials/Unpublished Memoirs

File of Investigation No. 374 on the murder of the Morozov brothers conducted by the Secret Political and the Special Departments of OGPU in the Urals (1932). The file constitutes more than two hundred pages with the secret title "T" ("Terror"); I only had access to a part of it. The important documents of the investigation were:

Interrogation Record for the File No...(no number mentioned), 4 September 1932.
Crime Scene Report signed by militia-man Titov, 6 September 1932.
File on the Slain Morozovs, Pavel and Fyodor, prepared by the Secret Political Department of Tavda OGPU.
Minutes of Meeting No. 4 Concerning the Organization of Kolkhoz, 12 September 1932.
Secret Declaration to "OO" (Special Section), by Spiridon Kartashov, 13 September 1932.
Special Note on the Terror Problem, No. 1858, 17 September 1932.
Interrogation Records for File No. 374, Morozova, Tatyana, 11 and 23 September 1932.
Indictment, prepared by the Secret Political Department of OGPU for the Trial, November 1932.
Some less important documents from File No. 374 are mentioned in the text.

Papers from the Department of Pioneer Work of the High Komsomol School and materials of the Historical Office of the Pioneer Organization of the Communist Youth League Central Committee (Moscow), in particular:

Pioneer Hero Catalogue, 1917–1983.
TASS Bulletin, No. 50 "P"—for Young Communist and Pioneer Press, Moscow, 22 December 1932. It has not been published in full.
"Registration at the Place of Gerasimovka", State Archives of Sverdlovsk Province, Irbit District, File No. 95–4.
Pozdnina, Elena (Bezborodova, her maiden name at that time), About Pavlik Morozov, *Memoirs*, December 1932, manuscript from Sverdlovsk Museum of Revolutionary History.
———. *Questionnaire*, 1967, manuscript from Tavda local museum.

Order of the Tavda City Council No. 186, 13 April 1978.

Yermakova, A., Pioneer-Hero, memoirs of Morozov's schoolmate, 1940, manuscript from Tavda local museum.

Personal Archives

Archive of Pavel Solomein (Ural, Sverdlovsk District), in the 1980s in possession of his widow and daughter. Of particular interest are:

Solomein, *Materials for Morozov's Biography*, the notebook, Gerasimovka, October-December 1932.

————, *Eyewitness Testimony*, the notebook, Gerasimovka, October-December 1932.

————, *Manuscripts and Letters*, Pervouralsk, 1932–1962.

Fomin, G., Letter to Solomein, Tavda, 1953.

Kassil, Lev, Letter to Pavel Solomein, 25 December 1936.

Savitskaya, Natalia, Questions by Writer O. Koryakov and Answers on Her Father Pavel Solomein, Pervouralsk, 1972.

Testimony on Tape

I made extensive use of tape recordings of interviews with the surviving witnesses and participants of the events in the thirteen cities and towns I visited. The testimony and unique archival documents were of historic interest and most valuable to me in my work. All the interviews were conducted in 1981–1983. What follows is a list of the main witnesses whose testimony I have on tape and quote in the book without specific reference:

Lazar Baidakov, Z. T. Bakhmach (Elizar Smirnov's widow), Vera Berkina, G. P. Ilyinskaya (citizen of Tavda), Zoya Kabina, Spiridon Kartashov, Alexander Khrabrovitsky (Moscow writer), Matrena Korolkova, Tatyana Morozova, Alexey Morozov, Pavlik Morozov (the protagonist's nephew), Grigory Parfenov (peasant), Elena Pozdnina, Ivan Potupchik, Dmitry Prokopenko, Elena Sakova, A. M. Selminsky (citizen of Tavda), V. E. Smirnov (Elizar Smirnov's son), Anna Tolstaya (witness of the trial), Grigory Yakovenko (investigator).

For more information about witnesses, see also "Cast of Characters."

Index